FUNDAMENTAL OF ARTIFICIAL NEURAL NETWORK AND FUZZY LOGIC

FUNDAMENTAL OF ARTIFICIAL NEURAL NETWORK AND FUZZY LOGIC

By

RAJESH KUMAR

M.Phil, M.Tech, Ph.D

Professor,

Head,

Instrumentation and Control Engg.

Graphic Era University

Dehradun, Uttarakhand

UNIVERSITY SCIENCE PRESS

(An Imprint of Laxmi Publications Pvt. Ltd.)

An ISO 9001:2015 Company

BENGALURU • CHENNAI • GUWAHATI • HYDERABAD

KOCHI • KOLKATA • LUCKNOW • RANCHI

NEW DELHI

Printed and bound in India
First Edition : 2009 *Reprint* : 2010; *Edition* : 2025
ISBN : 978-81-3180-710-1
UAN-9357-289-ART NEURAL NET FUZY LOGIC

Price: ₹ 289.00

Branches

✆	Bengaluru	080-26 75 69 30
✆	Chennai	044-24 34 47 26
✆	Guwahati	0361-254 36 69
✆	Hyderabad	040-27 55 53 83
✆	Kochi	0484-405 13 03
✆	Kolkata	033-40 04 77 79
✆	Lucknow	0522-430 36 13
✆	Ranchi	0651-224 24 64

PUBLISHED IN INDIA BY

UNIVERSITY SCIENCE PRESS
(An Imprint of Laxmi Publications Pvt. Ltd.)
An ISO 9001:2015 Company
113, GOLDEN HOUSE, GURUDWARA ROAD, DARYAGANJ,
NEW DELHI - 110002, INDIA

Corporate Office : B-33, Sector-5, Noida,
Gautambuddha Nagar (U.P.) - 201 301, INDIA
Telephone : +91-120-44 46 900
www.laxmipublications.com
info@laxmipublications.com

CONTENTS

PREFACE

Over the past decade, the application of Artificial Neural Network and Fuzzy Logic system to solving engineering problems like process control, modelling, communication, pattern recognition, speech recognition etc. has grown enormously. This supplement introduces the fundamentals necessary to implement and apply these soft computing approaches to engineering problem using MATLAB.

This book is intended as an introduction to the subject of artificial neural networks and fuzzy logic system, for readers at the junior or senior level as well as scientist and engineer.

I have used the material in research work and in teaching courses. The first part of this book gives a brief introduction to matlab. The book is organized so that the most frequently used neural networks and fuzzy logic are introduced very early, so that these can form the basis for initiating courses projects. In this book, the work has been done to study the implementation of fuzzy logic controller, artificial neural network controller in industrial process. The uses of fuzzy logic and artificial neural network are made the system more efficient.

Chapters 2–5 are essentially dependent of each other, how to design a neural networks for control or fault detection etc., how different parameters like learning rate, momentum factor, number of hidden nodes effect the network. Matlab implementation of the theory and practical implementation issues have been included in this book.

Although every attempt has been made to make this book error face yet I expect that some errors remain in the text, and welcome comments and corrections from readers.

—Author

ACKNOWLEDGEMENT

I wish to express my sincere and heartfelt thanks to my Ph.D. supervisors Dr. A.K. Ray, Professor, Department of Paper Technology, Saharanpur Campus, IIT, Roorkee and Dr. S. Mukherjee, Professor, Department of Electrical Engineering, IIT, Roorkee. I am highly indebted to Dr. A.K. Ray and Dr. S. Mukherjee whose astute research methodology and profound knowledge of the subject have greatly benefited me in easily grasping this interdisciplinary subject. I reaffirm my sincere thanks to them for their painstaking efforts in helping me complete this work.

I am highly obliged to Prof. Kamal Ghansala, Chairman, Graphic Era Institute of Technology, Dehradun for providing facilities of using MATLAB software.

The author thankfully acknowledges the Star Paper Mills Ltd., Saharanpur and Ballarpur Industry Limited, Yamuna Nagar, for permitting me to conduct In-plant studies and collection of data on head box of paper machine.

My sincere thanks are also due to my fellows Mr. Yogesh Kumar and Mr. Mohan Lal for their co-operation and their encouraging association during this work.

Author sincerely acknowledges the help, co-operation, perseverance and sacrifices rendered by my wife, Mrs. Mamta Raj and sons, Aditya Raj Haldia, and Prateek Raj Haldia during the entire period of preparation of this book.

This book is dedicated to Lord Buddha and My Parents whose love remained with me at every stage.

—Author

Chapter 1 ARTIFICIAL NEURAL NETWORK AND FUZZY LOGIC : PRELIMINARIES

1.1. INTRODUCTION

Use of artificial intelligence (AI) has become an indispensable tool for controlling various process parameters in process and allied industries.The AI includes mainly artificial neural network (ANN), Fuzzy logic (FL), Genetic Algorithm (GA) or any of their combinations. Typically these are Neuro-Fuzzy, Fuzzy-GA, Neuro-FL-GA etc. Out of the so many methodologies available, in overwhelmingly majority of cases ANN is found to be the most easiest one and is currently being applied in almost all process industries now-a-days for optimizing, simulating and controlling various processes and operations. This is being preferred over other deterministic modeling techniques as the chemical process system is mostly complex, bewildered and strongly nonlinear multi-variable in nature and cannot be solved easily by classical control system and deterministic dynamic modeling technique.

They first began to appear on the process-control scene in the early 1990s, but have been a research focus for more than 30 years. Neural networks are really empirical models that approximate the way we think neurons in the human brain work. Neural-net technology is not trying to produce computerized clones, but to model nature in an effort to mimic some of the brain's capabilities. Modeling for the purposes of this article, means developing a mathematical description of physical phenomena. The physics and chemistry of industrial processes are usually quite complex and sometimes poorly understood. Our process understanding, and our imperfect ability to describe complexity in mathematical terms, limit fidelity of first-principle models. Computational requirements for executing these complex models are a further limitation. It is often not possible to execute first-principle model algorithms at the high rate required for online control.

Nevertheless, rigorous first-principle models are commonplace design tools. Process control is another important model input are often not available as process measurements, making real-time application difficult. In fact, aspects often use models to infer unavailable measurements.

1.2. WHAT IS ANN ?

Artificial neural network (ANN) architectures are biologically inspired that is, they are made up of elements that perform in a manner that is analogous to the basic biological neuron or nerve cells. The artificial neurons are then organized in a manner that may (or may not) simulate the anatomy of the brain.

The standard artificial neuron is a processing element whose output is calculated by multiplying its input by a weight vector, summing the results, and applying an activation function to the sum. The activation function could be one of many types (sigmoid, hyperbolic, hard limit, symmetrical hard limit, and linear etc.). Neurons are grouped into layers and layers are grouped into networks to form highly interconnected processing structures. An input layer does no processing, it simply sends the inputs, modified by a weight, to each of the neurons in the next layer. This next layer can be a hidden layer or the output layer in a single layer design. The comparison between is shown in Table 1.1.

Table 1.1. Comparison of Biological vs. Artificial Neural Networks

Biological Human Neural System	*ANN Computer System*
Single Neuron, imprecise, noisy.	High digital precision.
Memory/cpu is the same thing.	Memory/cpu are separate.
Distributed storage and data representation.	Local storage of data. One item per address.
Computing time is independent of problem size.	Exponential increase of computing time.
Programming by training.	Software development.
Approximate solution based on fuzzy, noisy data.	Exact solution based on exact data.
Flexible/soft 3D structure.	Rigid, inorganic, flat 2D matter.
10^{10} neurons, 10^{12} synapses.	10^7 transistors. 10–100 fan-in/fan-out.
Metabolic Biochemistry.	Transformers and rectifiers from power sources.
10^{-12} watt/neuron.	10^{-5} watt/gate.
100 mv impulses with 1 ms duration.	5V with 10^{-9} sec switching.
Analog (?) computing.	Digital computing.
Massive Parallelism.	Sequential.
Destroy a few causes little if any degradation.	One transistor bit can cause total loss of performance.

1.3. WHY ARTIFICIAL NEURAL NETWORKS ?

The long course of evolution has given the human brain many desirable characteristics not present in von Neumann or modern parallel computers. These include

- Massive parallelism,
- Distributed representation and computation,
- Learning ability,
- Generalization ability,
- Adaptivity,
- Inherent contextual information processing,
- Fault tolerance, and
- Low energy consumption.

It is hoped that devices based on biological neural networks will possess some of these desirable characteristics.

Modern digital computers outperform humans in the domain of numeric computation and related symbol manipulation. However, humans can effortlessly solve complex perceptual problems (like recognizing a man in a crowd from a mere glimpse of his face) at such a high speed and extent as to dwarf the world's fastest computer. Why is there such a remarkable difference in their performance ? The biological neural system architecture is completely different from the von Neumann architecture (see Table 1.1). This difference significantly affects the type of functions each computational model can best perform. Numerous efforts to develop "intelligent" programs based on von Neumann's centralized architecture have not resulted in general-purpose intelligent programs. Inspired by biological neural networks, ANNs are massively parallel computing systems consisting of an extremely large number of simple processors with many interconnections. ANN models attempt to use some "organizational" principles believed to be used in the human.

1.3.1. Process Knowledge Critical

Empirical models circumvent the need for rigorous calculations and model inputs. Actual process data are used to develop relationships among key variables with adjustable parameters provided the best possible fit to the data. Second-order effect and process noise may be lumped into single input, or "fudge factor". Such empirical models are effective when employed over the range in which they were fitted to real process data, but cannot be reliably extrapolated. Empirical models can benefit from process understanding which will allow them to develop their models with a form similar to first principle models. Without any process understanding selecting a compact model that sufficiently represents reality is difficult, so the models become less robust and more subject to over fitting. To understand the value of using an ANN for empirical modeling, it is helpful to briefly compare an ANN with its biological origins. A natural neuron as shown in Fig. 1.1, is a nerve cell that consists of the following :

- The cell body contain the nucleus.
- One or more dendrites which as a rule, conduct impulses toward the cell body.
- The axon, which conduct impulse away from the cell body.
- Synapses, which are microscopic gaps between neurons where the termination of the axon of one neuron come into close proximity with the dendrites or cell body of another.

In the simplest scenario, natural neurons conduct impulse from receptor organs (such as eyes) to effectors organs (such as muscles). Impulses pass in one direction only. They enter the dendrites (inputs) and are weighted-that is, some impulses are stronger than others. Some impulses exited and other inhibit. The effects of all weighted inputs are summed. If the sum is equal to or greater than the threshold for the neuron then it first (gives output).

An artificial neuron (or node) handles three basic functions :

- Evaluates inputs and determining each one's strength.
- Calculates a total for the combined inputs and compares it with some threshold level.
- Determines the proper output.

Each artificial neuron can have multiple inputs. All of which are received simultaneously (see Fig. 1.2). Each connection between two neurons is given a weight value (*Wij*), which determine that input relative impact. (The initial weight for a neuron will change as the networks learn from various inputs and follow its rules for modification).

Several important activities take place within the design of an artificial neuron (think of it as being like the cell body). Each input signal is multiplied by a weight, and the results are summed together with a constant bias input, which resembles the threshold in a natural neuron. The sum of the input is then passed to a transfer function. If the sum of the input is greater than zero, the neuron generates an excitatory (positive signal). If the sum is less than zero, an inhibitory (negative) signal is generated. Both response types are significant.

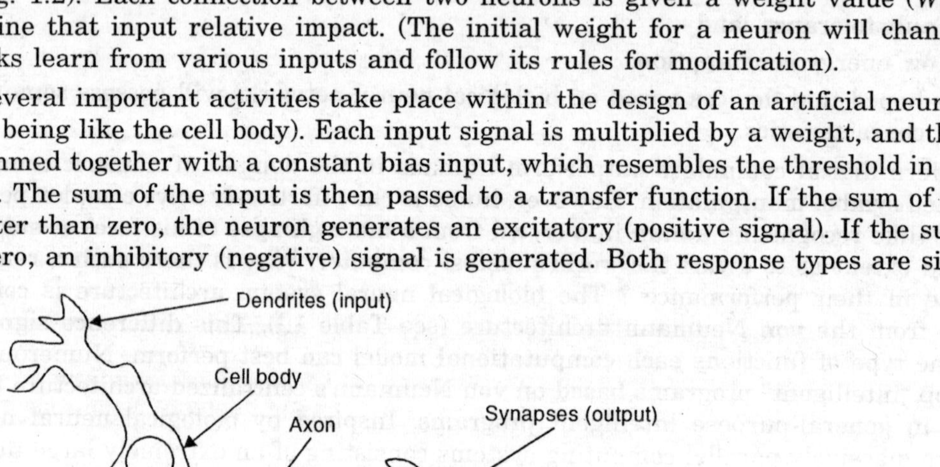

Fig. 1.1. *Artificial neural networks are created from nodes on natural neurons.*

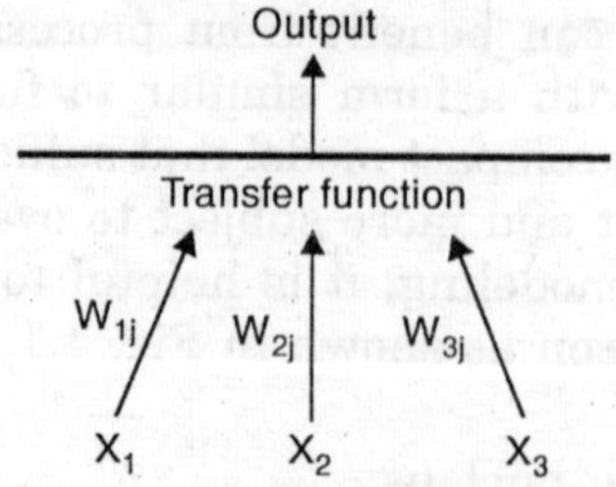

W1i = Synaptic weights

Xi = Input signals (x_1, x_2,............x_i)

Yi = Output signals (y_1, y_2,............y_i)

Li = Weighted sum of the inputs

= Σwij Xi

Fig. 1.2. *Nodes receives multiple inputs and give each a weight that changes as the network learns.*

The synaptic transfer function is generally nonlinear, though linear (straight link) functions are sometimes used in combination with nonlinear transfer functions. Often the transfer function of choice is a sigmoid, or S-shaped curve, such as that in Fig. 1.3. The curve approaches a minimum and maximum value at the asymptotes. Mathematically, this function is convenient because its derivatives are easy to calculate.

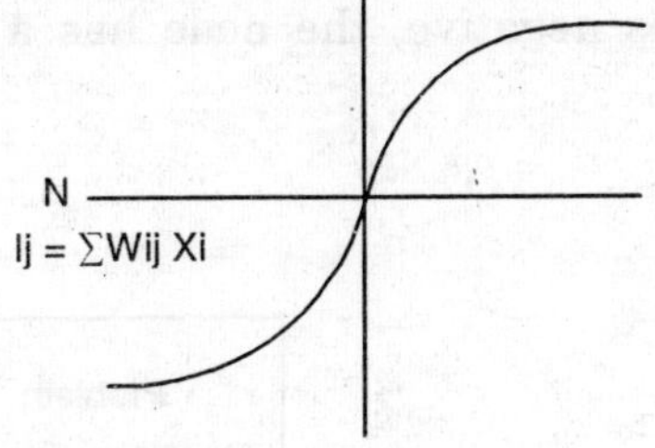

$$Yi = \frac{1-e^{ij}}{1+e^{ij}}$$

e = mathematical constant (Euler's number)

Ij = sum of inputs to the transfer functions

N = total number of inputs to this neuron including the bias

ij = an element of a vector or a matrix

Fig. 1.3. *Transfer functions are often smooth, sigmoidal curves.*

The output (*Yj*) of an artificial neuron can be used as the input to one or more other neurons. The human brain includes approximately one hundred billion (10^{11}) neurons. Typically each neuron can interact directly with 10,000 others, yielding a total of 10^{15} connections. Brainpower comes from the sheer numbers and multiple connections of so many neurons operating in concert. Can a computer be made in a similar fashions ? Fortunately we are not trying to create brains, but machines that model the biology enough to achieve useful end results.

1.3.2 Neural Network Models

Neural architectures are based on a computing threshold logic unit (TLU) with nodes associated with concepts and are weights representing similarity. The implementing elements, TLU consists of a single concept node with all the input signals and an output signal in Fig. 1.4.

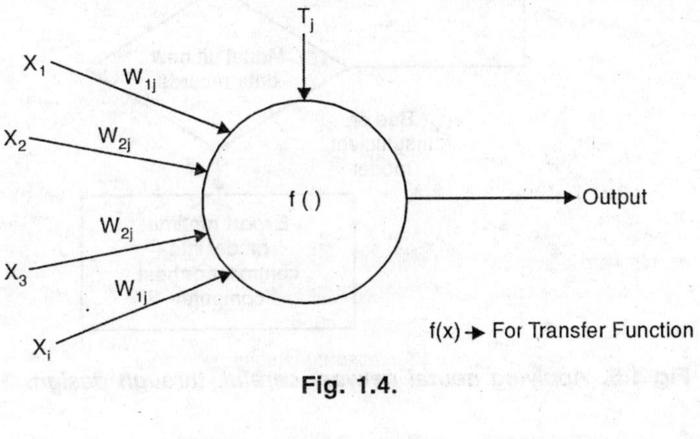

Fig. 1.4.

The output form a node is the internal threshold. The internal threshold for the *j*th node, denoted T_j, controls activation of that node. The node calculates all its $Xi\ W_{ij,s}$: sums the term together, and then calculates the total activation by subtracting the internal threshold value.

$$\text{Total activation} = X = f\,[\Sigma^{n}_{i=1} Xi\ W_{ij} - T_j]$$

If T_j is large and positive, the node has a high internal threshold, which inhibits node firing. Conversely, if threshold is negative, the node has a low internal threshold, which excites node firing.

1.3.3. Isn't Rigorous Better ?

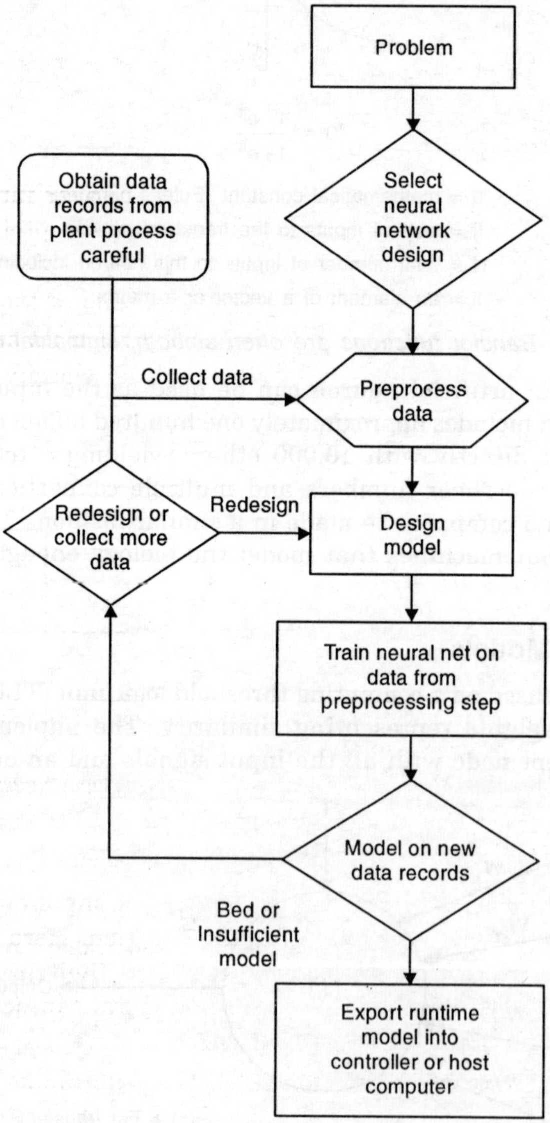

Fig 1.5. *Applying neural network careful, through design.*

Some process are well understood, allowing creation of very robust inferential models based on first principles describing the physics and chemistry of problems. However first principle model may suffer in accuracy due to noise and unmeasured second-order effects. They also often contain bias terms, or "fudge factors." Which must be adjusted based on occasional analyses.

For less understood process engineers have long used empirical models, which they generate by correlating process data with actual analysis. This approach is useful when the process is too complex to model in a practical way. Empirical modeling however brings many challenges, including selection of a suitable model form and conditioning of data. Empirical models can be exceptionally accurate when sufficient data are available, but they are not as robust as first principle models and are unreliable when used on data that are different from developing data.

1.4. TRANSFER FUNCTIONS

The transfer function in Fig. 1.6 may be a linear or a nonlinear function of *n*. A particular transfer function is chosen to satisfy some specification of the problem that the neuron is attempting to solve.

A variety limit transfer function, shown on the left side of Fig. 1.6, sets the output of the neuron to 0 if the function argument is less than 0, or 1 if its argument is greater than or equal to 0. We will use is function to create neurons that classify inputs into two distinct categories.

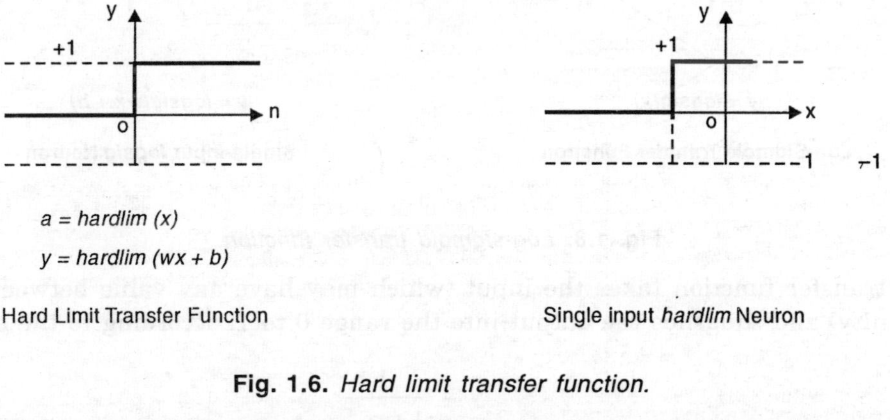

a = hardlim (x)

y = hardlim (wx + b)

Hard Limit Transfer Function

Single input *hardlim* Neuron

Fig. 1.6. *Hard limit transfer function.*

The graph on the right side of Fig. 1.6 illustrates the input/output characteristics of a single-input neuron that uses a hard limit transfer function. Here we can see the effect of the weight and the bias. Note that an icon for the hard limit transfer function is shown between the two figures. Such icons will replace the general *f* in network diagrams to show the particular transfer function that is being used.

The output of a *linear transfer function* is equal to its input :

$$y = x,$$

as illustrated in Fig. 1.7.

Neurons with this transfer function are used in the ADALINE networks, which are discussed in chapter 10.

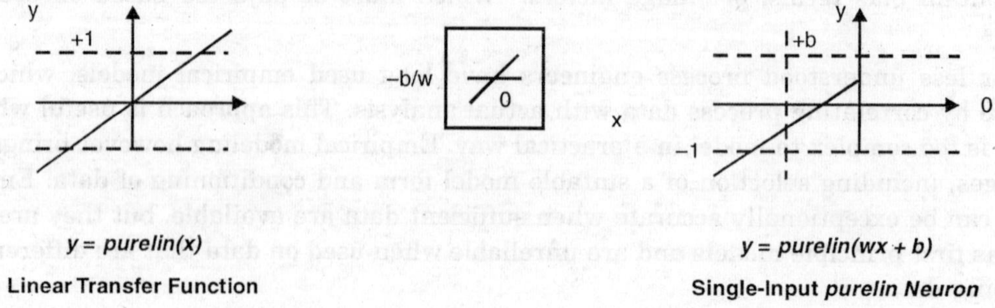

Fig. 1.7. *Linear transfer function.*

The output (a) versus input (p) characteristic of a single-input linear neuron with a bias is shown on the right of Fig. 1.8.

The log-sigmoid transfer function is shown in Fig. 1.8.

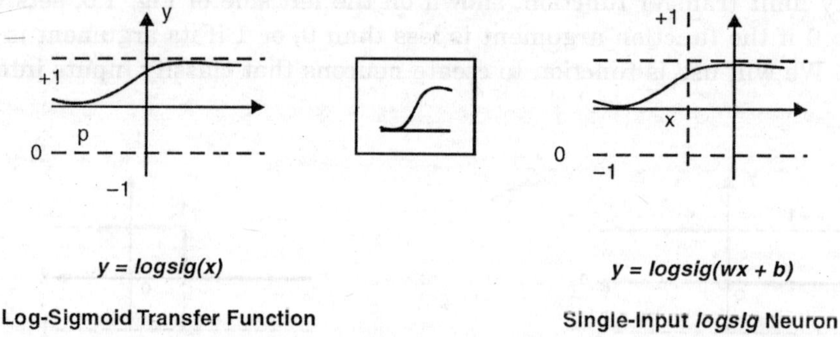

Fig. 1.8. *Log-sigmoid transfer function.*

This transfer function takes the input (which may have any value between plus and minus infinity) and squashes the output into the range 0 to 1, according to the expression :

$$y = \frac{1}{1 + e^{-x}}$$

The log-sigmoid transfer function is commonly used in multilayer networks that are trained using the backpropagation algorithm, in part because this function is differentiable.

Most of the transfer functions used in this book are summarized in Table 1.2. Of course, you can define other transfer functions in addition to those shown in Table 1.2, if you wish.

Table 1.2. Transfer Functions

Name	***Input/Output Relations***	***Icon***	***MATLAB Function***
Hard Limit	$y = 0 \quad x < 0$ $y = 1 \quad x \geq 0$	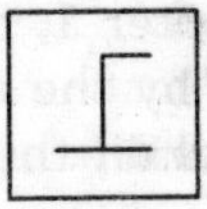	hardlim
Symmetrical Hard Limit	$y = -1 \quad x < 0$ $y = +1 \quad x \geq 0$		hardlims
Linear	$y = x$	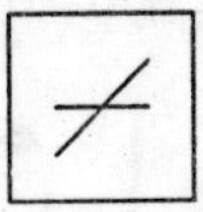	purelin
Saturating Linear	$y = 0 \quad x < 0$ $y = x \quad 0 \leq x \leq 1$ $y = 0 \quad x > 1$	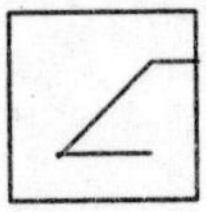	Satlin
Symmetric Saturating Linear	$y = -1 \quad x < -1$ $y = n \quad -1 \leq x \leq 1$ $y = 1 \quad x > 1$	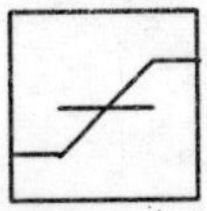	Satlins
Log-Sigmoid	$y = \dfrac{1}{1+e^{-x}}$		logsig
Hyperbolic Tangent Sigmoid	$y = \dfrac{e^x - e^{-x}}{e^x - e^{-x}}$	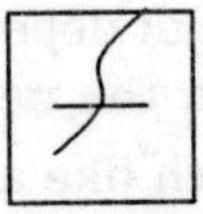	Tansig
Positive Linear	$y = 0 \quad x < 0$ $y = x \quad 0 \leq x$	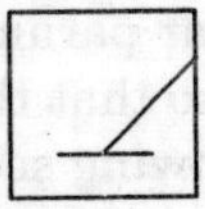	poslin
Competitive	$y = 1$ neuron with max n $y = 0$ all other neurons		compet

1.5. NEURAL NETWORK ARCHITECTURES

1.5.1. Neuron Model

Single-Input Neuron

A single-input neuron is shown in Fig. 1.9. The scalar input x is multiplied by the scalar *weight* w to form wx, one of the terms that is sent to the summer. The other input, I, is multiplied by a *bias* b and then passed to the summer. The summer output n, often referred to as the *net input*, goes into a *transfer function* f, which produces the scales neuron output a.

(Some authors use the term "activation function" rather that *transfer function* and "offset" rather than *bias*). If we relate this simple model back to the biological neuron that we discussed in chapter 1, the weight w corresponds to the strength of a synapse, the cell body is represented by the summation and the transfer function, and the neuron output a represents the signal on the axon.

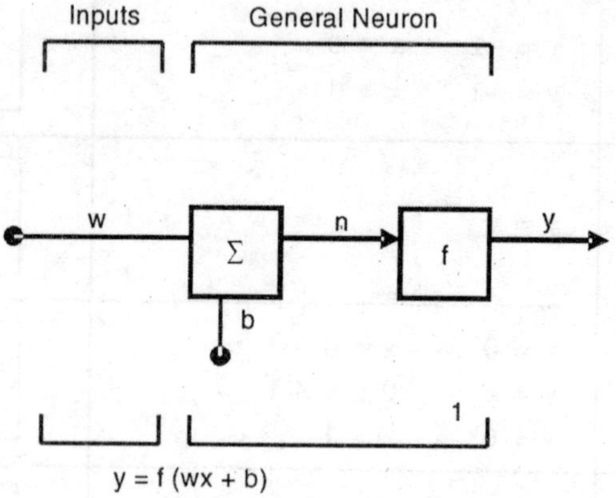

Fig. 1.9. *Single-Input neuron.*

The neuron output is calculated as

$$y = f\,(wx + b)$$

If, for instance, $w = 3$, $x = 2$ and $b = -1.5$, then

$$A = f\,(3\,(2) - 1.5) = f\,(4.5)$$

The actual output depends on the particular transfer function that is chosen. We discuss transfer functions in the next section.

The bias is much like a weight, except that it has a constant input of 1. However, if you do not want to have a bias in a particular neuron, it can be omitted. Note that w and x are both adjustable scalar parameters of the neuron. Typically the transfer function is chosen by some learning rule so that the neuron input/output relationship meets some specific goal. As described in the following section, we have different transfer functions for different purposes.

Single Layer Feedforward Network

This type of network comprises of two layers, namely the *input layer* and the *output layer*. The *input layer neurons* receive the input signals and the *output layer neurons* receive the output signals. The synaptic links carrying the weights connect every input neuron to the output neuron but not viceversa. Such a network is said to be *feedforward* in type or acyclic in nature. Despite the two layers, the network is termed single layer since it is the output layer, alone which performs computation. The input layer merely transmits the signals to the output layer. Hence, the name single layer *feedforward network*. Fig. 1.10 illustrates an example network.

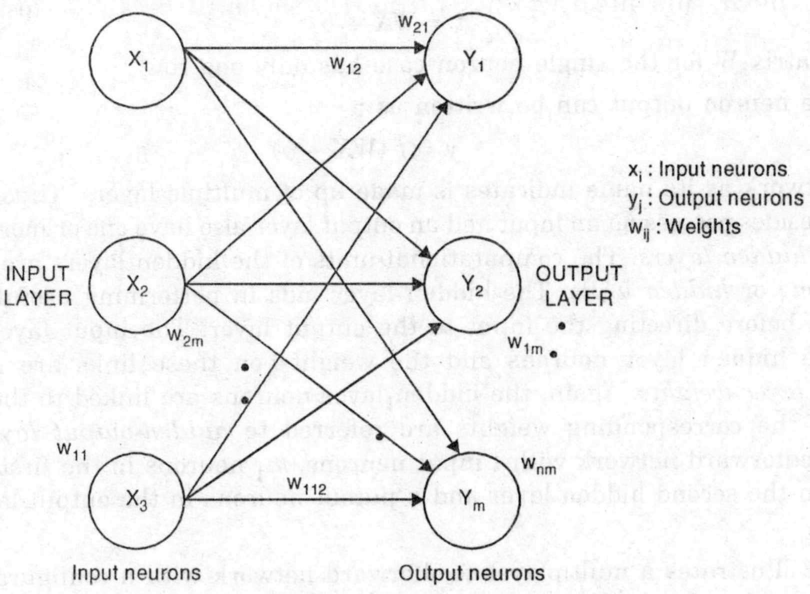

Fig. 1.10. *Single layer feedforward network.*

1.5.2. Multilayer Feedforward Network

Multiple-Input Neuron

Typically, a neuron has more than one input. A neuron with R inputs is shown in Fig. 1.11. The individual inputs $x_1, x_2 ..... x_R$ are each weighted by corresponding elements $w_{1.1}, w_{1.2} ... w_{1.R}$ of the weight matrix W.

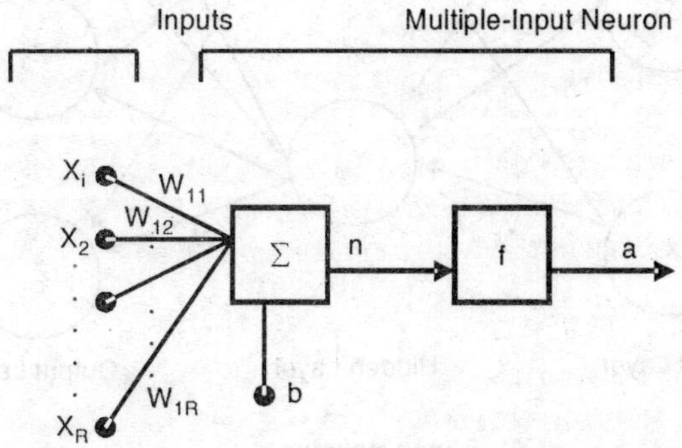

Fig. 1.11. *Multiple-input neuron.*

The neuron has a bias b, which is summed with the weighted inputs to form the net input n :

$$\eta = W_{11}X_1 + W_{12}X_2 + ... + W_{1R}\ X_R + b$$

This expression can be written in matrix form :

$$n = WX + b$$

where the matrix W for the single neuron case has only one row.

Now the neuron output can be written as :

$$y = f(WX + b)$$

This network as its name indicates is made up of multiple layers. Thus, architectures of this class besides possessing an input and an output layer also have one or more intermediary layers called *hidden layers*. The computational units of the hidden layers are known as the *hidden neurons* or *hidden units*. The hidden layer aids in performing useful intermediary computations before directing the input to the output layer. The input layer neurons are linked to the hidden layer neurons and the weights on these links are referred to as *input-hidden layer weights*. Again, the hidden layer neurons are linked to the output layer neurons and the corresponding weights are referred to *hidden-output layer weights*. A multilayer feedforward network with l input neurons, m_1 neurons in the first hidden layer, m_2 neurons in the second hidden layer and n putout neurons in the output layer is written as $1\text{-}m_1\text{-}m_2\text{-}n$.

Fig. 1.12 illustrates a multiplayer feedforward network with a configuration $1\text{–}m\text{–}n$.

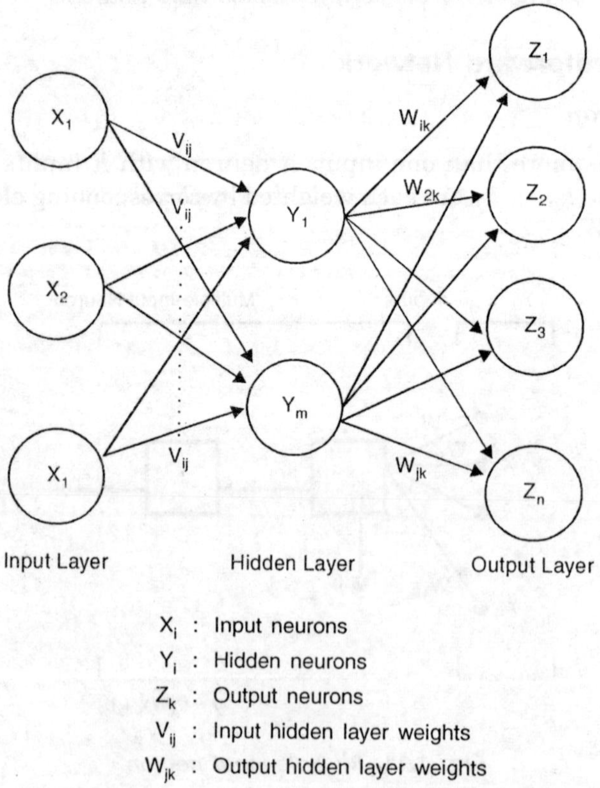

Fig. 1.12. *A multilayer feedforward network (l-m-n configuration).*

Obviously, there are many ways to combine artificial neurons to construct a network. One of the most common and most useful in the process industry is to connect the neurons to take a multiplayer network (MFN). Such as the one shown in Fig. 1.13. In this the neurons are combines to form three levels input, hidden and output.

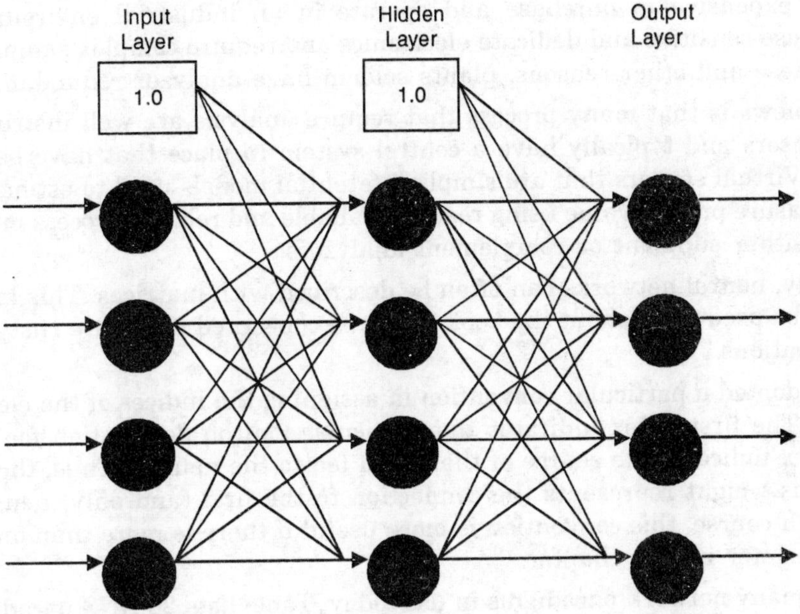

Fig. 1.13.

Bias neuron provide a constant input to each neuron in the network.It is a feedforward network because when fully concerned the output of each neuron in a layer act as a input to all the neurons in the next layer, with none sending outputs to neurons in their own layer or any previous layers. Given enough neurons, kolmogorov proved that some layered backpropagation network can implement any arbitrary complex, real-valued mapping from one space to another. (see piovoso. M.J and A.J. Owens, "Sensor data analysis Using Artificial Neural Networks". In chemical process control-CPCIV, edited by Y.Arkun and W.H.Ray, Padre Island, Tex, 1991, pp. 101-118. The hidden layer process information the input layer and sends the results to the output layer. The hidden layer is internal to the network and has no direct contact with the outside world. Hidden neurons usually have a sigmoidal transfer functions necessary to capture nonlinear information.The output layer sends out calculated values the neural net's output information. Typically the output layer consists of linear neuron that collects inputs from all the neurons in the hidden layer. Bias neurons are necessary in a feedforward network, as shown in Fig. 1.13. They are connected to each neuron except in the input layer. The bias neuron behave as other neuron in the same layer except they do not received input other neurons. They are constant source as that provide a value of 1.0. The neural network described above is fully connected three layers, feedforward backpropagation network. This neural network type has proven the most common and practical for process-industry applications. It is not the apply type of neural network, however the concept of using a neural network as a modeling tool can be applied to solve many types of problems. Sometimes the nature of the problem or the nature of the data suggests an alternate network design or training methodology.

Perhaps the most successful application of neural networks in the process industry is the virtual sensor. Many important process measurements, especially those involving quantitative analysis of products or intermediates, are difficult to obtain online. Despite the difficulty adequate process control or quality control requires determination of these physical or chemical properties. In such cases, plant personals must live with online analyzers that are frequently expensive to purchase and operate in an industrial environment. Online analyzers may use sensitive and dedicate electronics and require complex sample extractions systems. For these and other reasons, plants seldom have analyzer redundancy.

The good news is that many process that require analysis are well instrumented with a variety of sensors and typically have a control system in place that have been collecting data for years. Virtual sensors that are simply inferential models used to estimate or predict a difficult to measure process value using readily available and reliable process measurements, can step in to either supplant or complement analyzers.

Fortunately, neural networks can often be described with matrices. This kind of matrix expression will be used throughout the book. Don't be concerned if you are rusty with matrix and vector operations.

We have adopted a particular convention in assigning the indices of the elements of the weight matrix. The first index indicates the particular neuron destination for that weight. The second index indicates the source of the signal fed to the neuron. Thus, the indicates in $w_{1.2}$ say that this weight represents the connection to the first (and only) neuron from the second source. Of course, this convention is more useful if there is more than one neuron, as will be the base later in this chapter.

There are many network paradigms in use today. Table lists 26 ANS paradigms divided into four categories as shown in the CRC Critical Reviews in Artificial intelligence.

An Artificial Neutral Network is defined as a data processing system consisting of a large number of simply highly interconnected processing elements (artificial neurons) in an architecture inspired b the structure of the cerebral cortex of the brain (Tsoukalas and Uhrig, 1997). Generally an ANN structure can be represented using a *directed graph*. A *graph* G is an ordered 2-tuple (V, E) consisting of a set V of *vertices* and a set E of *edges*. When each edge is assigned an orientation, the graph is directed and is called *directed graph* or a *digraph*. Fig. 1.14 illustrates a digraph. Digraphs assume significance in Neutral Network theory since signals in NN systems are restricted to flow in specific directions.

The vertices of the graph may represent neurons (input/output) and the edges, the synaptic links. The edges are labeled by the weights attached to the synaptic links.

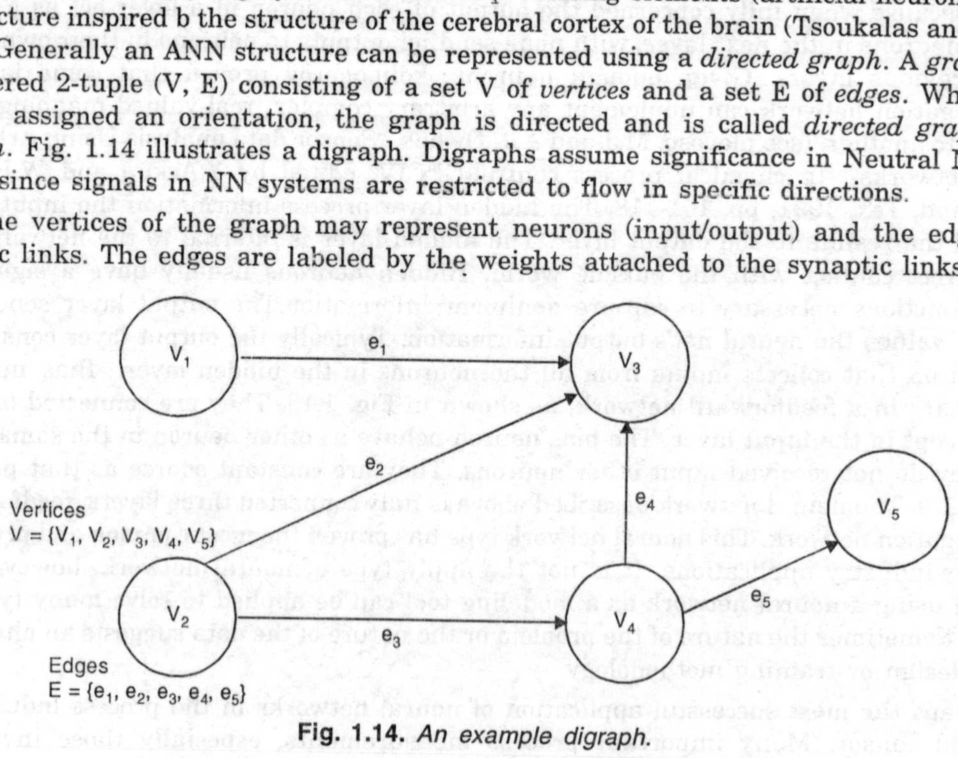

Fig. 1.14. *An example digraph.*

There are several classes of NN, classified according to their learning mechanisms. However, we identify three fundamentally different classes of Networks. All the three classes employ the digraph structure for their representation.

1.6. ARTIFICIAL NEURAL NETWORK LEARNING/TRAINING PROCESS

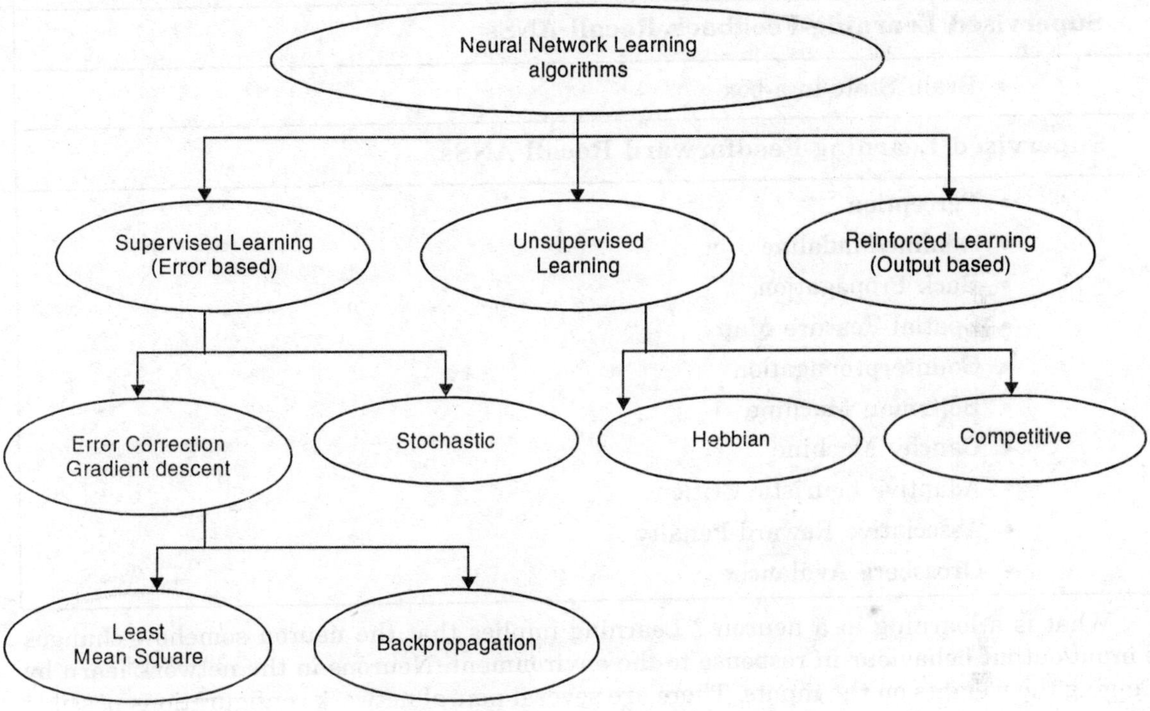

Fig. 1.15. *Classification of learning algorithms.*

Table 1.3. Artificial Neural systems (ANS) paradigms

Unsupervised Learning–Feedback Recall ANSs
▪ Additive Grossberg ANS ▪ Shunting Grossberg ANS ▪ Binary Adaptive Resonance ▪ Discrete Hopfield ANS ▪ Continuous Hopfield ANS ▪ Discrete Bidirectional Associative Memory ▪ Temporal Associative Memory ▪ Adaptive Bidirectional associative Memory ▪ Competitive adaptive Bidirectional Associative Memory ▪ Adaptive Inference Fuzzy Cognitive Map

Unsupervised learning-Feedforward Recall ANSs
• Learning Matrix • Drive Reinforcement ANS • Linear Associative Memory • Optimal Linear Associative Memory
Supervised Learning-Feedback Recall ANSs
• Brain State-in-a-box
Supervised Learning-Feedforward Recall ANSs
• Perception • Adaline/Madaline • Back Propagation • Spatial Feature Map • Counterpropagation • Boltzman Machine • Cauchy Machine • Adaptive heuristic Critic • Associative Reward-Penalty • Grossberg Avalanche

What is a learning in a neuron ? Learning implies that the neuron somehow changes its input/output behaviour in response to the environment. Neurons in the network learn by changing the weights on the inputs. There are several neural network configurations possible such as back-propagation learning is widely used for process applications.

Learning methods in Neural Networks can be broadly classified into three basic types : supervised, unsupervised, and reinforced.

1.6.1 Supervised Learning

In this, every input pattern that is used to train the network is associated with an output pattern, which is the target or the desired pattern. A teacher is assumed to be present during the learning process, when a comparison is made between the network's computed output and the correct expected output, to determine the error. The error can be used to change network parameters, which result in an improvement performance.

1.6.2 Unsupervised Learning

In this learning method, the target output is not presented to the network. It is as if there is no teacher to present the desired patterns and hence, the system learns of its own by discovering and adapting to structural features in the input patterns.

1.6.3 Reinforced Learning

In this method, a teacher though available, does not present the expected answer but only indicates if the computed output is correct or incorrect. The information provided helps the network in its learning process. A reward is given for a correct answer computed and a penalty for a wrong answer. But, reinforced learning is not one of the popular forms of learning.

Supervised and unsupervised learning methods, which are most popular forms of learning, have found expression through various rules. Some of the widely used rules have been presented below :

1.6.4 Hebbian Learning

This rule was proposed by Hebb (1949) and is based on correlative weight adjustment. This is the oldest learning mechanism inspired by biology.

In this, the input-output pattern pairs (*Xi, Yi*) are associated by the weight matrix *W*, known as the correlation matrix. It is computed as

$$W = \sum_{i=1}^{n} XiYi^T$$

Here, Y_i^T is the transpose of the associated output vector Y_i. Numerous variants of the rule have been proposed (Anderson, 1983; Kosko, 1985; Lippman, 1987; Linsker, 1988).

1.6.5 Gradient Descent Learning

This is based on the minimization of error *E* defined in terms of weights and the activation function of the network. Also, it is required that the activation function employed by the network is differentiable, as the weight update is dependent on the gradient of the error *E*.

Thus, if ΔW_{ij} is the weight update of the link connecting the ith and *j*th neuron of the two neighbouring layers, then ΔW_{ij} is defined as

$$\Delta W_{ij} = \eta \frac{dE}{dW_{ij}}$$

where, η is the learning rate parameter and dE/dW_{ij} is the error gradient with reference to the weight W_{ij}.

The Windrow and Hoffs Delta rule and Backpropagation learning rule are all examples of this type of learning mechanism.

1.6.6 Competitive Learning

In this method, those neurons which respond strongly to input stimuli have their weights updated. When an input pattern is presented, all neurons in the layer compete and the winning neuron undergoes weight adjustment. Hence, it is a "winner-takes-1l" strategy.

1.6.7 Stochastic Learning

In this method, weights are adjusted in a probabilistic fashion. An example is evident in stimulated annealing-the learning mechanism employed by Boltzman and Cauchy machines, which are a kind of NN systems.

1.7 APPLICATIONS OF NEURAL NETWORKS

A recent newspaper articles described the use of neural networks in literature research by Aston University. It stated that "the network can be taught to recognize individual writing styles, and the researchers used it to compare works attribute to Shakespeare and his contempories." A popular science television programme recently documented the use of neural network by an Italian research institute to test the purity of olive oil. These examples are indicative of the broad range of applications that can be found for neural networks. The applications are expanding because neural networks are good as solving problems, not just in engineering, science and mathematics but in medicine, business finance and literature as well.

Their application to a wide variety of problems in many fields makes them very attractive. Also, faster computer and faster algorithms have made it possible to use neural network to solve complex industrial problems that formerly required too much computation.

The following note and table of Neural Network Application are reproduced here from the Neural Network Toolbox for MATLAB with the permission of the MathWorks, Inc.

The 1998 DARPA Neural Network Study lists various neural network applications, beginning with the adaptive channel, equalizer in about 1984. This device, which is an outstanding commercial success, is a single neuron network used in long distance telephone systems to stabilize voice signals. The DRPA report goes on to list other commercial applications, including a small word organizer, a process monitor, a sonar classifier and a risk analysis system.

Neural networks have been applied in many fields since the DRPA report was written. A list of some applications mentioned in the literature given below :

Aerospace. High performance aircraft autopilots, flight path simulations, aircraft control systems, autopilot enhancements, aircraft component solutions, aircraft component fault detectors.

Automotive. Automobile automatic guidance systems, warranty activity analyzers.

Banking. Checks and other document readers, credit application evaluators.

Defense. Weapon steering target tracking, object discrimination. Facial recognition, new kinds of sensors, sonar, radar and image signal processing including data compression, feature extraction and noise suppression, signal/image identification.

Electronics. Code sequence prediction, integrated circuit chip layout, process control, chip failure analysis, machine vision, voice synthesis, nonlinear modeling.

Financial. Real state appraisal, loan advisor, mortgage screening, corporate bond rating, credit line use analysis, portfolio trading programme, corporate financial analysis, currency price prediction.

Insurance. Policy application evaluation, product optimization.

Manufacturing. Manufacturing process control, predict design and analysis, process and machine diagnosis, real time particle identification, visual quality inspection systems, beer testing, welding quality analysis, paper quality prediction, computer chip quality analysis, analysis of grinding applications, chemical product design analysis, machine maintenance analysis, project bidding, planning and management, dynamic modeling of chemical process systems.

Medical. Breast cancer cell analysis, EEG and ECG analysis, prosthesis design, optimization of transparent times, hospital expenses reduction, hospital quality improvement, and emergency room test advisement.

Oil and Gas. Exploration.

Robotics. Trajectory control, forklift robot, manipulator controllers, vision systems.

Speech. Speech recognition, speech compression, vowel classification, text to speech synthesis.

Securities. Market analysis, automatic bond rating, and stock trading advisory systems.

Telecommunications. Image and data compression, automated information services, real time translation of spoken language, customer language, customer payment processing systems.

Transportation. Truck brake diagnosis systems, vehicle scheduling, routing systems.

Process control. To control various process parameters like temperature, pressure, flow, level etc.

1.7.1 Characteristics of Neural Networks

(*i*) The NNs exhibit mapping capabilities, that is, they can map input patterns to their associated output patterns.

(*ii*) The NNs learn by examples. Thus, NN architectures can be 'trained' with known examples of a problem before they are tested for their 'inference' capability on unknown instances of the problem. They can, therefore, identity new objects previously untrained.

(*iii*) The NNs posses the capability to generalize. Thus, they can predict new outcomes from past trends.

(*iv*) The NNs are robust systems and are fault tolerant. They can, therefore, recall full patterns from incomplete, partial or noisy patterns.

(*v*) The NNs can process information in parallel, at high speed, and in a distributed manner.

1.7.2 Advantages and Disadvantages

Advantages

1. ANSs are not programmed. They learn by example with no requirement of prior knowledge.
2. ANSs are very robust in nature, and can operate even if portions of the input data are incorrect.

   The network can see through noise and distortions to obtain the true essence of real-world environment being viewed.
3. ANSs are capable of making generalizations to reach new conclusions based upon past experience.
4. ANSs can solve any problem involving the mapping of input data into input data.

Disadvantages

1. Learning takes time. Depending on the complexity of the ANS and the quantity of classification data (*i.e.,* training sets), the learning process can take hours, days or even weeks.
2. Even though the ANSs can see through noise and distortions most of the time, there will be cases where the network is tricked or sees an "optical illusion".
3. Being good at making generalizations and reaching new conclusions does not lead to being precise or logical. Consider the following problem :

$$2.14325 + 3.25617 = 5.39942$$

The ANS would conclude that adding the two numbers together will result in a number that is probably very close to 5.4. Now looking at a logical problem :

$$\text{IF } a = b \text{ AND } b = c \text{ THEN } a = c$$

The neural network would conclude that a is equal to a term is probably really close to term c. These advantages and disadvantages will be addressed later.

1.8. HISTORY OF ANN SYSTEM DEVELOPMENTS

History of neural networks	
1940s	First research in neural networks describes how biological systems might leam.
1957	Comell University : Visual pattern recognition system – perception
1959	Stanford University : Bemard Widrow developes adaptive linear element model which results in adaptive filters used to eliminate echos on telephone lines.
1969	Marvin Minsky and Seymour Papert publish a book stating perceptrons could not solve ¯Exclusive Or,¯ which results in neural network research losing favor.
1982	John Hopfield, CalTech, renews scientific community interest in neural networks with a presentation to the National Academy of Sciences.
1986	Dave Rumelhart and James McClelland develop Beackpropagation Neural Network.

1.9. WHERE DID FUZZY LOGIC COME FROM ?

The concept of Fuzzy Logic (FL) was conceived by Lotfi Zadeh, a professor at the University of California at Berkley, and presented not as a control methodology, but as a way of processing data by allowing partial set membership rather than crisp set membership or non-membership. This approach to set theory was not applied to control systems until the 70's due to insufficient small-computer capability prior to that time. Professor Zadeh reasoned that people do not require precise, numerical information input, and yet they are capable of highly adaptive control. If feedback controllers could be programmed to accept noisy, imprecise input, they would be much more effective and perhaps easier to implement. Unfortunately, U.S. manufacturers have not been so quick to embrace this technology while the Europeans and Japanese have been aggressively building real products around it.

1.9.1 What is Fuzzy Logic ?

In this context, FL is a problem-solving control system methodology that lends itself to implementation in systems ranging from simple, small, embedded micro-controllers to large, networked, multi-channel PC or workstation-based data acquisition and control systems. It can be implemented in hardware, software, or a combination of both. FL provides a simple way to arrive at a definite conclusion based upon vague, ambiguous, imprecise, noisy, or missing input information. FL's approach to control problems mimics how a person would make decisions, only much faster.

1.9.2 Fuzzy/Neural Complements

Fuzzy logic and neural networks, at first glance, may seem to have very little in common. The former is a generalized multi-value logic, while the latter consist of one or small, interconnected processing elements.

Just the opposite is true, however, where the two topics appear unrelated, they sometimes complement each other. On the other hand, from certain perspectives, the two topics are one and the same.

For example, a fuzzy IF-THEN statement and an appropriately defined neuron are the same concept expressed in two different manners. The parts of the conditional statement's antecedent correspond to the neuron's input, while the conditional statement consequent corresponds to the neuron's output.

Certainty factors (membership values) attached to the conditional are really weights, which we also find within a neuron. When the conditional antecedent is satisfied, the consequent is executed or fired. Similarly when the neuron inputs hold values sufficient for reaching the threshold value, the neuron's output is fired. Chaining together layer of conditionals, where the consequent of one layer form the antecedents of the next layer, is equivalent to linking layer of neurons into a network.

The differences between fuzzy logic and neural networks however, are what we can use to our advantage. The idea, of course, is to combine the two in a manner that give us the best of both techniques.

Here are just the few ways to exploit their complementary relationship :

- Neural network may be trained to generate membership values for a fuzzy logic membership function.
- Fuzzy logic functions may be used to fine tune a neural network training algorithm.
- Fuzzy logic functions or conditionals may encapsulate the input and/or output layers of a neural network. That is inputs are filtered through a fuzzy function before entering the neural network and/or outputs are filtered through a fuzzy function after being processed by the network.
- Fuzzy logic functions may access data stored within neural network-based (associative) memories.
- Fuzzy conditional statements may be used to activate subsets of a neural network-based system, and vice-versa.

Neither technique must be used exclusively in an application. Portions of the system may be implemented with fuzzy logic; other portions may be implemented with neural networks, fuzzy logic, conventional techniques, or hybrids.

This applies to both the hardware and the software of the system. The ability to train the weights of a neural network makes it a very flexible technique, suitable for use in the control laws of a control system, for example.

A network's capacity to recover from localized damage makes it invaluable for unstable environments. Although the algorithm used in the training phase of network may be time consuming, ever increasing hardware speeds may eventually permits real-time training. This kind of training "on the fly" may be useful in specialized applications.

Also fuzzy rules, by the very nature of the IF-THEN statement, are ideal for performing nonlinear control. In general, fuzzy logic and neural networks just add to the control engineer's repertoire of design techniques.

1.10. FUZZY LOGIC AND NEURAL NETWORKS

Fuzzy logic and neural networks may seem to have little in common. But, often just the opposite is true. Here's an overview of the basics.

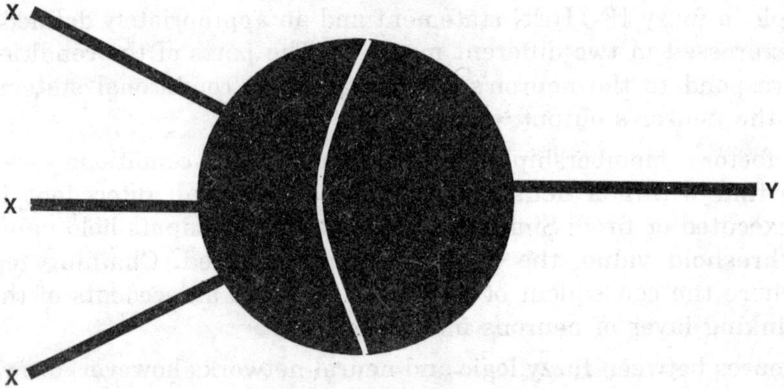

Fig. 1.16.

Combine fuzzy logic's fuzzy sets, fuzzy operators, fuzzy inference and fuzzy rules-like defuzzification-with neural networks and you can arrive at very unfuzzy real time control. (by *James R. Loos*)

Fuzzy logic, cursed with a very whimsical title, simply means multivalued logic, which include not only the conventional two valued (true/false) crisp logic, but also the logic of three or more values.

This means we can assign logic values of true, false and somewhere in between. This is where fuzziness comes in. Multi-valued logic avoid the black and white, all or nothing assignment of true or false to an assertion. Instead it permits the assignment of shades of gray.

When assigning bad value of true or false to an assertion, the numbers typically used are "1" or "0". This is the cased for programmed system. If "0" then "shades of gray" are any numbers between 0 and 1.

Therefore "nearly true" may be represented by 0.8 or 0.9, "nearly false" may be represented by 0.1 or 0.2, and "your guess is as good as mine" may be represented by 0.5. the flexibility available to us is limitless. We can associate any meaning, such as "nearly true", to any value of any granularity, such as 0.9999.

1.10.1 Fuzzy Sets

Fuzzy logic is actually built upon fuzzy set theory whereas a conventional set definitely does or definitely does not contain a particular element with a given degree of certainty. Actually this assigned certainty also exists for conventional sets.

In a conventional set, an element either does belong (certainty = 1) or does not belong (certainty = 0) to the set. In the case of fuzzy set, an element belongs to the set with a certainty of 0 (does not) or 1 (does) or any number between 0 and 1 (may be).

It is now apparent that the fuzzy set is actually a set of ordered pairs, each pair consisting of an element and its associated degree of certainty. Note that an element having a degree of 0 is not usually included in the specifications of a fuzzy set. A fuzzy set therefore may be defined in the following manner :

F = {(E1, C1), (E2, C2), (E3, C3).....(Ei, Ci)....(En, Cn)...

In this set "Ei" represents its corresponding certainty value. This certainty value is the same as the membership value or the degree of membership. The specification of the fuzzy set is a set of ordered pair known as the membership function.

Associated with any set conventional of fuzzy are its operations. Of course the set of real numbers has the operation of addition and multiplication, for example, while the crisp two valued logic sets, have the operations of AND or OR.

The AND operations requires two operands both of which must be "true" (1) to produce a true result, otherwise the result is "false" (0). The OR operations require two operands, but only one must be "true" to generate a "true" result.

These two operations allow us to make assertion in crisp logic and thus form a chain of reasoning inside a program. This combination of set members to form new quantities, new assertions or more properly, new sets, is known as assertion.

So we can combine crisp elements to form crisp results, but how do we combine fuzzy elements to form fuzzy results. The answer is : anyway we want.

Typically, a fuzzy set is provided with two operations that at least correspond to the AND or OR of crisp logic, but we have the luxury of defining those operations in a manner that bests fit the requirement of our applications. Some basic logic principles apply, but that's for another time.

For example the fuzzy counterparts of the crisp AND and OR functions may be defined as multiplication and addition respectively. Similarly we may use MIN and MAX for fuzzy replacement of crisp AND and OR.

Thus, not only may individual elements of a fuzzy set posses any of an infinite number of membership values but there is also a potentially infinite choice of fuzzy operators. In terms of flexibility this gives us a tremendous advantage over crisp logic. This is a very evident in the case of real time control.

1.10.2 Fuzzy Control

Describing the application of fuzzy logic to real time control requires the concepts of fuzzy rules and fuzzy inference. A fuzzy rule, also known as a fuzzy conditional statement or a fuzzy IF-THEN statement, says :

If x then y, where x specifies a logical conjunction of input variables and a corresponding membership value, and specifies an output variable and its corresponding membership value. Fuzzy rules have the following form :

If input 1 = high

And input 2 = low,

Then output = medium.

Three primitive functions are required to perform logical inferencing with the fuzzy rules just described. The first two, the fuzzy AND and the fuzzy OR, have been described However we get more specific about their implementation.

The fuzzy AND is the product of a rule's input membership values, generating a firing weights for the rule's output. The fuzzy OR is the normalized sum of the firing weight assigned to each rule that contributes to a particular conclusion, or fuzzy set.

Essentially, the OR calculates a single weight, $w(i)$, assigned to the membership function of such a conclusion. This is desirable for function approximation.

The AND and OR could have been defined as a minimum and a maximum respectively, or any of a number of other choices. It is upto the engineer to decide what implementation is best for a particular application.

A third primitive function needed here is defuzzification, which generates a crisp final output. Again, we have much freedom of choice for its implementation.

We are going to choose the so-called singleton method, using the weight $w(i)$ of each fuzzy output set I (conclusion) and the peak element. This is the spike or fuzzy singleton, $p(i)$, which is the element of the fuzzy output set I having the largest membership value.

The crisp output is the weighted average of the peak element values : (summation $[w(i)*p(i)])/(\text{summation}[w(i)])$.

To clarify what has just been said, here is a chronological recap of the events leading to a crisp control output :

1. For each rule, the input membership values go through the AND operation, creating a firing weight for the rule's output.
2. The firing weights of each rule contributing to a conclusion or fuzzy set go through to a conclusion or fuzzy set go through an OR operation. This creates a weight, $w(i)$, for the conclusion's output membership function.
3. The membership function weights, $w(i)$, and the corresponding peak values, $p(i)$, of all conclusions (fuzzy sets) of #2 go through a defuzzification function, generating a single crisp output.

These steps account for a single cycle of the control system. As in any control system, the cycle repeats endlessly.

A Control Example

The heart of a fuzzy real-time control system is its set of fuzzy rules. The following is an example of a fuzzy rule subset that leads to a single, crisp output of a speed control system. The output is defuzzified from a group of conclusions.

Here, the generated conclusions are for speed change (SC), while the input representing the state variables of the system, are speed error (SE), change in speed error (CSE), and operation mode (OM).

The input variables SE and CSE may have the value small (S), medium (M), or large (I). The input variable OM may have the value normal (N) or test (T). Finally the output variable SC may have the value (conclusion) of small (S), medium (m) or large (I).

If OM = N and SE = S

And CSE = S

Then SC = S

Else

If OM = N and SE = M

And CSE = S

Then SC = S

Else

If OM = N and SE = M

And CSE = M

Then SC = M

Else

If OM = N and SE = L

And CSE = M

Then SC = L

Else

If OM = T and SE = L

And CSE = L

Then SC = S

Else etc.....

In the example, above each IF-THEN rule posses a firing weight and contributes to the weight, $w(i)$, of one of the three conclusions of SC.

The conclusions are the fuzzy sets S, M and L. Their corresponding weights, $w(i)$ and peak element values, $p(i)$ determine the crisp output, calculated with the weighted average function described earlier.

Thus, if the rules contributing to S have a normalized weight of 0.5, the rules contributing to M have a normalized weight of 0.4, and the rules contributing to L have a normalized weight of 0.2, and S, M and L have peak element values of 2, 6 and 10, respectively, then the crisp output is (0.5*2 + 0.4*6 + 0.2*10/(0.5 + 0.4 + 0.2) = 4.9.

1.10.3 Neural Networks

Fuzzy logic and neural networks, as we shall see, complement each other in various ways. Neural networks for the engineer are just design techniques that draw inspiration from the workings of the brain. A neural network does not think, nevertheless neural networks do share some important characteristics with the brain. First, as it name suggest the neural network consist of a network that at least partially connected, simply processing elements.

In the biological brain, each processing element is called a neuron. These biological neurons have a body (consisting of a nucleus and a soma), a set of dendrites, an axon, and a set of synaptic buttons.

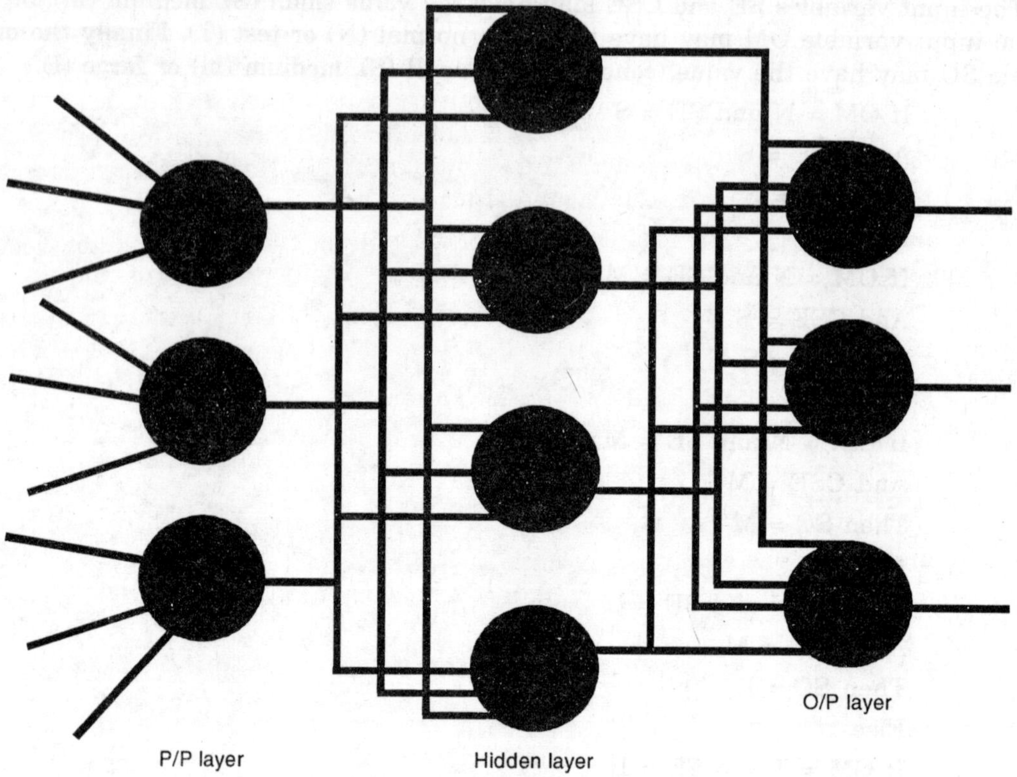

Fig. 1.17.

To the engineer or mathematician the important part are dendrites, which are really the input lines; the body which contain a transfer function; and the axon and synaptic buttons, which together form the output lines. A mathematical representation of a neuron is illustrated in Fig. 1.16.

In Fig. 1.17, the X 's represent input signals, the sigma (in the body) represents the transfer function, and the Y represents the output signal.

Not shown is the weight that is associated with each input line. Each weight, $w(i)$, is used along with the corresponding input, $x(i)$, by the transfer function which in turn, generates a value that is compared to a threshold.

If the generated value exceeds that threshold, the neuron fires, or sends a "1" or some other value representing a high assertion over the output line. If the threshold is not exceeded, the neuron sends a "0" or some value representing a low assertion over its output line. Having described a single processing element (Fig. 1.17) that a network is simply interconnection of this element. Three layers of element are illustrated above, where the output lines of one layer feed into the input lines of the succeeding layer.

How does a neural network operate ? Before addressing that question it is appropriate to first describe the actual task performed by a neural network.

In all cases, the job of any neural network can be reduced to single operation pattern recognition. Referring to the three layered Fig. 1.17 pattern recognition is simply an association between the input lines on the left side and the output lines on the right side.

For example each of the nine input lines may carry value of "1" or "0" (or "true or false" if you prefer). Therefore, in this case there are 512 (2**9) possible input combinations or patterns.

Each time a pattern is present on the input lines (100110011, for example), each of the three output lines carries the value of "1" or "0" (say, 010). Note that appearance of same input pattern always produces the same output.

Because there are more possible input patterns than output combinations, more than one input pattern may generated the same output.

For each output combination, the input patterns that produce it may be gathered into a single set. Thus, such set of input patterns form categories, identified by their corresponding output combinations.

So, now we can examine how a neural network actually works. As just explain, the input lines each carries values of "1" or "0". Note that each input line has an associated weight.

Recalling the working of a single neuron these input values enter each neuron, where they are combined, along with their weights, in some arbitrary fashion to form a value. If this value exceeds the predefined threshold, the neuron's output line is set to "1"; otherwise it is set to "0"

This process is performed for each neuron in the first (left-most) layer of Fig. 1.2. The output of the first layer neuron represent the inputs of the second (middle) layer neurons, where again, the thresholding process takes place.

Finally the second layer outputs form the third layer inputs. And thresholding operations within the third layer neurons generate the output for the entire network.

Note that the first layer is known as the input layer, the second layer is the hidden layer, and the third layer is the output layer. What we have just described is the propagation of signals through this layer of the neutral network.

1.10.4 Neural Power

The source of a neural network's power and flexibility rests in its set of weight. The neural network of Fig. 1.2 posses a maximum of 32 weights (nine in the input layer, twelve in the hidden layer, and twelve in the output layer). We say "maximum" because assigning a "0" weight is equivalent to severing the connection which alters the architecture of the network.

The weights are vital because the valued assigned to each weight of the neural network affect the functionally of the network. Specifically the weights and the architecture of the network determine which patterns the network recognizes and the categorization of those patterns.

So, how do we determine the value assigned to a network set of weight ?

Before the neural network is deemed ready for daily use, it must be subjected to a training phase. Training as its name suggests, consists of a series of repetitions.

A repetition contains the following chronological order : (1) present an input pattern to the network; (2) from the input lines, propagate the signals through all layers of the network and finally to the output lines; (3) compare the output signals to the expected output signals. If they are equal, do nothing. Otherwise, adjust the weight of the neural network according to some predefined function.

These repetitions are continued for each input pattern of the training set. If after the presentation of all training set patterns, the weight has converged to relatively stable value, training is complete. However, if the weights appear instable, the same training set is resubmitted to the network, and the training phase continues.

The predefined function that adjust the weight may take an endless number of forms. An important requirement of such a training function, as suggested above, is that it be convergent.

Also, from a practical viewpoint the training function should be computationally inexpensive, *i.e.*, fast. Speed is specially important should we ever want to train or retrain a network.

Before we turn to the application of neural networks, it is important to return to the analogy of the brain. The weight of the network represent distributed knowledge.

The 33 weights of the Fig. 1.17 network, for example, provide the ability to perform pattern recognition.

Also, with some weight removed, even to the point where the network is no longer functional, retraining may be performed on the remaining weight. Think of it with some sort of rehabilitation.

Therefore, this distribution knowledge and the resulting ability to survive and recover from localized damage is an obvious advantage for many applications. Therefore real time control system designed around neural networks have the resiliency to survive in hostile environments.

SOLVED EXAMPLES

Q. 1.1. *The input to a single-input neuron is 2.0, its weight is 2.3 and its bias is –3.*

(i) What is the net input to the transfer function ?

(ii) What is the neuron output ?

Ans.

(*i*) The net input is given by :

$N = wp + b = (2.3)(2) + (-3) = 1.6$

(*ii*) The output cannot be determined because the transfer function is not specified.

Q. 1.2. *What is the output of the neuron of Q. 1.1 if it as the following transfer functions ?*

(i) Hard limit

(ii) Linear

(iii) Log-sigmoid

Ans.

(*i*) For the hard limit transfer :

$$a = \text{hardlim}\,(1.6) = 1.0$$

(*ii*) For the linear transfer function :

$$a = \text{purelin } (1.6) = 1.6$$

(*iii*) For the log-sigmoid transfer function :

$$a = \text{logsig } (1.6) = \frac{1}{1+e^{-1.6}} = 0.8320.$$

Q. 1.3. *Given a two-input neuron with the following parameters : b = 1.2, W = [3 2] and p = [–5 6]^T, calculate the neuron output for the following transfer functions :*

(*i*) *A symmetrical hard limit transfer function.*

(*ii*) *A saturating linear transfer function.*

(*iii*) *A hyperbolic tangent sigmoid (tansig) transfer function.*

Ans. First calculate the net input n :

$$N = Wp + b = [3\ 2]\ [-5] + (1.2) = -1.8$$

Now find the outputs for each of the transfer functions :

(*i*) a = hardlims (–1.8) = –1

(*ii*) a = satin (–1.8) = 0

(*iii*) a = tansig (–1.8) = –0.9468.

Q. 1.4. *A single-layer neural network is to have six inputs and two outputs. The outputs are to be limited to and continuous over the range 0 to 1. What can you tell about the network architecture ? Specifically :*

(*i*) *How many neurons are required ?*

(*ii*) *What are the dimensions of the weight matrix ?*

(*iii*) *What kind of transfer functions can be used ?*

(*iv*) *Is a bias required ?*

Ans. The problem specifications allow you to say the following about the network :

(*i*) Two neurons, one for each output, are required.

(*ii*) The weight matrix has two rows corresponding to the two neurons and six columns corresponding to the six inputs. (The product Wp is a two-element vector.)

(*iii*) Of the transfer functions we have discussed, the logsig transfer functions would be most appropriate.

(*iv*) Not enough information is given to determine if a bias is required.

EXERCISE

1. What do you meant by transfer function ? Explain all transfer functions which are mostly used in various applications.
2. Explain biological and artificial neural networks. Define soma, dendrites, axon, activation function.

Chapter 2

FUNDAMENTAL MODELS OF ARTIFICIAL NEURAL NETWORK

2.1. BACKGROUND ON NEURAL NETWORK TECHNOLOGY

The limitation of the single layer neural network was a major factor for the "quiet years" of the 1970's in the history of backpropagation. The discovery and widespread dissemination of an effective general method of training a multilayer neural network played a major role in the re-emergence of neural networks as a tool for solving a wide variety of problems.

A method of propagating the error back to the hidden units had been discovered by Werbos in 1974, but had not gained wide publicity. This method was discovered independently by David Parker (1985) and by Le Cun (1986) again. It is similar to an earlier algorithm in optimal control theory developed by Bryston and Ho (1986). Parker's work was later refined by psychologists David Rumelhart of the University in the Parallel Distributed Processing Group and they publicized it.

2.2 BACK PROPAGATION

The backpropagation network can be used to solve problems in any areas. One such application is the NET talk which learnt to read English aloud. As is the case with most neural networks, the aim is to train the net to achieve a balance between the net's ability to respond (memorization)and the ability to give reasonable responses to the input that is similar' but not identical to the one used in training (generalization).

The training to a backpropagation net involves three stages; the feedforward of the input training pattern, the calculation and backpropagation of the associated error and the weight adjustments. After the net has been trained, its application involves only the feedforward phase.

A multilayer net can learn only input patterns to an arbitrary accuracy. More then one hidden layer can also be used through one is sufficient. The weight adjustment is based on the generalized delta rule. A weight in a neural network is a segment of the information about the input signal that has to be stored.

Figure 2.1 shows example of a single biological neuron and a simplified network of nerve cell that might typically be found in a brain. The input area of a cell is a set of inward branching fibers called dendrites. The dendrites are connected to the cell body, soma, which acts as a summing junction. The output area of the cell is the long fiber denoted as the axon connected to a set of outward branching fibers called boutons. As the cell body receives weighted inputs, a summation takes place and the activity level of the cell increases until a threshold is reached, triggering an output impulse that travels along the axon and branches to the end of the boutons.

The connection points between boutons and either other cell dendrites or somas are known as a synapses.

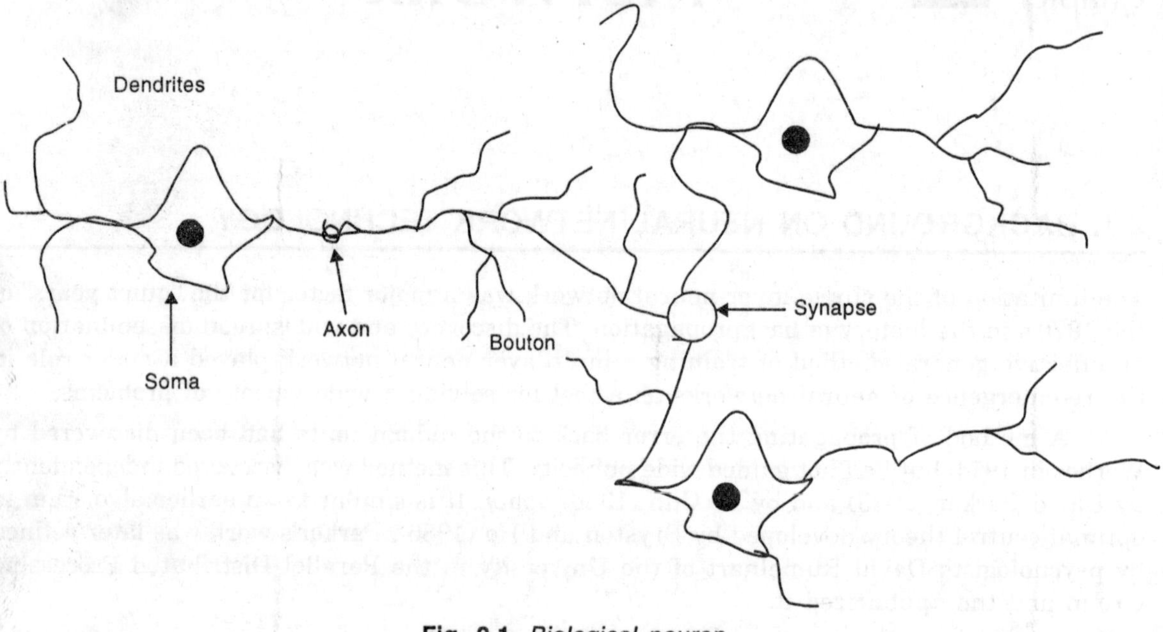

Fig. 2.1. *Biological neuron.*

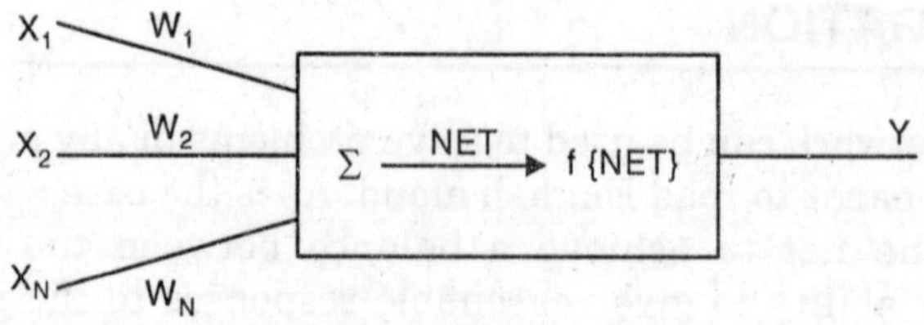

Fig. 2.2. *Artificial Neuron.*

Figure 2.2 shows the neuron model used to simulate the first order characteristics of the biological neuron. A set of inputs are applied, each representing either an input from outside the network are the output of another neuron within the network. Each input is multiplied by a weight of factor which is analogous to the synapatic strength of the biological neuron.

The weighted inputs are then summed to determine the activation level of the neuron. The output can be represented mathematically as :

$$Y = f\{X_1W_1 + X_2W_2 + \dots X_NW_N\}$$

which reduces to : $Y = f(\Sigma XnWn)$

$n = 1$

where : Y = output from a neuron

X = nth input to a neuron

Wn = nth weight applied to nth input

$f()$ = transfer function

2.2.1 Fundamentals of Back Propagation Learning

The most common form of learning utilized in neural networks today is error correction learning. Previously, mathematicians and computer scientists looked down upon error-correction learning, primarily because the technique did not work on neural networks with hidden layers. It is applied only to two-layer neural networks because we could not define how much error came from the hidden modes, and hence could not determine the weight factors for those nodes. Through a technique known as back propagation, however we can now apply error-correction learning to neural network with hidden layers. Another challenge in error-correction learning is determining the value of the learning rate, η_p. Historically, values for η_p have been restricted such that $0 < \eta < 1$, and some researchers have identified values for η, that yield stable solutions.

2.2.2. Requirements for Back Propagation Learning

Back propagation requires a perception neural network, defined as a network with only feed forward interlayer connections (no interlayer or recurrent connection). Each layer must feed sequentially into the next layer. Theories do exist for back-propagation on neural networks with multiple hidden layers, connections that skip over layers, recurrent connections, and even feedback connections (Simpson, 1990). However, for simplicity, we shall investigate only the three-layer, *A*, *B*, and *C*. Feeding into layer *a* is the input vector *I*. Thus layer *a* has *L* nodes, a_i (i = 1 to *L*), one node for each input parameter. Layer *B*, the hidden layer, has *m*

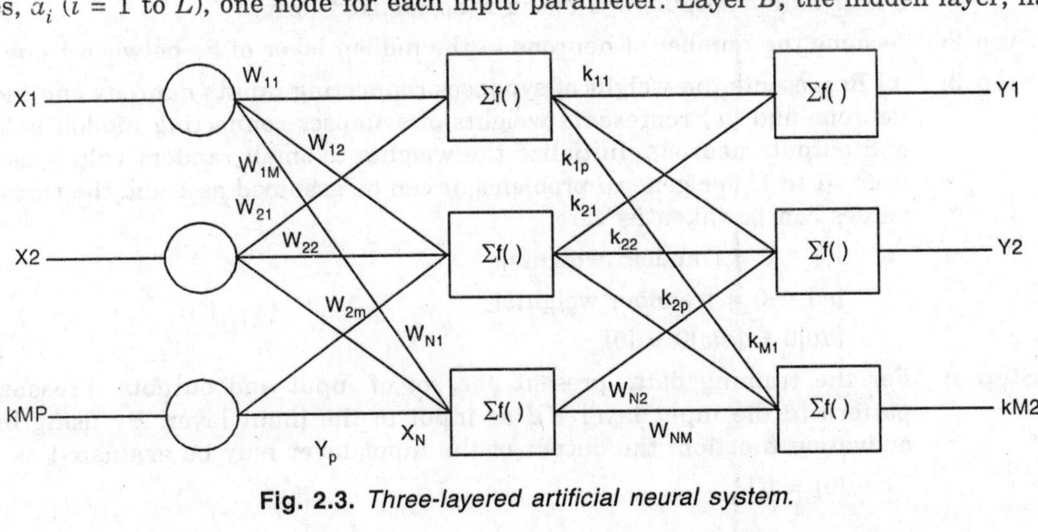

Fig. 2.3. *Three-layered artificial neural system.*

nodes, b_j (j = 1 to m). Note that in the drawing, $L = m = 3$; in practice, though, L and m need not be equal. Each layer may have a different number of nodes. Layer C, the output layer, has n nodes, c_k (k = 1 to n), again with one node for each output parameter. The interconnecting weight between the ith node of layer A and the jth node of layer B is denoted as v_{ij}, and that between the jth node of layer B and the kth node of layer C is w_{jk}. Finally, each node has an internal threshold value. For layer A, the threshold is T_{Ai}, for layer B, T_{Bi}, and for layer C, T_{ck}.

When in operation the network is supplied with a group of inputs. The updating of activation values propagates forward from the input neurons, through the hidden layer of neurons to the output neurons that provide the network response. The outputs can be mathematically represented by :

$$Y_p = f\left(\sum_{m=-1}^{M}\left(\left(f\sum_{n=-1}^{N} X_n W_{nm}\right)\right) * K_{mp}\right)$$

Y_p = The pth output of the network

X_n = The nth input to the network

W_{nm} = The mth weight factor applied to the nth input to the network

K_{mp} = The pth weight factor applied to the mth output of the hidden layer

$F(\ )$ = Transfer function (*i.e.,* sigmoid, etc.)

The ANS becomes a powerful tool that can be used to solve difficult process control applications with both advantages and disadvantages. When properly applied, the disadvantages are not really limitations when their meaning and implications are understood and addressed by the control system,

ALGORITHM

(Backpropagation Learning Algorithm)

Step 1: Normalize the inputs and the outputs with respect to their maximum values. It is proved that the neural networks work better if input and outputs lie between 0–1. For each traning pair, assume there are 'l' inputs given by 1*1{*I*}*I* and '*n*'outputs *n**1{*o*}*o* in a normalized form.

Step 2: Assume the number of neurons in the hidden layer of lie between 1 < *m* < 2l

Step 3: [*v*] Represents the weight of synapses connecting inputs neurons and hidden neurons and [*w*] represents weights of synapses connecting hidden neurons and outputs neurons. Initialize the weights to small random values usually from –1 to 1. For general problems, it can be assumed as 1 and the threshold values can be taken as zero.

[*v*] ^ 0 = [random weights]

[*w*] ^ 0 = [random weights]

[*dv*]0 = [*dw*]0 = [0]

Step 4: For the training data, present one set of input and outputs. Present the pattern to the input layer {*I*}*I* as input to the input layer. By using linear activation function, the output of the input layer may be evaluated as

$$\{0\} = \{I\}_I$$

Step 5 Compute the inputs of the hidden layer by multiplying corresponding weights of the synapses as

$$\{I\}_H = \{I\}_I$$

$$m*1 \; m*l \; l*1$$

Step 6: Let the hidden layer unit evaluate the output using the sigmoid function as

$$\left|\; \{\ 1\backslash(1 + e\ \wedge\ - \text{Ion})\ \} \;\right|$$

Step 7: Compute the inputs to the layer by multiplying corresponding weights of the synapses as

$$\{I\}_o = [w]\ \wedge\ T\ \{o\}_H$$

$$n*1 \; n*m \; m*1$$

Step 8: Let the output layer unit evaluate the output using sigmoid function as

$$\{0\}_o = \left|\; \{\ 1\backslash 1 + e\text{-}In\ \} \;\right|$$

Step 9: Calculate the error and the difference between the network output and the desired output for the ith training set as

$$E\wedge p = \sqrt{}E(T_j - O_{oj})\wedge 2/n$$

Step 10: Find $\{d\}$ as

$$\{d\} = \left|\; \{\ (T_k - O_{ok})\ O_{ok}\ (1 - O_{ok})\ \} \;\right|$$

$$n*1$$

Step 11: Find $[y]$ matrix as

$$[y] = \{o\}H<d>$$

$$m*n \; m*l \; l*n$$

Step 12: Find $[dW]\wedge t{+}1 = a[dW\}\wedge t + n[y]$

$$M*n \; m*n \; m*n$$

Step 13: Find $\{e\} = \{w\}\ \{d\}$

$$M*1 \; m*n \; n*1$$

$$\left|\; \{\ ei\ (O_{hi})\ (1 - O_{hi})\ \} \;\right|$$

*m*1 m*1*

find [*x*] matrix as

[*x*] = {*o*}*I*<*d*> ={*I*}<*d*>

*l*m 1*l l*l l*m*

Step 14: Find [*dv*]^*t*+*n*[*x*]

*L*m l*m l*m*

Step 15: Find

[*v*]^*t*+1 = [*dv*]^*t*+1

[*w*]^*t*+1= [*dw*]^*t*+1

Step 16: Find error rate = Σ*ep*/*n* set'

Step 17: Repeat steps 4–16 until the convergence in the error rate is less than the tolerance value.

Example : There are two inputs and one output as shown in figure 2.4, calculate weight changes using back propagation algorithm with the help of supervised learning and unsupervised learning.

S. No.	*Inputs*		*Outputs*
	I1	*I2*	
1.	.4	–0.7	0.1
2.	0.3	–0.5	0.05
3.	0.6	0.1	0.3
4.	0.2	0.4	0.25
5.	0.1	–0.2	0.12

The value lie between-1 to 1 and hence, there is no need to normalize the value. Assume two neurons in the hidden layer. The neural network architecture is shown in the figure 2.4.

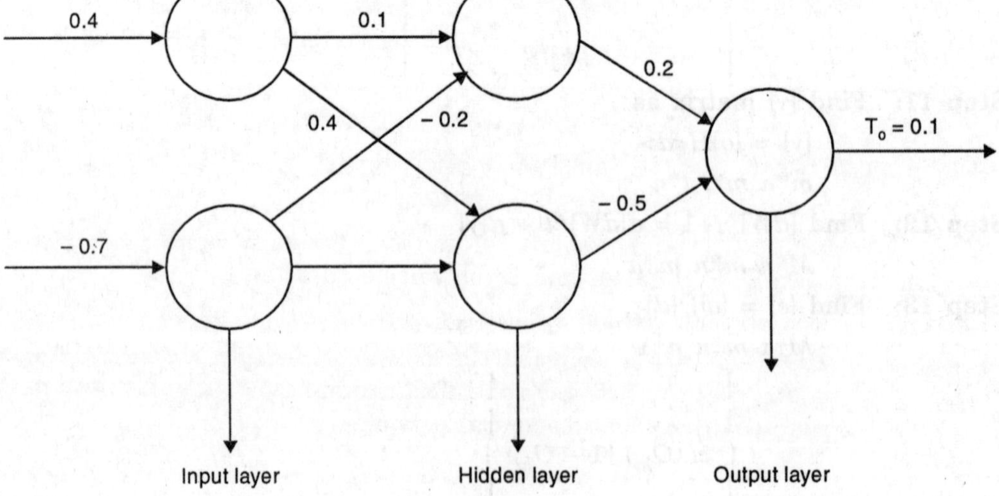

Fig. 2.4

Step 1: $\{0\}_i = \{I\}_i = |0.4|$
{-0.7}
| |

Step 2: Initialize the weights as
$[v]$^0 = |0.1 0.4|
|–0.2 0.2|$_{2*2}$; $[w]$^o = {0.2}
{–0.5}$_{2*1}$

Step 3: Find $\{I\}H$ = $[v]$^$T\{O\}I$ as
= |0.1 –0.2| {0.4} {0.18}
|0.4 0.2| {-0.7} = {0.02}

Step 4: $\{o\}$ = |1̸ 1+e^–0.18| = {0.5448}
|1̸1+e^–0.02 | {0.505}

Step 5: $\{I\}o$ = $[w]T$ $\{o\}$ H = <0.2–0.5> {0.5448} = – 0.14354
{0.505}

Step 6: $\{0\}o$ |1̸ 1+e^0.14354| = 0.4642

Step 7: Error $\{To\text{-}Oo\}$^2 = 0.13264

Step 8: Let us adjust the weight.
Find first d = $(To\text{–}On)(Oo)(1\text{–}Oo)$
(0.1–0.462) (0.4642) (0.5358) = – 0.09058
$[y]$ = $\{o\}H$<d> = {0.5448}
{0.505} <–0.09058>

Step 9: $\{e\}$ = $[w]$ $\{d\}$ = {0.2} = {–0.09058} = {–0.00449}
{-0.5} {0.01132}

Step 10: $\{e\}$ = {(–0.018116) (0.5448) (1–0.5448)}
{(0.04529) (0.505) (1–0.505)} = {–0.00449}
{0.01132}

Step 11: $\{x\}$ = $\{O\}$ t<d> = {0.4} [–0.001077 0.002716]
[0.0031343 –0.004754]

Step 12: $[v]$ = [0.1 0.4] + [–0.001077 0.002716]
[–0.2 0.2] [0.001885 –0.004754]

Step 13: With the updated weights $[v]$ and $[w]$, errors is calculated again and next training set is taken and error will be adjusted.

Step 14: Iterations are carried out till we get the error less than the tolerance.

Step 15: Once weights are adjusted the network is ready for inference. Computer program neuro net is developed for training the data and inferring the result using back propagation neural network.

MATLAB PROGRAM

Supervised training :

% Matlab program

```
%To train Artificial Neural Network by Rajesh Kumar
clear
fid=fopen('rajesh.txt','w');
maxerr=1.0;
saveerr=1.0;
b=1;
in=input('Enter number of Input Nodes : ');
ih=input('Enter number of hidden Nodes : ');
io=input('Enter number of output Nodes : ');
sqerr=0;
v=rand(ih,in);
w=rand(io,ih);
alpha=input('Enter alpha : ');
learn=input('Enter Learning rate : ');
tri=input('Enter Number of Training Sets : ');
disp('Enter Inputs : ');
for t=1 :tri
 for i=1 :in
 imat(t,i,1)=input('');
 end
 disp('Enter Outputs : ');
 for i=1 :io
 omat(t,i,1)=input('');
 end
end
imaxx=max(imat);
omaxx=max(omat);
imax=max(imaxx);
omax=max(omaxx);
inii=imat/imax;
toi=omat/omax;
j=1;
fprintf(fid,'Initial Weights randomly generated : ');
fprintf(fid,'\n');
fprintf(fid,'Weights(in->hid) : ');
fprintf(fid,'%f ',v);
fprintf(fid,'\n');
fprintf(fid,'Weights(hid->out) : ');
fprintf(fid,'%f ',w);
```

```
hold on;
.......
Programme based on algorithm (say, backpropagation, RBF etc.)
.......
 fprintf(fid,'\n');
 fprintf(fid,'Training set :%d',t);
 fprintf(fid,'\nIncremented Weights(in->hid) : ');
 fprintf(fid,'%f ',v);
 fprintf(fid,'\n');
 fprintf(fid,'Incremented Weights(hid->out) : ');
 fprintf(fid,'%f ',w);
 end
 j=j+1;
end
disp('See the Weights in out.txt!!');
if(b==1)
 disp('Enter Inputs to the trained Neural Network : ');
.......
Programm for testing data
.....

end
```

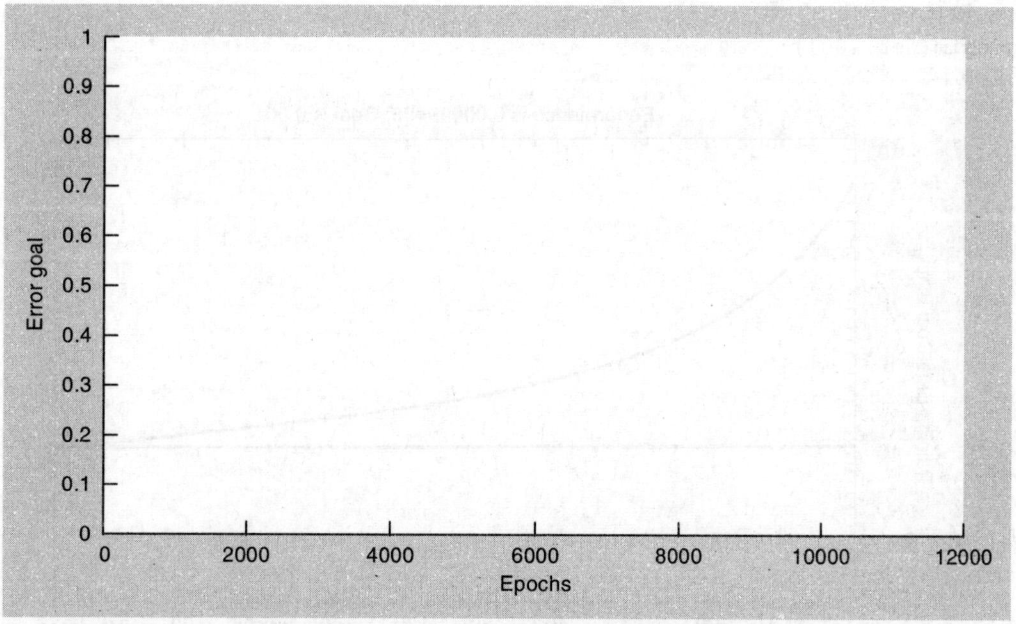

Fig. 2.5. *Error goal Vs epochs during training.*

Updated Weights after training are as under :

Weights between input and hidden layer

Input 1 .1962 .1981 .1263 .1033 .1599 .1956

Input 2 .1962 .1981 .1263 .1033 .1599 .1956

Weights between hidden and output layer

.1340

.1151

.1190

.1172

.1350

.1352

Unsupervised training :

```
% Made by Rajesh Kumar
net=newff([min. max. value of input1; min. max. value of input2.],
[12 1],{'logsig','logsig'},'traingd');
net.trainparam.show=100;
net.trainparam.lr=.6;
net.trainparam.epochs=5000;
net.trainparam.goal=1e-3;
t=[ Normalized target values];
p=[Input1 patterns; Input2 patterns];
net=train(net,p,t);
a=sim(net,p);
gensim(net,.001);
```

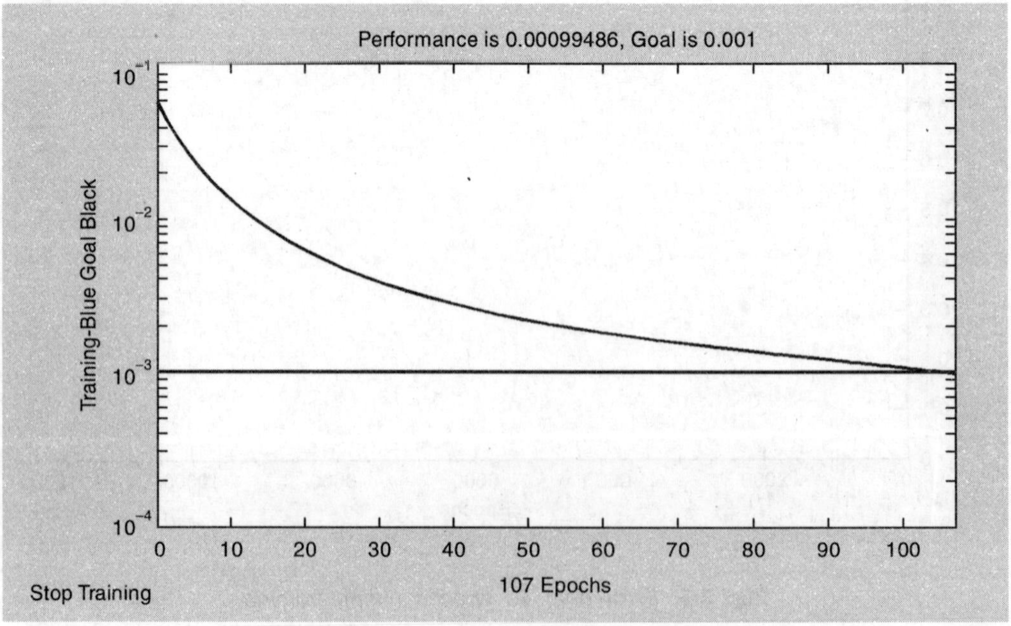

Fig. 2.6. *Error goal Vs Epochs during training.*

TRAINGD, Epoch 0/5000, MSE 0.0576822/0.001, Gradient 0.145183/1e-010
TRAINGD, Epoch 100/5000, MSE 0.00106794/0.001, Gradient 0.00431359/1e-010
TRAINGD, Epoch 107/5000, MSE 0.000994986/0.001, Gradient 0.0040048/1e-010
TRAINGD, Performance goal met.

Neural network model :

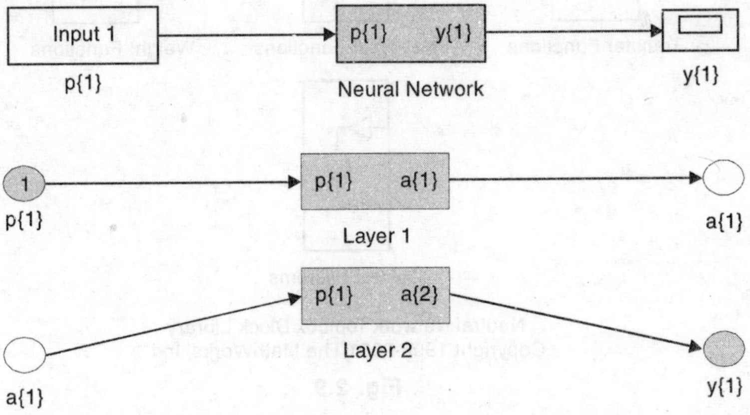

Fig. 2.7

Weights

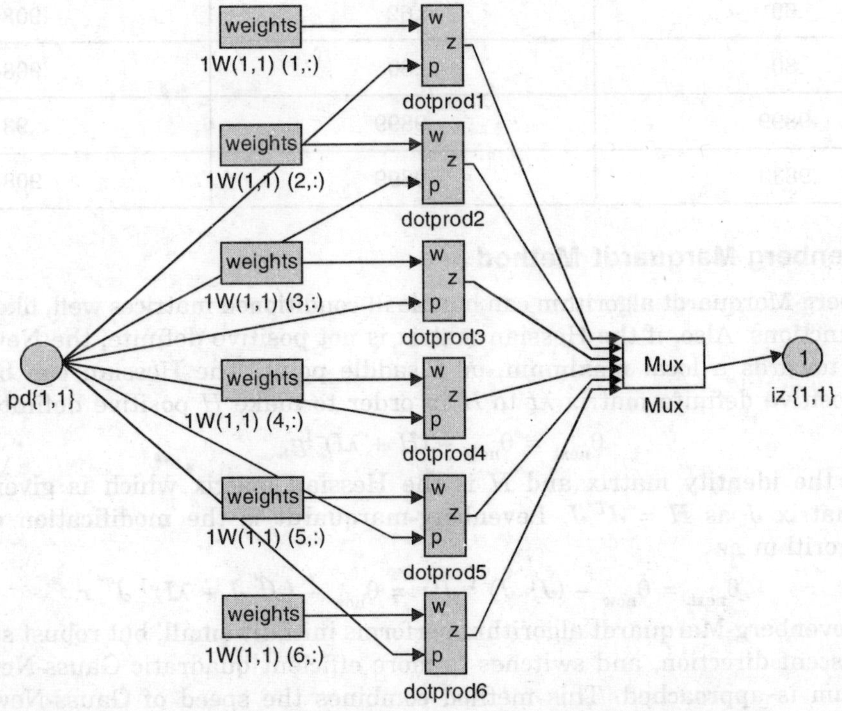

Fig. 2.8. *Artificial neural network model using Matlab simulink (unsupervised training).*

(*a*) Neural network model (*b*) Input layer and hidden layer (*c*) Weights between input and hidden layer.

Transfer functions :

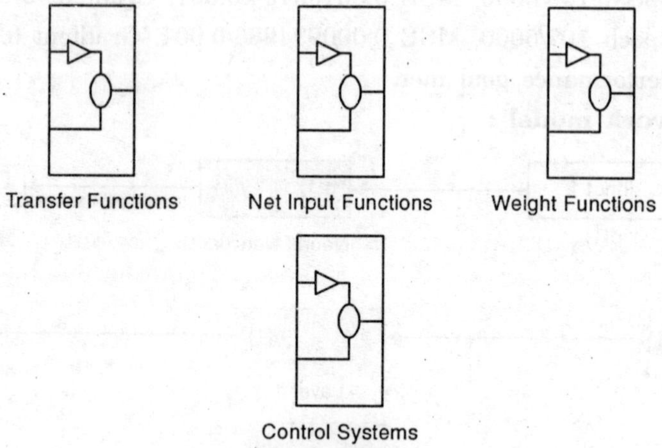

Neutral Network Toolbox Block Library
Copyright 1992-2001 The MathWorks, Inc.

Fig. 2.9

Validation :

Input 1	*Input 2*	*Output*
.69	.62	.9084
.80	.80	.9084
.9899	.9899	.93
.9833	.9899	.9084

2.2.3. Levenberg-Marquardt Method

The Levenberg-Marquardt algorithm can handle ill-conditioned matrices well, like nonquadratic objective functions. Also, if the Hessian matrix is not positive definite, the Newton direction may point towards a local maximum, or a saddle point. The Hessian can be changed by adding a positive definite matrix λI to H in order to make H positive definite.

Thus, $$\theta_{next} = \theta_{now} - (H + \lambda I)^{-1} g,$$

where I is the identity matrix and H is the Hessian matrix which is given in terms of Jacobian matrix J as $H = J^T J$. Levenberg-marquardt is the modification of the Gauss-Newton algorithm as

$$\theta_{next} = \theta_{now} - (J^T J)^{-1} J^T r = \theta_{now} - (J^T J + \lambda I)^{-1} J^T r.$$

The Levenberg-Marquardt algorithm performs initially small, but robust steps along the steepest descent direction, and switches to more efficient quadratic Gauss-Newton steps as the minimum is approached. This method combines the speed of Gauss-Newton with the everywhere convergence of gradient descent, and appears to be fastest for training moderate-sized feedforaward neural networks.

2.2.4 Forward-Propagation and Back-Propagation

During training, a forward pass takes place. The network computes an output based on its current inputs. Each node I computes a weighted sum a_i of its inputs and passes this through a nonlinearity to obtain the node input y_i. The error between actual and desired network outputs is given by

$$E = \frac{1}{2}\sum_{p}\sum_{i}\left(d_{pi} - y_{pi}\right)^2$$

where p indexes the pattern in the training set, I indexes the output nodes, and d_{pi} and y_{pi} are, respectively, the desired target and actual network output for the error with respect to the weights is the sum of the individual pattern errors and is given as

$$\frac{dE}{dW_{ij}} = \sum_{p}\frac{dE_p}{dW_{ij}} = \sum_{p,k}\frac{dE_p}{da_k}\frac{da_k}{dW_{ij}}$$

where the index k represent all outputs nodes. It is convenient to first calculate a value δ_i for each node i as

$$\delta_i = \frac{dE_p}{da_i} = \sum_{k}\frac{dE_p}{dy_k}\frac{dy_k}{da_i}$$

which measures the contribution of a_i to the error on the current pattern. For simplicity, pattern index p are omitted on y_i, a_i and other variables in the subsequent equations.

For output nodes, dE_p/da_k, is obtained directly as

$$\delta = -(d_{pk} - y_{pk})\, f \quad \text{(for output node).}$$

The first term in this equation is obtained from error equation, and the second term which is

$$\frac{dy_k}{da_k} = f'(a_k) = f'_k$$

is just the slope of the node nonlinearity as its current value. For hidden nodes, δ_i is obtain indirectly as

$$\delta_i = \frac{dE_p}{da_i} = \sum_{k}\frac{dE_p}{da_k}\frac{da_k}{da_i} = \sum_{p}\delta k\frac{da_k}{da_i}$$

where the second factor is obtained by noting that if the node I connects directly to node k then $da_k/da_i = f'_i w_{ki}$, otherwise it is zero. Thus,

$$\delta_i = f'i\sum_{k} w_k\,\delta_k$$

for hidden nodes.

In other words, δ_i is a weighted sum of the δ_k values of nodes k to which it has connections w_{ki}. The way the nodes are indexed, all delta values can be updated through the nodes in the reverse order. In layered networks, all delta values are first evaluated at the output nodes based on the current pattern errors, the hidden values is then evaluated based on the output delta values, and so on backwards to the input layer.

Having obtained the node deltas, it is an easy step to find the partial derivatives dE_p/dW_{ij} with respect to the weights. The second factor is da_k/dw_{ij} because a_k is a linear sum, this is zero if $k = i$; otherwise

$$\frac{da_i}{dw_{ij}} = X_j$$

The derivative of pattern error E_p with respect to weight w_{ij} is then

$$\frac{dE_p}{dw_{ij}} = \delta_i x_j$$

First the derivative of the network training error with respect to the weights are calculated. Then a training algorithm is performed. This procedure is called back-propagation since the error signals are obtained sequentially from the output layer back to the input layer.

2.2.5 Weight Update Algorithm

The reason for updating the weights is to decrease the error. The weight update relationship is

$$\Delta w_{ij} = \frac{\eta dE_p}{dw_{ij}} = \eta\left(d_{pi} - y_{pi}\right) f_i x_j$$

where the learning rate $\eta > 0$ is a small positive constant. Sometimes η is also called the step size parameter.

The *Delta Rule* is weight update algorithm in the training of neural networks. The algorithm progresses sequentially layer by layer, updating weights as it goes. The update equation is provided by the gradient descent method as

$$\nabla w_{ij} = w_{ij}(k+1) - w_{ij}(k) = -\eta \frac{dE_p}{dw_{ij}}$$

$$\frac{dE_p}{dw_{ij}} = -\left(d_{ij} - y_{pi}\right)\frac{dy_{pi}}{dw_{ij}}$$

for linear output unit, where

$$y_{pi} = \sum_i w_{ij} x_i$$

and $$\frac{dy_{pi}}{dw_{ij}} = x_i$$

so, $$\nabla w_{ij} = w_{ij}(k+1) - w_{ij}(k) = \eta\,(d_{pi} - y_{pi})\,x_i$$

The adaptation of those weights which connects the input units and the ith output unit is determined by the corresponding error $e_i = 1 \sum (d_{pi} - y_{pi})^2$.

2.3 EFFECT OF PARAMETERS

2.3.1 Input and Output Selection

Just as with any control problem. The inputs and outputs and their interrelationships and depend ness must be considered. With the use of today's distributed control systems, this is a wealth of information available. In many cases, there is a temptation to simply everything. The secret to a good neural network application is to fit the data to the problem without over-fitting. Because the training process creates a statistical map of inputs to outputs, having inputs that do not relate to a desired output forces the network to determine that there is no relationship and set the weights for non-related input to zero. This penalty carries over to the network operation in that there are now a number of needless multiplications by 0 that must be performed.

Another case of over-fitting is having two inputs that represent the sane basic information. For example, if both the process variable of a flow loop and the valve position of the flow control valve are used as inputs to the network, the effect is that of having one input entered twice. This is due to the fact that the network uses normalized data, so when both signals are converted to relative values between 0 and 1, the valve position and flow measurement represent the same basic data and, in effect, bias the network with relation to that signal.

2.3.2 Hidden Nodes and Hidden Layers

The number of hidden layers and hidden nodes is a very important issue due to the physical number of calculations that must be made in both the training and operational mode. There has been a great deal of work in the area of determining how many hidden layers produce the best results. In general, for the class of feedforward networks, of which backpropagation is one, it has been shown that a network with multiple hidden layers can be replaced by an equivalent network with a single hidden layer. The problem then becomes one of determining how many hidden nodes are required in the single hidden layer. One commonly used method is to train different networks with varying numbers of hidden nodes and test their predicted accuracy, such as :

$$\text{No. of hidden nodes} = \frac{\text{No. of inputs} + \text{No. of outputs}}{2}$$

and

$$\text{No. of hidden nodes} = \frac{\left[(\text{No. of inputs})^2 + (\text{No. of outputs})^2\right]^{0.5}}{2}$$

and others. A method that provides the most accurate results is to train different networks with varying numbers of hidden nodes and then test their prediction accuracy. As the number of hidden nodes increases, the accuracy increases until a point is reached where the network is over-parameterized. Figure 2.10 illustrates this. When the curve reaches the bottom of the knee, that number of hidden nodes is the proper number.

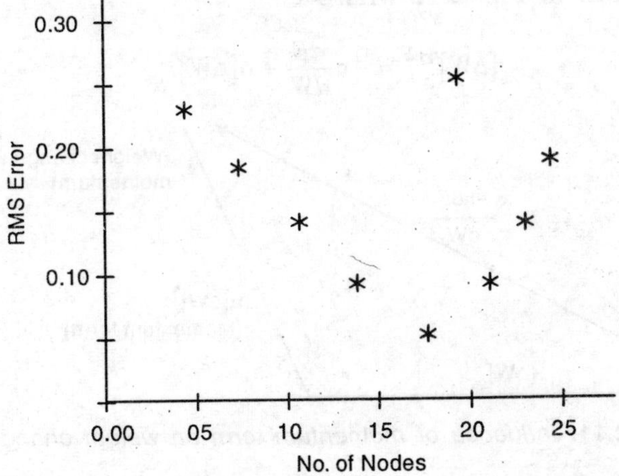

Fig. 2.10. *RMS error vs. no. nodes in hidden layer.*

2.3.3 Accuracy

During training the accuracy of a network refers to how close the output of the network has to be to the target to be considered trained. Many this is referred to as the "training threshold" or "learning threshold". There are a number of ways to represent learning threshold (LT), one in particular is :

$$LT = 0.8.\ (\Sigma\varepsilon^2/2)$$

Where ε is the normalized error between the network output and the actual output for a particular set within the training set. A value of I would mean any output is acceptable and a value of 0 would mean that exact match is required. Another way to express the learning threshold is in terms of RMS error, such that the network is determined to be trained when the individual RMS error for all the training set predictions is less that the specified learning threshold. Regardless of whether the shell program uses one of the above, or some other acceptable definition of learning threshold, it is important for the user to understand the relationship between the learning threshold and the accuracy of the data collected to create the training set. The matching of the learning threshold to the data accuracy will generate the network that will produce output with the most possible accuracy. If the selected learning threshold is tighter then the accuracy of the data, the network will train and pass through the optimum point and begin to map the inaccuracy of the data itself.

2.3.4 Learning Coefficient η

The learning coefficient cannot be negative because this would cause the change of weight vector to move away from ideal weight vector position. If the learning coefficient is zero, no learning takes place and hence, the learning coefficient must be positive. If learning coefficient is equal to 2 then the network is unstable and if the learning coefficient is greater than 1, the weight vector will overshoot from its ideal position and oscillate. Hence, the learning coefficient must be between zero and one. Larger values for the learning coefficient are used when input data patterns are close to the ideal otherwise small values are used. If the nature of the input data patterns is not known, it is better to use moderate values.

2.3.5 Momentum Coefficient α

We have already seen that another method of reducing the training time is the use of momentum factor because it enhances the training process. The influence of the momentum on weight change is shown in Fig. 2.11 where

$$[\Delta W]^{n+1} = -\eta\frac{dE}{dW} + \alpha[\Delta W]^n$$

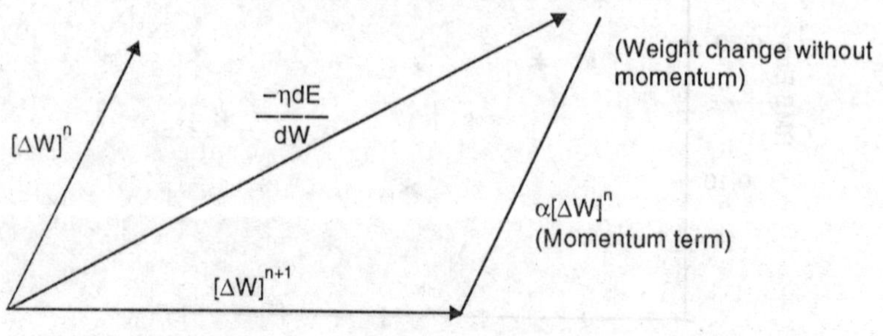

Fig. 2.11. *Influence of momentum term on weight change.*

The process works for many problems but not so well in others. The momentum also overcomes the effect of local minima. The use of momentum term will often carry a weight change process through one or local minima and get it into global minima. This is perhaps its most important function. There is a substantial number of advanced algorithms or other procedures that have been proposed as a means to speed up the training of backpropagation networks. Sejnowski and Rosenberg (1987) proposed a similar momentum method that used exponential smoothening. Parker (1987) proposed a method called "second order" back-propagation that uses second derivative to produce more accurate estimation of weight change. The computational requirements were great and were generally viewed as not being cost effective compared to other methods. The main drawback of the BPN is the long and sometimes uncertain training time. This may be due to poor choice of training coefficients and the initial random distribution of weights. However in most cases failure to train BPN is usually due to local minima or network paralysis where training virtually ceases due to operation in the flat region of sigmoidal function. Backpropagation should never be used in situation where inputs are continuously changing because then the process may never converge.

This method is applied to one example and error rate is given for different values of learning coefficient in table 2.1.

Table 2.1. Error rate for different η.α

Iteration	*Error*	*Remark*	η	α
1	1	0.256		0.6
0.9	5	0.095		
6	0.290	STOP	0.3	0.9
1	0.085			
4	0.009			
5	0.056	STOP	0.15	0.9
1	0.009			
4	0.001			
5	0.006	STOP	0.075	0.9
1	0.001			
4	0.005	STOP		

2.3.6. Training Technique and Computing Time

A great deal of effort has gone into the development of training algorithms and techniques to speed up the training process, as was pointed out by the Caudill. Unless the user is developing a custom ANS, training techniques are a function of the shell selected. The actual training algorithms are beyond the scope of this text and will not be addressed.

In terms of pure computing speed, many significant advances have been made in the development of commercially available accelerator cards. The cards are capable of increasing processing speed 50 to 100 times. Neural network chips are also being used. As applications for these cards and chips are developed and applied, problems that required a day of training will be reduced to matter of minutes.

2.3.7. Robustness

ANS are one of the most robust control functions the author has used when compared with traditional supervisory and optimization techniques. There are cases where an ANS has continued to operate and produce acceptable results with fifteen percent of the input data out of range. This is due to the fact that the one level of the ANS is operating based upon its perception of certain features of the entire input data set. This is analogous to picking someone out of a group of people getting of a plane based upon race, hair color, height, relative size, and a description of the clothes they will be wearing.

These attributes are great for the controller engineer, but it must be realized that the ANS is not absolutely precise. Potential ANS applications include those where human intelligence functions effortlessly and conventional computational techniques have proven to be cumbersome or inadequate.

2.3.8. Inferences and Generations

A true beauty of the ANS is its ability to see through noise chaos and distortions to be obtained the true essence of the real world environment being viewed. This is one of the attributing factors to the robustness described in the previous section. Even when part of the picture is missing or obscured, the ANS can make correct inferences or generalization to complete the picture. Figure illustrates the above in a very simple way when an ANS is compared to a rule-based system. Given is a set of pictures of boxes that represent a database that will be used to develop two system : first a set of rules to recognize boxes; and second, a trained ANS to recognize boxes. A picture of the box, with a portion of the outline covered, is then presented and both systems are asked if the picture shows a box. The rule base system, which can only compare to the pictures contain in its database, would reply that the picture is absolutely not a box. However, an ANS trained with the same limited database would reply that there is probably a box in the picture.

2.3.9. Local Minima

Tsoukalas and Uhrig (1997) have recommended a procedure for getting over the problem of local minima. One of the most practical solutions involves the introduction of a "shock" which changes all weights by specific or random amounts. If this fails then the most practical solution is to rerandomize the weights and start the training all over.

Second method of backpropagation is used until the process seems to stall. Simulated annealing is then used to continue training until local minima has been left behind. After this, simulated annealing is stopped and BPN continues until global minimum is reached. In most of the cases, only a few simulated annealing cycles of this two-stage process are needed. Usually in such a procedure, the final training step is BPN to minimize the overall error of the process.

2.4. MC-CULLOCH-PITTS NEURON NETWORK

The definition of a synthetic neuron model based on the highly simplified considerations of the biological model was firstly formulated by Mc Culloch and Pitts in 1943. The Mc Culloch and Pitts model of the neuron is shown in figure 2.9.

$$f(y) = \begin{pmatrix} 1 \text{ if } y_{in} >= \theta \\ 0 \text{ if } y_{in} < \theta \end{pmatrix}$$

where y_{in} is the total input signal received by the neuron Y, and θ is the threshold.

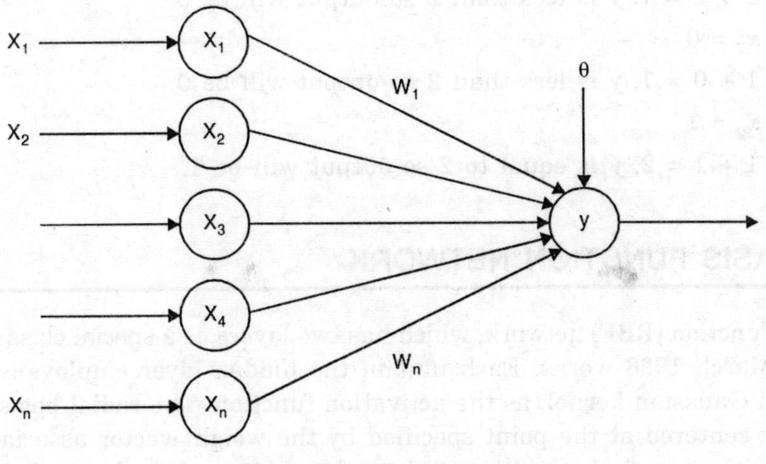

Fig. 2.12. *Mc-Culloch neuron.*

where, $y = w_1x_1 + w_2x_2 \ldots\ldots\ldots w_nx_n$.

☞ **A Mc-Culloch neuron model to implement AND function.**

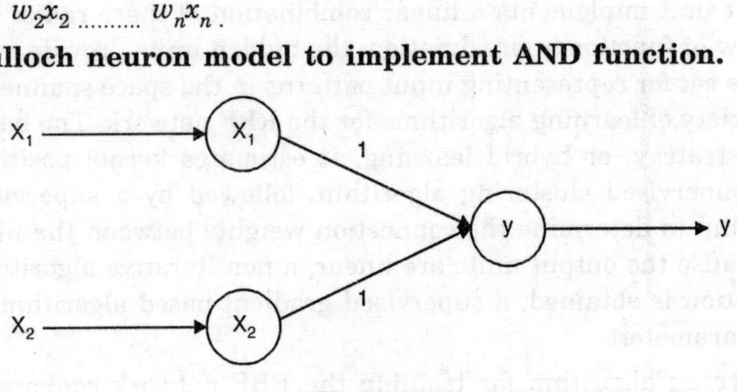

Fig. 2.13

X_1	X_2	Y
0	0	0
0	1	0
1	0	0
1	1	1

The threshold for the neuron, y is the sum of maximum value of input 1 and maximum value of input 2. So $y = 1 + 1 = 2$.

$$f(y) = \begin{cases} 1 \text{ if } y_{in} >= 2 \\ 0 \text{ if } y_{in} < 2 \end{cases}$$

(1) if $x_1 = 0$, $x_2 = 0$

then $y = 0 + 0 = 0$, y is less than 2 so output will be 0.

(2) if $x_1 = 0, x_2 = 1$
then $y = 0 + 1 = 1$, y is less than 2 so output will be 0.

(3) if $x_1 = 1, x_2 = 0$
then $y = 1 + 0 = 1$, y is less than 2 so output will be 0.

(4) if $x_1 = 1, x_2 = 1$
then $y = 1 + 1 = 2$, y is equal to 2 so output will be 1.

2.5 RADIAL BASIS FUNCTION NETWORK

The Radial Basis Function (RBF) network, which has two layers, is a special class of multilayer feed-forward net-March 1996 works. Each unit in the hidden layer employs a radial basis function, such as a Gaussian kernel, as the activation function. The radial basis function (or kernel function) is centered at the point specified by the weight vector associated with the unit. Both the positions and the widths of these kernels must be learned from training patterns. There are usually many fewer kernels in the RBF network than there are training patterns. Each output unit implements a linear combination of these radial basis functions. From the point of view of function approximation, the hidden units provide a set of functions that constitute a basis set for representing input patterns in the space spanned by the hidden units. There are a variety of learning algorithms for the RBF network. The basic one employs a two-step learning strategy, or hybrid learning. It estimates kernel positions and kernel widths using an unsupervised clustering algorithm, followed by a supervised least mean square (LMS) algorithm to determine the connection weights between the hidden layer and the output layer. Because the output units are linear, a non iterative algorithm can be used. After this initial solution is obtained, a supervised gradient-based algorithm can be used to refine the network parameters.

This hybrid learning algorithm for training the RBF network converges much faster than the back-propagation algorithm for training multilayer perceptrons. However, for many problems, the RBF network often involves a larger number of hidden units. This implies that the runtime (after training) speed of the RBF network is often slower than the runtime speed of a multilayer perceptron. The efficiencies (error versus network size) of the RBF network and the multilayer perceptron are, however, problem- dependent. It has been shown that the RBF network has the same asymptotic approximation power as a multi layer perceptron.

2.5.1 Issues

There are many issues in designing feed-forward net

- how many layers are needed for a given task,
- how many units are needed per layer,
- how will the network perform on data not included in
- how large the training set should be for "good" generalization.
- training set (generalization ability), and

Although multilayer feed-forward networks using backpropagation have been widely employed for classification and function approximation, 2 many design parameters still must be determined by trial and error. Existing theoretical results provide only very loose guidelines for selecting these parameters in practice.

A radial basis function network (RBF) has been proven to be a universal function Approximator [park and sandberg 1991]. Therefore, it can perform similar function mappings as a MLP but its architecture and functionally are very different. A RBF network is a two layer network that has different types of neurons in the hidden layer and the output layer. The hidden layer, which corresponds to a MLP hidden layer, is a non linear, local mapping. This layer contains radial basis function neurons which most commonly use a Gaussian activation function($g(x)$). These functions are centered over receptive fields. Receptive fields are areas in input space which activate the local radial basis neurons.

$$G_j(x) = exp[-(x - \mu_j)^2/\sigma_j^2]$$

Where x is the input vector

μ_j is the center of a region called a receptive field

σ_j is the width of the receptive field

$G_j(x)$ is the output of the jth neuron.

The output layer is a layer of standard linear neurons and performs a linear transformation of the hidden node outputs. This layer is equivalent to a linear output layer in a MLP, but the weights are usually solved for using a least algorithm rather trained for using backpropagation. The output layer may, or may not, contain biases. A RBF is a local network that is trained in a supervised manner.

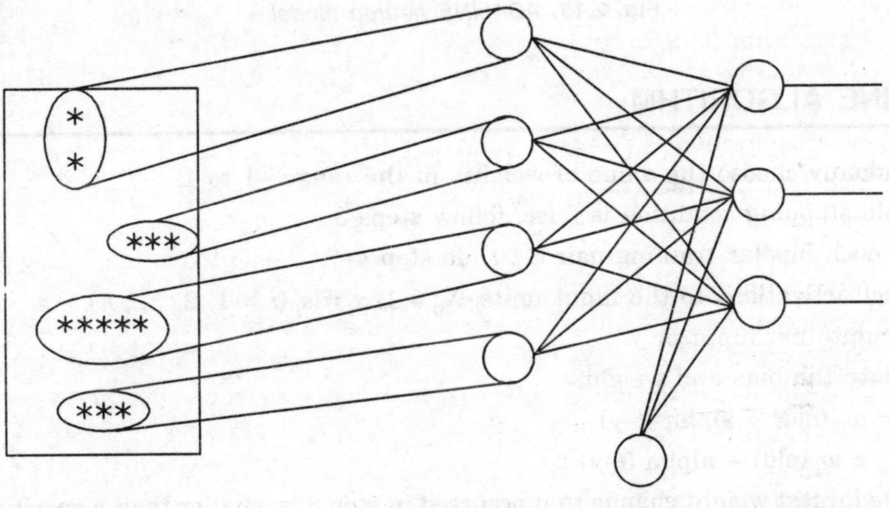

Fig. 2.14. *Radial basis network.*

2.6. ADALINE NETWORK

In the early 1960's a device called ADALINE(For ADAptive LINEar combiner) was introduced, and a new, powerful learning rule called the widrow-Hoff learning rule was developed by

Benard Widrow and Marcian Hoff (1960, 1962). The rule minimized the summed square error during training involving pattern classification. Early applications of ADALINE and its extension to MADALINE (for many ADALINES) include pattern recognition, weather forecasting and adaptive control. The network is shown in Fig. 2.15.

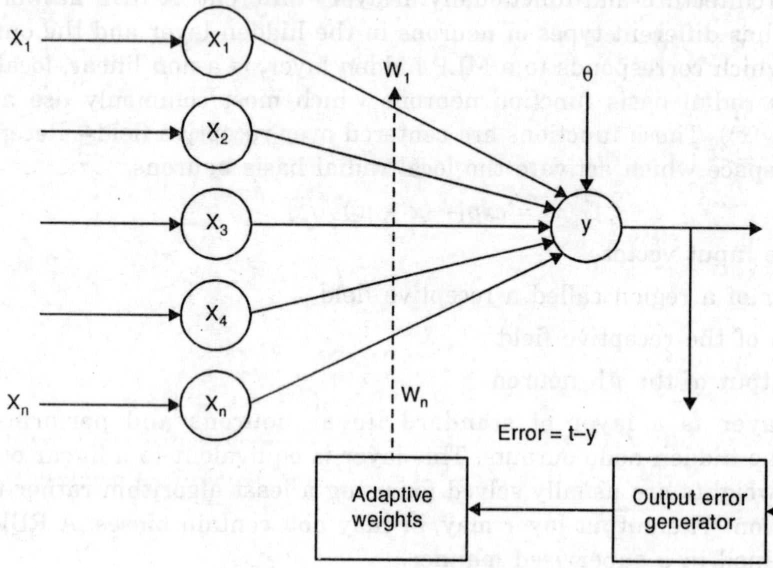

Fig. 2.15. *ADALINE neuron model.*

2.7 ADALINE ALGORITHM

1. Randomly choose the value of weights in the range –1 to 1.
2. While stopping condition is false, follow steps 3.
3. For each bipolar training pair $S : t$, do step 4–7.
4. Select activations to the input units. $X_0 = 1, x_i = s_i$ $(i = 1, 2, ..., n)$.
5. Calculate net input or y.
6. Update the bias and weights.

   $W_0 = w_0$ (old) + alpha $(t–y)$

   $W_{new} = w_i$ (old) + alpha $(t–y)\ x_i.$
7. If the largest weight change that occurred in step 3 is smaller than a specified value, stop else continue.

2.8 MADALINE NETWORK

The MADALINE system has a layer of ADALINE the is connected to a layer of Madaline.

$$f(x) = \begin{pmatrix} 1 \text{ if } x >= 0 \\ -1 \text{ if } x < 0 \end{pmatrix}$$

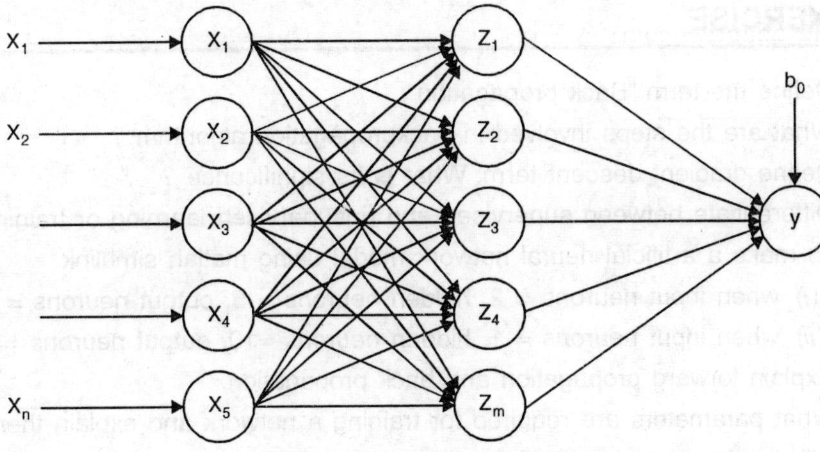

Fig. 2.16. *Madaline model.*

1. First layer is input layer, second layer is adaline layer, third layer is madaline layer, Randomly select the values of adaline weights and madaline weights equal to v, the value of momentum in the range 0 to 1.
2. While stopping condition is false, follow steps 3 to 9.
3. For each bipolar training pair $S : t$, follows 4 to 8.
4. Set the activations for the input, $x_i = s_i$.
5. Calculate the input to each adaline unit, $z_{in} = b + \text{sum } (w_1x_1 + w_2x_2 \ldots)$.
6. Calculate the output of each adaline unit, $z = f\ (z_{in})$.
7. Calculate output of madaline unit, $y_{in} = b_0 + \text{sum } (z)$, $y = f\ (y_{in})$.
8. Calculate the error and update weights.

   If $t = y$, no weights are updated, $t = 1$, update weights on the adaline unit,

   B (new) = b (old) + alpha $(1 - z_{in})$

   W (new) = w (old) + alpha $(1 - z_{in})\ x_i$.

   If t is not equal y and $t = -1$, then the update weights on all adaline unit that have positive net input. For madaline unit,

   B (new) = b (old) + alpha $(1 - z_{in})$

   W (new) = w (old) + alpha $(1 - z_{in})\ x_i$.
9. For stopping condition.

2.9 COUNTER PROPAGATION NETWORK

The application of a counter propagation neural network (CPNN) to detect single faults and their magnitudes. The performance of CPNN has been evaluated by considering a variety of faults occurring in a non-isothermal continuous stirred tank reactor (CSTR). The result presented here indicates that CPNN provides an attractive alternative to error-back propagation (EPB) networks due to its faster learning ability for fault detection and diagnosis. In detail, see chapter 4.

EXERCISE

1. Define the term "Back propagation".
2. What are the steps involved in backpropagation algorithm ?
3. Define gradient descent term. What is its significance ?
4. Differentiate between supervised and unsupervised learning or training method.
5. To make a artificial neural network model using matlab simulink.
   (*i*) when input neurons = 2, hidden neurons = 5, output neurons = 2.
   (*ii*) when input neurons = 1, hidden neurons =10, output neurons = 2.
6. Explain forward propagation and back propagation.
7. What parameters are required for training a network and explain them.
8. What is learning threshold ?
9. What are the main components of a biological neuron ? Differentiate biological and artificial neuron network.
10. Explain briefly about intelligent control. Give few applications in industries.
11. Implement OR function using Mc-Culloch neuron network. When weights are 2, 2.
12. Implement NOT function using Mc-Culloch neuron network. When weights is 1.
13. Implement NAND function using Mc-Culloch neuron network. When weights are 2, –1

    Say $y = 2x_1 - x_2$.

□□□

Chapter **3** **ASSOCIATED MODELS**

3.1 LEARNING OF ARTIFICIAL NEURAL NETWORK (ANN)

The ability to learn is a fundamental trait of intelligence. Although a precise definition of learning is difficult to formulate, a learning process in the ANN context can be viewed as the problem of updating network architecture and connection weights so that a network can efficiently perform a specific task.

The network usually must learn the connection weights from available training patterns. Performance is improved over time by iteratively updating the weights in the network. ANNs' ability to automatically *learn from examples* makes them attractive and exciting. Instead of following a set of *rules* specified by human experts, ANNs appear to learn underlying rules (like input-output relationships) from the given collection of representative examples. This is one of the major advantages of neural networks over traditional expert systems.

To understand or design a learning process, you must first have a model of the environment in which a neural network operates, that is, you must know what information is available to the network. We refer to this model as A learning Paradigm. Second, you must understand how network weights are updated, that is, which learning rules govern the updating process. A learning algorithm refers to a procedure in which learning rules are used for adjusting the weights. There are three main learning paradigms : supervised, unsupervised, and hybrid. In supervised learning, or learning with a "teacher," the network is provided with a correct answer (output) for every input pattern. Weights are determined to allow the network to produce answers as close as possible to the known correct answers. Reinforcement learning is a variant of supervised learning in which the network is provided with only a critique on the correctness of network outputs, not the correct answers themselves. In contrast, unsupervised learning, or learning without a teacher, does not require a correct answer associated with each input pattern in the training data set. It explores the underlying structure in the data, or correlations between patterns in the data, and organizes patterns into categories from these correlations. Hybrid learning combines supervised and unsupervised learning. Part of the weights are usually determined through supervised learning, while the others are obtained through unsupervised learning. Learning theory must address three fundamental and practical issues associated with learning from samples : capacity, sample complexity, and computational complexity. Capacity concerns how many patterns can be stored, and what functions and decision boundaries a network can form., Sample complexity determines the number of training patterns needed to train the network to guarantee a valid generalization.

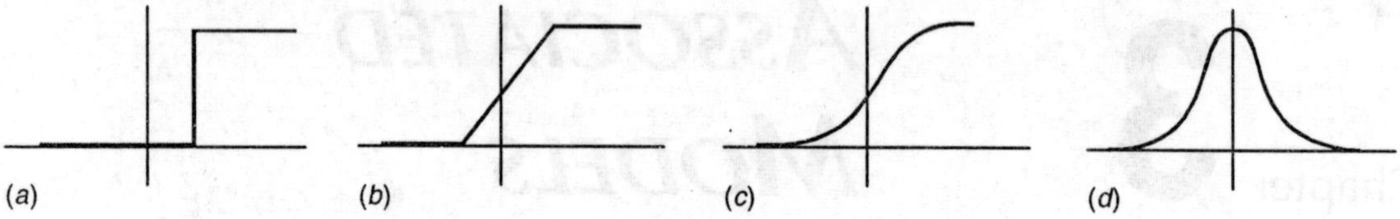

Fig. 3.1

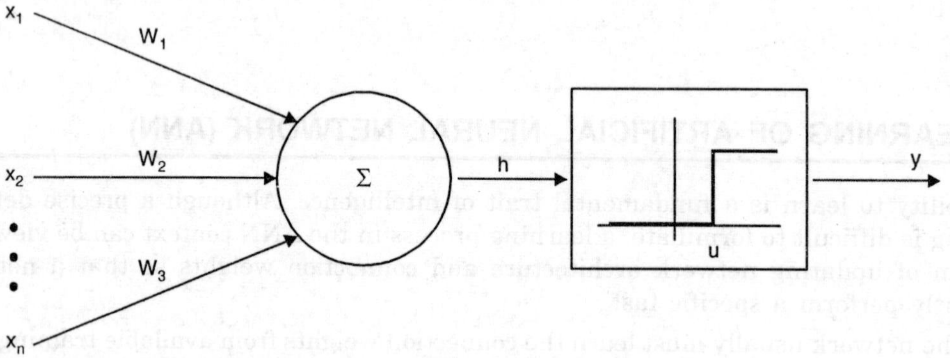

Fig. 3.2

Too few patterns may cause "over-fitting" (wherein the network performs well on the training data set, but poorly on independent test patterns drawn from the same distribution as the training patterns. Computational complexity refers to the time required for a learning algorithm to estimate a solution from training patterns. Many existing learning algorithms have high computational complexity. Designing efficient algorithms for neural network learning is a very active research topic. The activation functions and single layer network are shown in Fig. 3.1 and 3.2 respectively.

There are four basic types of learning rules : error correction, Boltzmann, Hebbian, and competitive learning.

3.1.1. Error-Correction Rules

In the supervised learning paradigm, the network is given a desired output for each input pattern. During the learning process, the actual output y generated by the network may not equal the desired output d. The basic principle of error-correction learning rules is to use the error signal (d-y) to modify the connection weights to gradually reduce this error. The perceptron learning rule is based on this error-correction principle. A perceptron consists of a single neuron with adjustable weights, w, j = 1, 2, ..., n and threshold U, as shown in Figure 3.2. Given an input vector x = (xl, x, ..., xJt, the net input to the neuron is

Perceptron learning algorithm

1. Initialize the weights and threshold to small random numbers.
2. Present a pattern vector $(x_1, x_2, ..., x_n)^t$ and evaluate the output of the neuron.
3. Update the weights according to

$w_j(t+1) = w_j(t) + \eta(d - y)x_j$,

where d is the desired output, t is the iteration number and η $(0.0 < \eta < 1.0)$ is the gain (step size).

$$v = \sum_{j=1}^{n} w_j x_j - u$$

The output y of the perceptron is + 1 if $v > 0$, and 0 otherwise. In a two-class classification problem, the perceptron assigns an input pattern to one class if $y = 1$, and to the other class if $y = 0$. The linear equation

$$\sum_{j=1}^{n} w_j x_j - u = 0$$

defines the decision boundary (a hyper plane in the n-dimensional input space) that halves the space. Rosenblatt developed a learning procedure to determine the weights and threshold in a perceptron, given a set of training patterns (see the "Perceptron learning algorithm" sidebar). Note that learning occurs only when the perceptron makes an error. Rosenblatt proved that when training patterns are drawn from two linearly separable classes, the perceptron learning procedure converges after a finite number of iterations. This is the perceptron convergence theorem. In practice, you do not know whether the patterns are linearly separable. Many variations of this learning algorithm have been proposed in the literature. Other activation functions that lead to different learning characteristics can also be used. However, a single-layer perceptron can only separate linearly separable patterns as long as a monotonic activation function is used. The back-propagation learning algorithm (see the "Back-propagation algorithm sidebar") is also based on the error-correction principle.

3.1.2. Boltzmann Learning

Boltzmann machines are symmetric recurrent networks consisting of binary units (+ 1 for "on" and –1 for "off"). By symmetric, we mean that the weight on the connection from unit i to unit j is equal to the weight on the connection from unit j to unit i ($w_i = w_i$. A subset of the neurons, called visible, interact with the environment; the rest, called hidden, do not. Each neuron is a stochastic unit that generates an output (or state) according to the Boltzmann distribution of statistical mechanics. Boltzmann machines operate in two modes : clamped, in which visible neurons are clamped onto specific states determined by the environment; and free-running, in which both visible and hidden neurons are allowed to operate freely. Boltzmann learning is a stochastic learning rule derived from information-theoretic and thermodynamic principles. The objective of Boltzmann learning is to adjust the connection weights so that the states of visible units satisfy a particular desired probability distribution. According to the *Boltzmann learning rule*, the change in the connection weight w_g is given by

$$\Delta w_{ij} = \eta(\overline{\rho}_{ij} - \rho_{ij}),$$

where η is the learning rate, and ρ_{ij} are the correlations between the states of units i and J when the network operates in the clamped mode and free-running mode, respectively. The values of p_{li} and p, are usually estimated from Monte Carlo experiments, which are extremely slow. Boltzmann learning can be viewed as a special case of error-correction learning in which error IS measured not as the direct difference between desired and actual outputs, but as the difference between the correlations among the outputs of two neurons under clamped and free running operating conditions.

3.1.3. Hebbian Rule

The oldest learning rule is Hebb's postulate of learning. Hebb based it on the following observation from neurobiological experiments : If neurons on both sides of a synapse are activated synchronously and repeatedly, the synapse's strength is selectively increased. Mathematically, the Hebbian rule can be described as

$$w_{ij}(t+1) = w_{ij}(t) + \eta y_i(t)\, x_i(t),$$

where x_i and y_j, are the output values of neurons i and J, respectively, which are connected by the synapse w_g and η is the learning rate. Note that x_i is the input to the synapse. An important property of this rule is that learning is done locally, that is, the change in synapse weight depends only on the activities of the two neurons connected by it. This significantly simplifies the complexity of the learning circuit in a VLSI implementation. A single neuron trained using the Hebbian rule exhibits an orientation selectivity. Figure 3.3 demonstrates this property. The points depicted are drawn from a two-dimensional Gaussian distribution and used for training a neuron. The weight vector of the neuron is initialized tow, as shown in the figure.

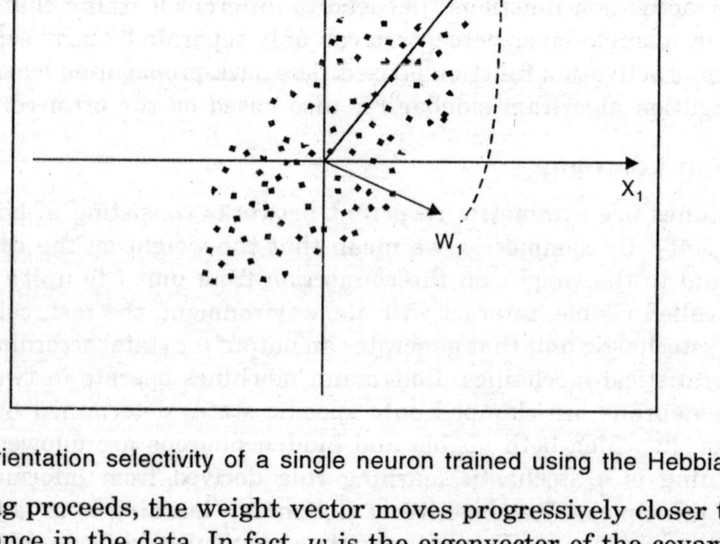

Fig. 3.3. Orientation selectivity of a single neuron trained using the Hebbian rule.

As the learning proceeds, the weight vector moves progressively closer to the direction w of maximal variance in the data. In fact, w is the eigenvector of the covariance matrix of the data corresponding to the largest eigen value.

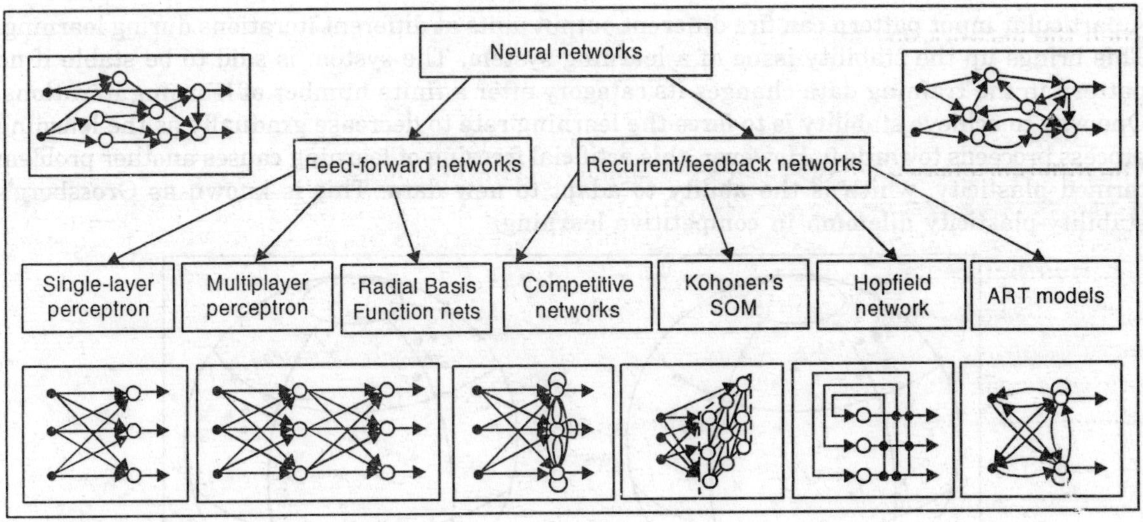

Fig. 3.4

3.1.4. Competitive Learning Rules

Unlike Hebbian learning (in which multiple output units can be fired simultaneously), competitive-learning output units compete among themselves for activation. As a result, only one output unit is active at any given time. This phenomenon is known as *winner-take-all*. Competitive learning has been found to exist in biological neural networks. Competitive learning often clusters or categorizes the input data. Similar patterns are grouped by the network and represented by a single unit. This grouping is done automatically based on data correlations. The simplest competitive learning network consists of a single layer of output units as shown in Figure 3.4. Each output unit i in the network connects to all the input units (+) via weights, $w, j = 1, 2, ..., n$. Each output unit also connects to all other output units via inhibitory weights but has a self-feedback with an excitatory weight. As a result of competition, only the unit i with the largest (or the smallest), net input becomes the winner, that is, $w_i{}^*.x \geq w_i.x$, $\forall i$, or $\|w_i{}^* - x\| \leq \|w_i - x\|$, $\forall i$. When all the weight vectors are normalized, these two inequalities are equivalent. A simple competitive learning rule can be stated as

$$\Delta w_{ij} = \begin{cases} \eta\left(x_j^u - w_{i^*j}\right), & i = i^*, \\ 0, & i \neq i^*. \end{cases}$$

Note that only the weights of the winner unit get updated. The effect of this learning rule is to move the stored pattern in the winner unit (weights) a little bit closer to the input pattern. Figure 3.5 demonstrates a geometric interpretation of competitive learning. In this example, we assume that all input vectors have been normalized to have unit length. They are depicted as black dots in Figure 3.5. The weight vectors of the three units are randomly initialized.

Their initial and final positions on the sphere after competitive learning are marked as *Xs* in Figures 3.5*a* and 3.5*b*, respectively. In Figure 3.5, each of the three natural groups (clusters) of patterns has been discovered by an output unit whose weight vector points to the center of gravity of the discovered group. You can see from the competitive learning rule that the network will not stop learning (updating weights) unless the learning rate q is 0.

A particular input pattern can fire different output units at different iterations during learning. This brings up the stability issue of a learning system. The system is said to be stable if no pattern in the training data changes its category after a finite number of learning iterations. One way to achieve stability is to force the learning rate to decrease gradually as the learning process proceeds towards 0. However, this artificial freezing of learning causes another problem termed plasticity, which is the ability to adapt to new data. This is known as Grossberg's stability-plasticity dilemma in competitive learning.

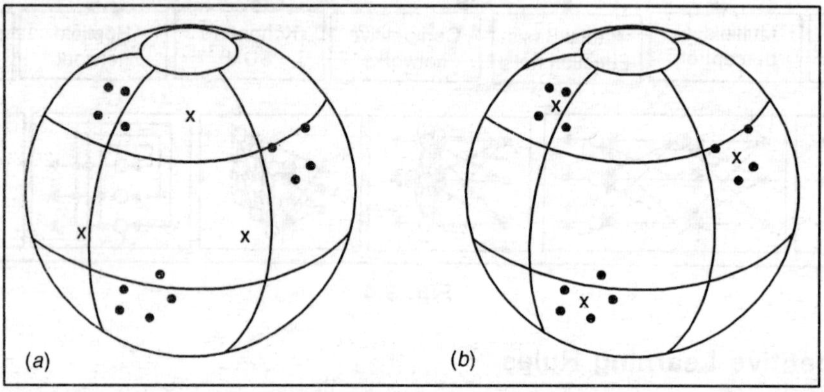

Fig. 3.5. *An example of competitive learning : (a) before learning; (b) after learning.*

The most well-known example of competitive learning is vector quantization for data compression. It has been widely used in speech and image processing for efficient storage, transmission, and modeling. Its goal is to represent a set or distribution of input vectors with a relatively small number of prototype vectors (weight vectors), or a codebook. Once a codebook has been constructed and agreed upon by both the transmitter and the receiver, you need only transmit or store the index of the corresponding prototype to the input vector. Given an input vector, its corresponding prototype can be found by searching for the nearest prototype in the codebook.

Table 3.1. Well known learning algorithms

Paradigm	*Learning rule*	*Architecture*	*Learning algorithm*	*Task*
Supervised	Error-correction	Single-or multilayer perceptron	Perceptron learning algorithms Back-propagation Adaline and Madaline	Pattern classification Function approximation Prediction, control
	Boltzmann	Recurrent	Boltzmann learning algorithm	Pattern classification
	Hebbian	Multilayer feed-forward	Linear discriminant analysis	Data analysis Pattern classification
	Competitive	Competitive	Learning vector quantization	Within class categorization Data compression
		ART network	ARTMap	Pattern classification Within-class Categorization

Unsupervised	Error-correction	Multilayer feed-forward	Sammons projection	Data analysis
	Hebbian	Feed-forward or competitive	Principal component analysis	Data analysis Data compression
		Hopfield Network	Associative memory learning	Associative memory
	Competitive	Competitive	Vector quantization	Categorization Data compression
		Kohonen's SOM	Kohonen's SOM	Categorization Data analysis
		ART networks	ART1, ART2	Categorization
Hybrid	Error-correction and competitive	RBF network	RBF learning algorithm	Pattern classification Function approximation Prediction, control

3.2. KOHONEN'S SELF-ORGANIZING MAPS

The self-organizing map (SOM) has the desirable property of topology preservation, which captures an important aspect of the feature maps in the cortex of highly developed animal brains. In a topology-preserving mapping, nearby input patterns should activate nearby output units on the map. Figure 3.4 shows the basic network architecture of Kohonen's SOM. It basically consists of a two dimensional array of units, each connected to all n input nodes. Let wg denote the n-dimensional vector associated with the unit at location (i, j) of the 2D array. Each neuron computes the Euclidean distance between the input vector x and the stored weight vector wy. This SOM is a special type of competitive learning network that defines a spatial neighborhood for each output unit. The shape of the local neighborhood can be square, rectangular, or circular. Initial neighborhood size is often set to one half to two thirds of the network size and shrinks over time according to a schedule (for example, an exponentially decreasing function). During competitive learning, all the weight vectors associated with the winner and its neighboring units are updated (see the "SOM learning algorithm" sidebar). Kohonen's SOM can be used for projection of multivariate data, density approximation, and clustering. It has been successfully applied in the areas of speech recognition, image processing, robotics, and process control. The design parameters include the dimensionality of the neuron array, the number of neurons in each dimension, the shape of the neighborhood, the shrinking schedule of the neighborhood, and the learning rate.

3.3. ADAPTIVE RESONANCE THEORY MODELS

Recall that the stability-plasticity dilemma is an important issue in competitive learning. How do we learn new things (plasticity) and yet retain the stability to ensure that existing knowledge is not erased or corrupted ? Carpenter and Grossberg's Adaptive Resonance Theory models (ART1, ART2, and ART Map) were developed in an attempt to overcome this dilemma." The network has a sufficient supply of output units, but they are not used until deemed necessary. A unit is said to be committed (uncommitted) if it is (is not) being used. The learning algorithm updates the stored prototypes of a category only if the input vector is sufficiently similar to them. An input vector and a stored prototype are said to resonate when they are sufficiently similar. The extent of similarity is controlled by vigilance parameter, p, with $0 < p < 1$, which also determines the number of categories. When the input vector is not sufficiently similar to any existing prototype in the network, a new category is created, and an uncommitted unit is assigned to it with the input vector as the initial prototype. If no such uncommitted unit exists, a novel input generates no response. We present only ART1, which takes binary (0/1) input to illustrate the model. Figure 3.6 shows a simplified diagram of the ARTl architecture. It consists of two layers of fully connected units. A top-down weight vector w_j, is associated with unit j in the input layer, and a bottom-up weight vector bar of (w_i) is associated with output unit i; bar of (w_i) is the normalized version of w.

$$\overline{w_i} = \frac{w_i}{\varepsilon + \sum_j w_{ji}}$$

where ε is a small number used to break the ties in selecting the winner. The top-down weight vectors w_j's store cluster prototypes. The role of normalization is to prevent prototypes with a long vector length from dominating prototypes with a short one. Given an n-bit input vector x, the output of the auxiliary unit A is given by

$$A = Sgn_{0/1}\left(\sum_j x_j - n\sum_i O_i - 0.5\right)$$

where Sgn, (x) is the signum function that produces + 1 if $x >= 0$ and 0 otherwise, and the output of an input unit is given by

$$V_j = Sgn_{0/1}\left(x_j + \sum_i w_{ji} O_i + A - 1.5\right)$$

$$= \begin{cases} x_j, & \text{if no output } O_j \text{ is "on"}, \\ x_j \wedge \Sigma_i w_{ji} O_i, & \text{otherwise.} \end{cases}$$

A reset signal R is generated only when the similarity is less than the vigilance level. (See the "ART1 learning algorithm" sidebar.) The ARTl model can create new categories and reject an input pattern when the network reaches its capacity. However, the number of categories discovered in the input data by ARTl is sensitive to the vigilance parameter.

3.4. HOPFIELD NETWORK

Hopfield used a network energy function as a tool for designing recurrent networks and for understanding their dynamic behavior.' Hopfield's formulation made explicit the principle of storing information as dynamically stable attractors and popularized the use of recurrent networks for associative memory and for solving combinatorial optimization problems.

A Hopfield network with n units has two versions : binary and continuously valued. Let v, be the state or output of the ith unit. For binary networks, v, is either + 1 or – 1, but for continuous networks, v, can be any value between 0 and 1. Let w, be the synapse weight on the connection from units i to j. In Hopfield networks, $w = w$, ~, Vi, j (symmetric networks), and $w = 0$, Vi (no self-feedback connections). The network dynamics for the binary Hopfield network are

$$v_i = Sgn\left(\sum_j w_{ij}v_j - \theta_i\right) \quad ...(a)$$

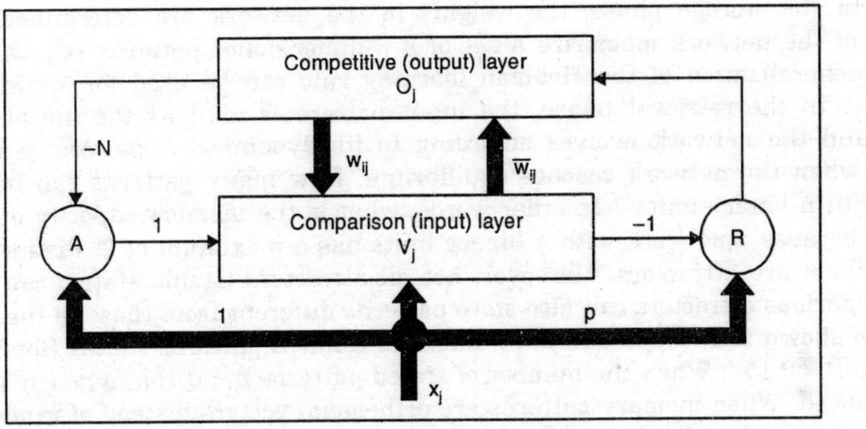

Fig. 3.6. *ART1 Network.*

ART1 learning algorithm

1. Initialize $w_0 = 1$, for all i, j. Enable all the output units.
2. Present a new pattern x.
3. Find the winner unit i^* among the enabled output units $\overline{w}_i \cdot x \geq \overline{w}_i \cdot x, \forall i$
4. Perform vigilance test

   $r = \dfrac{w_i \cdot x}{\sum_i x_i}$

   If $r \geq \rho$ (resonance), go to step 5. Otherwise, disable unit i and go to step 3 (until all the output units are disabled).
5. Update the winning weight vector w_{ji}, enable all the output units, and go to step 2.

   $\Delta w_{ji} = \eta\,(V_i - w_{ji})$
6. If all output units are disabled, select one of the uncommitted output units and set its weight vector to x. If there is no uncommitted output unit (capacity is reached), the network rejects the input pattern.

The dynamic update of network states in Equation 4 can be carried out in at least two ways : synchronously and asynchronously. In a synchronous updating scheme, all units are updated simultaneously at each time step. A central lock must synchronize the process. An asynchronous updating scheme selects one unit at a time and updates its state. The unit for updating can be randomly chosen. The energy function of the binary Hopfield network in a state $v = (v_1, v_2, ..., v_J)^T$ is given by

$$E = -\frac{1}{2}\sum_i \sum_j w_{ij}v_iv_j$$

The central property of the energy function is that as network state evolves according to the network dynamics (Equation a), the network energy always decreases and eventually reaches a local minimum point (attractor) where the network stays with a constant energy.

3.5. ASSOCIATIVE MEMORY

When a set of patterns is stored in these network attractors, it can be used as an associative memory. Any pattern present in the basin of attraction of a stored pattern can be used as an index to retrieve it. An associative memory usually operates in two phases : storage and retrieval. In the storage phase, the weights in the network are determined so that the attractors of the network memorize a set of p n-dimensional patterns $\{x^1, x^2, ..., x^p\}$ to be stored. A generalization of the Hebbian learning rule can be used for setting connection weights w_{li}. In the retrieval phase, the input pattern is used as the initial state of the network, and the network evolves according to its dynamics. A pattern is produced (or retrieved) when the network reaches equilibrium. How many patterns can be stored in a network with n binary units ? In other words, what is the memory capacity of a network ? It is finite because a network with n binary units has a maximum of 2“ distinct states, and not all of them are attractors. Moreover, not all attractors (stable states) can store useful patterns. Spurious attractors can also store patterns different from those in the training set. It has been shown that the maximum number of random patterns that a Hopfield network can store is P = 0.15~. When the number of stored patterns $p < 0.15n$, a nearly perfect recall can be achieved. When memory patterns are orthogonal vectors instead of random patterns, more patterns can be stored. But the number of spurious attractors increases asp reaches capacity. Several learning rules have been proposed for increasing the memory capacity of Hopfield networks. Note that we require $n2$ connections in the network to store pn-bit patterns.

3.5.1 Energy Minimization

Hopfield networks always evolve in the direction that leads to lower network energy. This implies that if a combinatorial optimization problem can be formulated as minimizing this energy, the Hopfield network can be used to find the optimal (or suboptimal) solution by letting the network evolve freely. In fact, any quadratic objective function can be rewritten in the form of Hopfield network energy. For example, the classic Traveling Salesman Problem can bc formulated as such a problem.

APPLICATIONS :

We have discussed a number of important ANN models and learning algorithms proposed in the literature. They have been widely used for solving the seven classes of problems described in the beginning of this article. Table 2 showed typical suitable tasks for A” models and learning algorithms. Remember that to successfully work with real-world problems, you must deal with numerous design issues, including network model, network size, activation function, learning parameters, and number of training samples. We next discuss an optical character recognition (OCR) application to illustrate how multilayer feedforward networks are successfully used in practice. OCR deals with the problem of processing a scanned image of text and transcribing it into machine-readable form. We outline the basic components of OCR and explain how ANNs are used for character classification.

3.5.2 An OCR System

An OCR system usually consists of modules for preprocessing, segmentation, feature extraction, classification, and contextual processing. A paper document is scanned to produce a gray-level or binary (black-and-white) image. In the preprocessing stage, filtering is applied to remove noise, and text areas are located and converted to a binary image using a global or local adaptive thresholding method. *En* the segmentation step, the text image is separated into individual characters. This is a particularly difficult task with handwritten text, which contains a proliferation of touching characters. One effective technique is to break the composite pattern into smaller patterns (over-segmentation) and find the correct character segmentation points using the output of a pattern classifier. Because of various degrees of slant, skew, and noise level, and various writing styles, recognizing segmented characters is not easy. This is evident from figure 3.7, which shows the size-normalized character bitmaps of a sample set from the NIST (National Institute of Standards and Technology) hand-print character database.

SCHEMES

Figure 3.8 shows the two main schemes for using A NNs in an OCR system. The first one employs an explicit feature extractor (nor necessarily a neural network). For instance, contour direction features are used in figure 3.8. The extracted features are passed to the input stage of a multilayer feed-forward network This scheme is very flexible in incorporating a large variety of features. The other scheme does not explicitly extract features from the raw data. The feature extraction implicitly takes place within the intermediate stages (hidden layers) of the *A*". A nice property of this scheme is that feature extraction and classification are integrated and trained simultaneously to produce optimal classification results. It is not clear whether the types of features that can be extracted by this integrated architecture are the most effective for character recognition. Moreover, this scheme requires a much larger network than the first one. A typical example of this integrated feature extraction-classification scheme is the network developed by Le Cun et aLzo for zip code recognition. A 16 × 16 normalized gray-level image is presented to a feed-forward network with three hidden layers. The units in the first layer are locally connected to the units in the input layer, forming a set of local feature maps. The second hidden layer is constructed in a similar way. Each unit in the

Fig. 3.7. *A sample set of character in NIST data base.*

second layer also combines local information coming from feature maps in the first layer. The activation level of an output unit can be interpreted as an approximation of the a posteriori probability of the input pattern's belonging to a particular class. The output categories are ordered according to activation levels and passed to the postprocessing stage. In this stage, contextual information is exploited to update the classifier's output. This could, for example, involve looking up a dictionary of admissible words, or utilizing syntactic constraints present, for example, in phone or social security number.

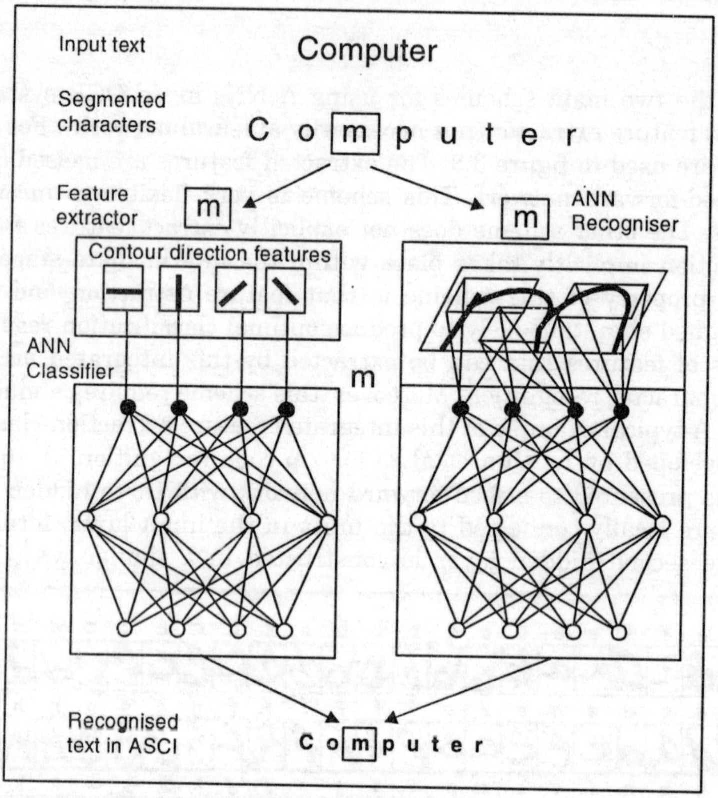

Fig. 3.8. *Two schemes for using ANNs in an OCR system.*

3.5.3 Results

ANN's work very well in the OCR application. However, there is no conclusive evidence about their superiority over conventional statistical pattern classifiers. At the First Census Optical Character Recognition System Conference held in 1992, 18 more than 40 different handwritten character recognition systems were evaluated based on their performance on a common database. The top 10 performers used either some type of multilayer feed-forward network or a nearest neighbor-based classifier. ANN's tend to be superior in terms of speed and memory requirements compared to nearest neighbor methods. Unlike the nearest neighbor methods, classification speed using ANN's is independent of the size of the training set. The recognition accuracies of the top OCR systems on the NIST isolated (presegmented) character data were above 98 percent for digits, 96 percent for uppercase characters, and 87 percent for lowercase characters. (Low recognition accuracy for lowercase characters was largely due to the fact that the test data differed significantly from the training data, as well as being due to "ground-truth errors.) One conclusion drawn from the test is that OCR system performance on isolated characters compares well with human performance. However, humans still outperform OCR systems on unconstrained and cursive handwritten documents.

3.6 DEVELOPMENTS IN ANN'S HAVE STIMULATED

A lot of enthusiasm and criticism. Some comparative studies are optimistic, some offer pessimism. For many tasks, such as pattern recognition, no one approach dominates the others. The choice of the best technique should be driven by the given application's nature. We should try to understand the capacities, assumptions, and applicability of various approaches and maximally exploit their complementary advantages to develop better intelligent systems. Such an effort may lead to a synergistic approach that combines the strengths of A"s with other technologies to achieve significantly better performance for challenging problems. As Minsky recently observed, the time has come to build systems out of diverse components. Individual modules are important, but we also need a good methodology for integration. It is clear that communication and cooperative work between researchers working in ANNs and other disciplines will not only avoid repetitious work but (and more important) will stimulate and benefit individual disciplines.

EXERCISE

1. What are the types of Learning rules ?
2. What is Boltzmann Learning ?
3. Explain Hebbian rule.
4. Discuss Kohonen's self-organising Maps.
5. What do you mean by an OCR system ?.
6. What is ANN? Discuss in details.

□□□

Chapter 4 APPLICATIONS OF ARTIFICIAL NEURAL NETWORK

4.1 USE OF NEURAL NETWORKS ON VLE DATA PREDICTION

The neural network model is employed to predict the vapour-liquid equilibrium (VLE) data for six different binary systems having different chemical features and solution types (Azatrope-Nonazeaotrope) in various conditions (isothermal or isobaric). A model based on a feed-forward back propagation neural network is proposed. Only half of the experimentally determined VLE data are assigned to the designed framework as training pattern in order to estimate the VLE data of the whole system in given conditions. The VLE data are also calculated by the UNIFAC model, a calculation method widely used in this field. The mean deviations from the experimental data are determined for both the models. It is observed that the data found by neural network gives an excellent agreement with the experimental data, while the UNIFAC model show deviations, particularly at low pressures. In fact the neural network model can be treated as a potent means for VLE data prediction in a fast and reliable way, compared to the conventional thermo dynamical models.

4.1.1 Introduction

In chemical industry the vapour-liquid equilibrium (VLE) data are mostly important for the design of distillation, where the liquid mixtures are separated into their components. The correlation of these data is found thermodynamically by various interpretations of the Gibbs-Duhem equation, because it is troublesome and time consuming to get them experimentally. The Wilson, NRTL, and UNIQUAC are the local composition models, and UNIFAC and ASOG are the main group contribution methods based on UNIQUAC and Wilson, respectively, implicating the local composition concept. Some of the models such as, UNIFAC-Lyngby, UNIFAC-Dortmund, and UNIQUAC-A were modified for special cases. Another type of estimation methods are the Margules and van Laar equations, which are empirical models of solution behavior, derived from excess gibbs energy function. These models represent the excess Gibbs energy function in different types of mathematical expressions and are used, both in vapour-liquid and liquid-liquid equilibrium calculations. The common feature is that the models used the liquid phase activity co-efficient to achieve the equilibrium data. Therefore, these methods are called activity co-efficient models, in general, and include two or more energy parameters with respect to a particular system. A set of specific parameters measured with respect to any system is valid exclusively for such a particular system (it cannot predict differences between isomers for example). On the other hand, because of the complexity of mathematical functions in same models, determination of the energy parameters is mathematically difficult. Furthermore for a defined system the energy parameters determined by a known model given by different sources in the literature, is found to be sometimes different. In fact, any doubt about the VLE estimates causes the design to be made at higher reflux ratio than may be necessary, leading to increased energy usage in distillation method. Although these models have limited flexibility in the fitting of data, they are adequate for most engineering purposes. But these uncertainties cause errors in activity co-efficient data, especially in equilibrium data.

The neural network model, proposed in this paper, is an alternatively intensive used method for most of prediction problems in engineering calculations and/or for different purposes. Many studies have claimed neural networks potent applicability for analysis of some complex systems. Neural networks have succeeded in coping with a few biological and chemical problems such as, control of bioreactors with unstable parameters, prediction of secondary dimensional structure of proteins, analysis of overlapped spectrum or chromatography, property prediction of compounds, phase equilibrium predictions in aqueous two phase extraction, and design of a combined mixing rule for the prediction of vapour-liquid equilibria.

The neural network is unable to offer parameters such as, the second viral co-efficient in thermodynamic meanings or any energy parameter in a detailed mechanism. For the purpose of gaining promising predictability, an approach based on optimum neural network architecture should be determined.

4.1.2 Thermodynamic Basis

For any vapour-liquid system in equilibrium the equality of fug cities of pure components leads to,

$$Y_i \cdot \varnothing_i' \cdot P = x_i \cdot \gamma_i \cdot f_i^\circ \qquad \text{...(1)}$$

Where y_i is the mole fraction of component i in vapour phase, x_i is the mole fraction in liquid phase, $\varnothing_i'$ is the fugacity co-efficient of I in the vapour phase, P is the total pressure, γ_i is the activity co-efficient of I in the fluid phase and f_i° is the standard-state fugacity of the pure I component. The standard-state fugacity is considered the fugacity of pure liquid i (f_i) at system temperature and pressure and is given by :

$$Fi = P_i^s \varnothing_i'^s \exp \frac{\left(ViL_{(P-Pis)}\right)}{RT} \qquad \text{...(2)}$$

Where for pure liquid, P_i^s is the saturation (vapour) pressure, $\varnothing_i^s$ is the fugacity co-efficient at saturation, and v_i^L is the molar liquid volume, at temperature T. The exponential is known as the Poynting factor. Substituting in Eq. (1) for f_i by Eq. (2) and solving for γ_i gives :

$$\gamma_i = \frac{y_i \cdot \varnothing_i' \cdot P}{x_i \cdot P_i^s} \qquad \text{...(3)}$$

where $\varnothing_i' = \dfrac{\varnothing_i}{\varnothing_i^s} \cdot \exp \dfrac{\left[-v_i^L \left(P - P_i^s\right)\right]}{RT}$

At low pressures, vapour phases usually approximate ideal gases. For which $\acute{\emptyset}_i = \acute{\emptyset}_i^s = 1$ and the pointing factor, represented by the exponential, differs from unity by only a few parts per thousand and their influence in Eq. (4) nullifies. Thus the assumption that $\acute{\emptyset}_i = 1$ introduces some error for low-pressure VLE data, the Eq. (3) gets reduce to :

$$\gamma_i = \frac{y_i \cdot P}{x_i \cdot P_i^s}$$

4.1.3 Neural Network Model

A neural network mimics the structure of human synapse connections to imitate the work of the brain. Typical structure of a neural network consist of multiple layers, each of them has a group of computing neurons, as shown in figure 4.1. Each of the neuron in one layer is completely connected with others in the adjacent layers but not with ones in the same layer. The first layer merely stores and transports the values of the input features to the next layer, the last layer calculates the output values, and between them are the hidden layers.

One typical neuron in such a neuron net is shown in figure 4.2. the inputs X are the products of the incoming neuron values L and synaptic weights w. The output y is then determined by applying the resulting input value to the activation functions. There are many activation functions available to be adopted for a net. In this work the log sigmoid function is preferred.

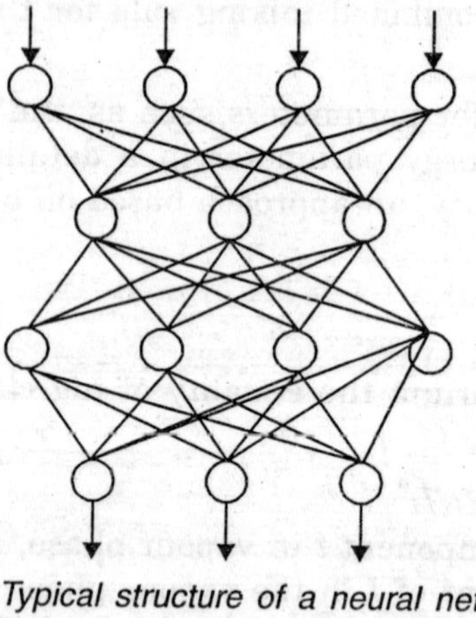

Fig. 4.1. *Typical structure of a neural net consisting of multiple layers.*

As a result of this preference the input values can be any values in the range of $-\infty$ and $+\infty$, but the output values are limited between 0 and 1.

$$Y = f\left(\sum_{i=0}^{N} L_i W_i\right)$$

$$f(X) = \frac{1}{1+e^{-x}}$$

here N is the number of incoming values from different neurons, L is the vector of incoming neurons, and w is the synaptic weights between incoming values and selected neuron.

4.1.4. Experimental Procedure

The feature of the neural network has been adapted to deal with the prediction of the VLE data of six various systems (Table 4.1). Four of the systems were taken from literature. All of the systems present various chemical structures and different solution types (Azeotrope-Nonazeotrope) under various conditions (isothermal or isobaric). The isobaric (MIBK) systems at 53.33 and 80.0 kPa were determined experimentally.

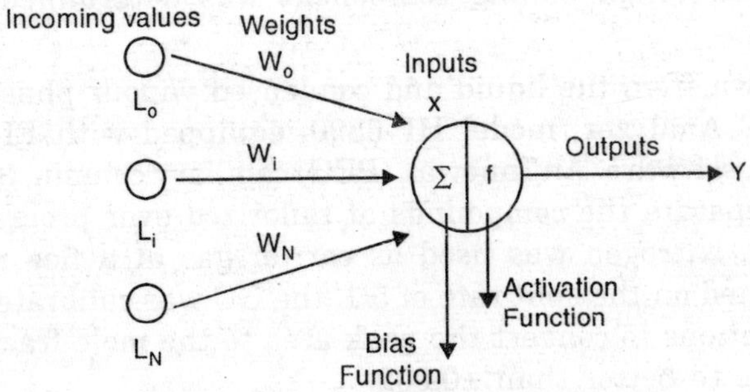

Fig. 4.2. *A neuron model.*

Table 4.1. The binary systems

System source	*Solution type*	*Condition*	*Data*
Isopropanol + MIBK	Normal	Isobaric,53.33kPa	Experimental
Isopropanol + MIBK	Normal	Isobaric,80.0kpa	Experimental
n-hexane+1.2-dichloroethane	Min.azeotrope	Isothermal,323.15K	Experimental
n-heptane+1.2-dichloroethane	Min.azeotrope	Isothermal,323.15K	Experimental
1,2-dichloroethane+n-octane	Normal	Isothermal,323.15K	Experimental
Acetone + chloroform	Max. azeotrope	Isobaric,101.32kPa	Experimental
*Methyl isobutyl ketone			

Isopropanol and methyl isobutyl ketone were used in Merck quality. An all-glass dynamic recirculating vapour-liquid equilibrium apparatus, developed by Fisher Scientific Co., equipped with temperature and pressure controllers were used in the experimental equilibrium data determinations. The still allows good mixing and flowing of both vapour and liquid phases through an extended contact line, which guaranties an intense phase exchange and their separation, once the equilibrium is reached. The equilibrium temperature was measured using a mercury glass thermometer (Fisher certificated) within an accuracy of ± 0.05 K. The temperature control of the heating was achieved by a digital thermometer provided with a pt-100 sensor. The total pressure of the system was controlled by an electronic manometer. The VLE tests were run at 40, 66.66 and 101.32 ± 0.02 kPa pressures respectively. The equilibrium conditions were checked by the reproducibility of the results Gas Chromatography (GC) analysis of liquid samples taken from two phases.

Approximately, 100 mL low boiling component (Isopropanol) was put in the boiler of the apparatus. The pressure was set via the controller and the heaters were then actuated. On reaching the boiling point the equilibrium temperature of the pure low boiling component was determined. The 2–2.5 mL high boiling component (Methyl isobutyl Ketone) was then added to the boiler and waited for the equilibrium conditions. The attainment of the constant temperature for about 1h was the sign of equilibrium reached. In equilibrium, samples were taken out from liquid and condensed vapour phases for analyzing with GC. Thus, in a known pressure (P) the liquid and vapour phase compositions (x_1, x_2 y_1, y_2) of a mixture at the equilibrium temperature (T) were determined experimental. By adding a few mL high boiling component each time and repeating and while continuing this procedure the equilibrium data of the high boiling component enriched mixtures were determined as well. Finally the boiling point of the pure high boiling component was determined after recharging the apparatus.

Samples withdrawn from the liquid and condensed vapour phases were analyzed with a Hewlett-Packard GC Analyzer, model HP-6890, equipped with FI-detector, and coupled with HP Chem.-Station software. An Innowax (PEG) capillary column, 30 m × 320 μm × 0.5 μm in size, was used to separate the compounds at tailorized over programs available for each binary system studied. Nitrogen was used as carrier gas at a floe rate of 0.8 mL/min all injections were performed on the split rate of 5/1. the GC was calibrated with gravimetrically prepared standard solutions to convert the peak area to the mole fraction composition. Mole fractions were accurate to better than ±0.002.

4.1.5 Application of Neural Network

The adaptation of the neural network model to the VLE data prediction was performed by using the MATLAB program (version 6.0), a widely used calculation and programming agent in engineering applications. The VLE problem was handled as a generalization problem and the neural network calculation employed a feed-forward algorithm to calculate the output, along with back-propagation to recursively correlate the weights. The learning process by adjusting the weights of the model was the most important part to establish a predictable neural network. As objective function in the learning process the total squared error in each vector was taken as :

$$\text{Total squared error} = \sum_{i=1}^{n} \left(Y_i^{\text{expt1}} - Y_i^{\text{cal}}\right)^2$$

Here Y_i^{exptl} is the experimental value, Y_i^{cal} the calculated value, and n the experimental number.

Only half of the experimentally determined VLE data points of six various binary mixtures were assigned into the designed framework as training patterns, in order to estimate the whole systems. The results were verified by examining the distribution of output errors and the dynamic response of the learning process.

In the application the low boiling component concentrations in the liquid phase (x_1) are given as input set values, and as a result the low boiling component concentrations in the vapour phase (y_i) and the liquid phase activity co-efficients (γ_1, γ_2) are taken as output set values.

4.1.6 Results and Discussion

The experimental activity co-efficients, γ_1 and γ_2,were calculated using the experimental $T_{x1\text{-}y1}$ values of related binary system. The pure component vapour pressures (P_i^s) in this equation were calculated through the Antoine equation using the constants A_i, B_i, and C_i.

The experimentally observed values of activity co-efficients (γ_i) and vapour phase concentrations (y_i) were compared with estimated values from UNIFAC original model and designed neural network model. In the UNIFAC model the group-volume a surface area parameters of the mentioned chemicals were taken as well. Table 4.2 and 4.3 present a quantitative assessment of the predictions achieved for each method with respect to mean deviation. Mean deviation was taken as :

$$\text{Mean deviation}_n = \overline{\Delta Y_i} = \sum_{k=1} |Y_{i.k}(\text{exptl}) - Y_{i.k}(\text{cal cd})| \ln.$$

According to table 4.2 the isobaric Isopropanol Methyl Isobutyl Ketone systems at 53.33 and 80.0 kPa and the isothermal 1, 2-dichloroethane + *n*-octane system at 323.15 K are attracting attention with a mean deviation above 0.1 with respect to UNIFAC calculated activity co-efficients. These deviations are shown in more detail by plotting experimentally observed γ_i values against the estimates in figure 4.3–4.5 respectively. The neural network model has shown excellent results for all systems with its flexible configuration.

For evaluating the appropriateness of the models to the Azeotrope systems, it is useful to show the *x-y* plots (vapour-liquid equilibrium curve) of the Azeotrope systems *n*-hexane + 1, 2-dichloroethane at 323.15 K, *n*-heptane + 1, 2-dichloroethane at 323.15 K and acetone + chloroform at 101.32 kPa. At these systems the Azeotropic point, where the equilibrium curve intersect the diagonal is, in fact important, representing the separation concentration of the systems with normal distillation method. It was seen that both the models show satisfactory results for Azeptrope systems.

Table 4.2. Mean deviation between experimental and calculated activity co-efficients

System	*UNIFAC*		*Neural network*	
	γ_1	γ_2	γ_1	γ_2
Isopropanol+MIBK,53.33kPa	0.1006	0.1400	0.0553	0.0119
Isopropanol+MIBK,80.0kPa	0.1412	0.1782	0.0234	0.0360
n-hexane+1,2-dichloroethane	0.0630	0.0543	0.0238	0.0142
n-heptane+1,2-dichloroethane	0.0475	0.0382	0.0261	0.0304
1,2-dichloroethane+n-octane	0.0233	0.1051	0.0310	0.0452
Acetone+chloroform	0.0198	0.0104	0.0163	0.0094

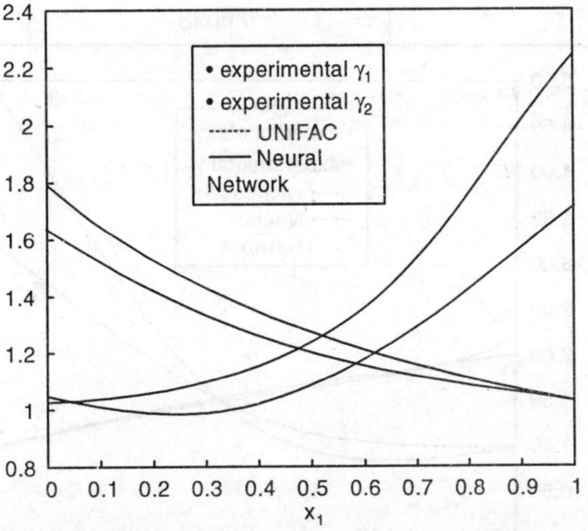

Fig. 4.3. *Comparison of calculated and experimental activity co-efficients of isopropanol + methyl isobutyl ketone system at 53.33 kPa.*

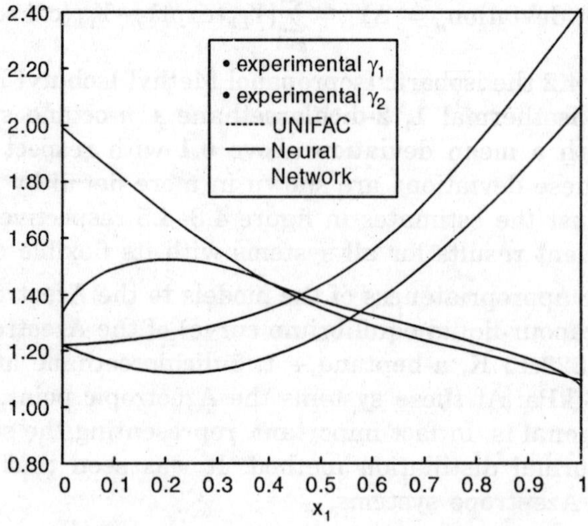

Fig. 4.4. *Comparison of calculated and experimental activity co-efficients of Isopropanol + Methyl Isobutyl Ketone system at 80.0 kPa.*

Table 4.3. Mean deviations between experimental and calculated vapour

System	Phase concentration	
	UNIFAC	***Neural network***
	Y_1	y_1
Isopropanol+MIBK, 53.33kPa	0.0135	0.0111
Isopropanol+MIBK, 80.0kPa	0.0258	0.0114
n-hexane+1,2-dichloroethane	0.0163	0.0095
n-heptane+1,2-dichloroethane	0.0077	0.0135
1,2-dichloroethane+n-octane	0.0094	0.0082
Acetone+chloroform	0.0028	0.0114

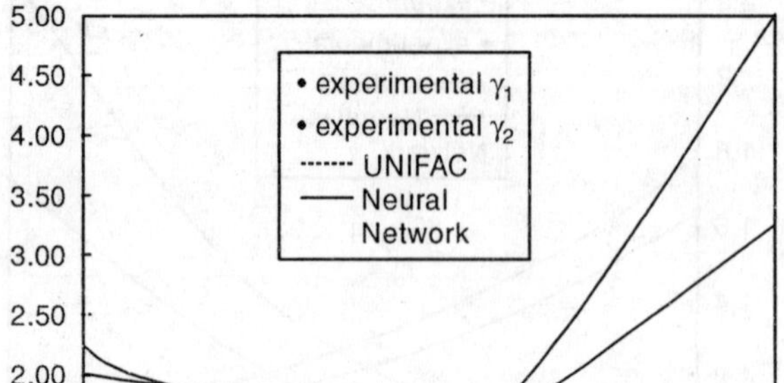

Fig. 4.5. *Comparison of calculated and experimental activity co-efficients of 1, 2-dichloroethane + n-octane system at 323.15 K.*

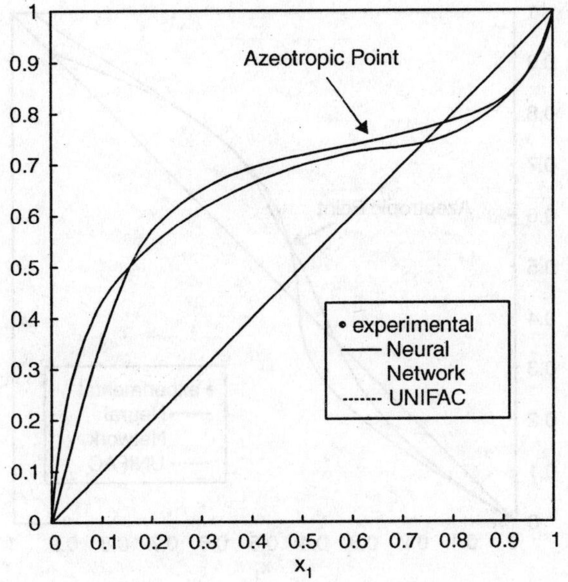

Fig. 4.6. *Comparison of calculated and experimental vapour phase compositions of the system n-hexane + 1, 2-dichloroethane at 323.15 K.*

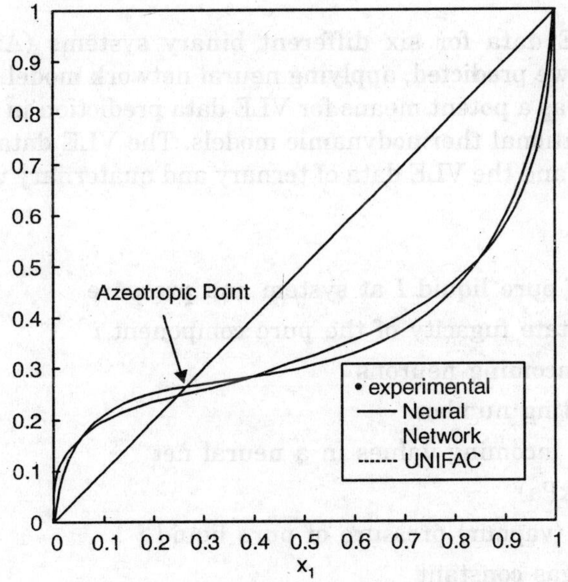

Fig. 4.7. *Comparison of calculated and experimental vapour phase compositions of the system n-heptane + 1, 2-dichloroethane at 323.15 K.*

In UNIFAC method, despite the care taken for pressure indirectly through the temperature, it seems insufficient at low pressures. On the contrary, neural network model shows a good agreement at all conditions presenting minimum deviations and giving satisfying results.

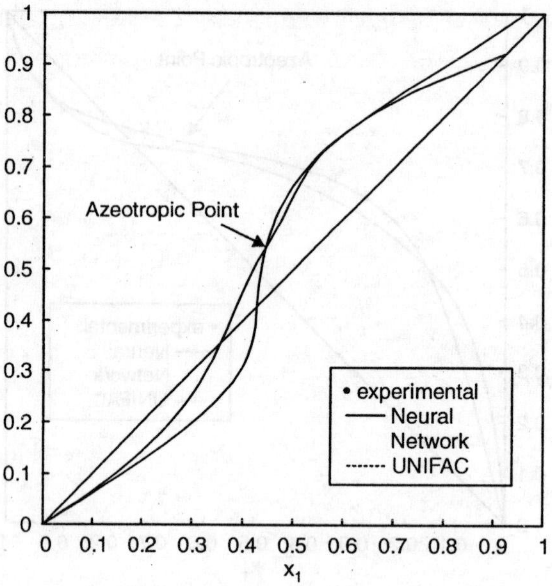

Fig. 4.8. *Comparison of calculated and experimental vapour phase compositions of the system acetone + chloroform at 101.32 kPa.*

4.1.7 Conclusion

In this study the VLE data for six different binary systems (Azeotrope-Nonazeotrope, Isothermal or Isobaric) we predicted, applying neural network model. It has seen that neural network can be treated as a potent means for VLE data prediction in a fast and reliable way, compared to the conventional thermodynamic models. The VLE data of binary systems in a wide range of pressure, and the VLE data of ternary and quaternary will be the future course of our study.

Nomenclature

f_i : fugacity of pure liquid I at system and pressure

f_i^{o} : standard-state fugacity of the pure component i

L : vector of incoming neurons

n : experimenting number

N : number of incoming values in a neural net

P : pressure (kPa)

P_i^s : saturation (vapour) pressure of pure liquid i

R : universal gas constant

T : temperature (K)

V_i^L : molar liquid volume of pure component i

w : synaptic weights

x_i : mole fraction of component i in liquid phase

y_i : mole fraction of component i in vapour phase

$\overline{\Delta Y_i}$: mean deviation

$\varnothing_i^s$: fugacity co-efficient of pure component i at saturation

$\varnothing_i^{\wedge}$: fugacity co-efficient of component i in the vapour phase

γ_i : activity co-efficient of i in the fluid phase

Appendix A : Neural Network Program for Prediction VLE Data

```
Clear
NNTWARN OFF
% This program is tested with MATLAB version 6.0 release 12.
% Definitions:
% Training set file: The file consisting the data for training the neural network
(x, y, T, gamma1, gamma2 vectors).
% Input set file: The file consisting the data to be used as input set
for neural network.
(vector x).
% Output set file: The file where the output set of the neural network will be
saved.

% loading data
R=input ('Training set file name:', 's');
S=input ('Input set file name:', 's')
G=input ('Output set file name:', 's')

PPP=load (R);[lpx lpy] = size(PPP);
PPP11=load(S);[lpx111py11] = size(PPP11);
% building input vector [P]….
X1=PPP(1:1px,1);
P=x1;
X11=PPP11(1:1px11,1);
P11=x11';

%building target vector [T]…
y1=PPP(1:1px,3);
temperature=PPP(1:1px,5)/1000;
gama1=PPP(1:1px,6)/10;
gama2=PPP(1:1px,7)/10;
T=[y1'; temperature';gama1';gama2'];
%defining hidden neurons….
h1=8;
%building weight co-efficients randomly….
w1-rand(1,h1)';w2=rand(h1,4)';
b1=rand(h1,1);b2=rand(4,1);
%training…
df=500;
```

```
me=10000;
eg=0.0005;
1r=0.02;
tp=[de me eg 1r];


[w1, b1, w2, b2, ep,tr]=trainbpx(w1,b1, 'logsig',w2,b2, 'logsig', P,T,tp);

%processing output data…
TTy=simuff(P,w1,b1, 'logsig',w2,b2, 'logsig');

%displaying normalized output data…
outoput=TTy11;
output(:,2)=output(:,2)*1000;
output(:,3)=output(:,3)*10;
output(:,4)=output(:,4)*10;
output2(1:1px11,1)-x11;
output2(2:,2)=output(:,1);
output2(:,3)=output(:,2);
output2(:,4)=output(:,3);
output2(:,5)=output(:,4);
disp
('.............................................................')

disp('x1 y1 T gamma1 gamma2')
disp(output2)

%fid=fopen(output2.txt, 'w');
fid=fopen(G, 'w');
fprintf(fid, ' ......\n');
fprintf(fid, '\n');
fprintf(fid, '%8.5f %8.5f %8.5f %8.5f %8.5f\n', output2');
fclose(fid);
% save output2
```

4.2 COUNTER PROPAGATION NEURAL NETWORKS FOR FAULT DETECTION AND DIAGNOSIS

The application of a Counter Propagation Neural Network (CPNN) to detect single faults and their magnitudes. The performance of CPNN has been evaluated by considering a variety of faults occurring in a non-isothermal Continuous Stirred Tank reactor (CSTR).

The result presented here indicates that CPNN provides an attractive alternative to Error-Pack Propagation (EBP) networks due to its faster learning ability for fault detection and diagnosis.

4.2.1 Introduction

The term "process fault" in its broadest sense indicates those process, symptoms that results from the physical change in the process, such as deviation in flow, fluid level temperature and pressure from their normal operating range. Fault refers also to the physical changes themselves, such as leaks, blockages, fouling erosion, corrosion wear, scaling and foaming. Even changes in the unmeasured process parameters such as heat or mass-transfer co-efficients are assumed to be faults. Such undesirable process behavior can occur due to the occurrence of just one (single) fault or their simultaneously presence (multiple faults). Especially for nonlinear systems, the relationship between performance pattern (measured process variables) and fault causes becomes complex. The objective of fault detection and diagnosis is to recognize the abnormal process behavior patterns and to find the corresponding causes of faults. The task can be viewed as a pattern association problem where one wishes to recognize deviations, disturbances or equipment/sensor malfunctions and associate them with their respective origins.

Artificial Neural Networks (ANN) due to their ability to learn and generalize nonlinear functional relationship(s) between input-output variables provide a flexible mechanism for learning and recognition of process faults. A neural network can store knowledge by learning from historical fault information and has the characteristics of associative memory *i.e.,* during learning the network memorizes the fault patterns, and in the post-training stage when shown a new input pattern, it associates that pattern with the appropriate memorized one. Some networks (*e.g.,* error-back-propagation) can also interpolate the memorized patterns so that the predictions corresponding to the inputs not learned explicitly can be made. The process information to be learned by the network could be *e.g.,* the steady-state values of variables under normal as well as faulty conditions. Such a database can be easily generated using either the process model, past data of fault occurrence or quality control program design to identify the faults. When operated in the predictive mode employing new data, the trained neural network can classify faults and also provides stable and highly sensitive fault diagnosis.

ANSs use a variety of architectures and notable ones being the feedforward are commonly utilized for pattern recognition tasks while the recurrent networks characterize the nonlinear dynamic feedback systems. Amongst these the feedforward networks trained using the Error Back Propagation (EBP) algorithm seems to be the most popular approach for process fault detection. Several researchers have shown how the EBP algorithm can be used to detect and diagnose process faults. These studies have shown that the networks trained with EPB formalism posses the ability to learn the input-output patterns from a set of training examples and can often successfully generalize this knowledge to diagnose new cases of faults.

While it is true that the EBP formalism posses excellent pattern recognition, interpolation and generalization abilities, it is faced with difficulties such as entrapment into a local minima during network training, long training times, and several runs that are necessary to optimize network's structural and functional parameters such as the number of hidden layers, number of neurons in each hidden layer and momentum and learning co-efficients. Krammer and Leonard (1990) have detailed limitations of EBP network in the context of fault detection and diagnosis. They observe that the EBP networks though effectively separate the training examples into different classes, the partitioning may not be the most plausible. Also, the EBP networks are unable to detect a pattern that falls in a region with no training data. As a result, a novel fault pattern falling in such regime gets misclassified as one of the known faults or sometimes even as normal. Other network formalisms; namely, Radial Basis Function (RBF) and Adaptive Resonance Theory-2 (ART2) networks have also been employed for fault detection and diagnosis task. The RBF networks are distant based classifiers and known to have improved generalization and faster learning abilities. Neural networks based on ART possess the stability-plasticity property due to which a trained network, without forgetting the learned information (stability) can learns new patterns (plasticity). Kavuri and Venkatasubramaniam (1993) have developed a two-stage fault classifier which uses fuzzy clustering with ellipsoidal units. This algorithm in the first stage determines the number of hidden layer neurons and also the initial estimates of network weights. The second stage uses EBP methodology to tune the network weights. This two-stage approach avoids the need to optimize the network structure by trial and error means and also the local minima.

Although the Rbf networks fare better than the EBP networks at extrapolation, they do not always guarantee an optimal solution (equivalent of finding the global minimum) to classification problems. Moreover determining the optimal architecture of RBFNs as in EBP networks is not straightforward and does require trial and error approach. Other networks models (*e.g.*, ART) that have been used for fault diagnosis purposes have, in general complex training algorithms and yet not applied extensively. With this background, in this paper we present results of the study wherein the Counter Propagation Neural Network (CPNN) has been employed for performing fault diagnosis of nonisothermal Continuous Stir Tank Reactor (CSTR). The CPNNs are associated with them advantages like the training algorithm is simple and fast and also that the optimal network architecture can be determined beforehand. Moreover a CPNN is not faced with entrapment into local minima problem which means that the network is guaranteed to find the correct response (or the nearest stored response) to any given input.

4.2.2 Counterpropagation Neural Networks

Counterpropagation networks invented by Hecht-Nielsen (1987) are suitable for statistical analysis, functional approximation and as look-up tables. The CPNN architecture is a combination of two well-known algorithms; the self-organizing map of Kohonen (1984) and the Grossberg's outstar. The CPNN architecture (Fig. 4.9) consists of three layers of neurons namely : input, Kohonen, and Grossberg layers. The neurons of input and Kohonen layers, as well as Kohonen and Grossberg layers are fully connected. Although the Kohonen and Grossberg can be identified as the hidden and output layers of EBP networks, the difference lies in the way the Kohonen layered is trained and functions. To be specific, the Kohonen layers neurons compete with each other and only the winner neuron is allowed to get activated and change its weights. This mode of neuron operation is referred to as winner-takes-all.

The Kohonen and Grossberg layers of CPNN undergo unsupervised and supervised training, respectively. Upon presenting the input and corresponding output patterns to the network, the interlayer weights are gradually adjusted. The process is repeated till the network when presented with a certain input pattern correctly generates the corresponding

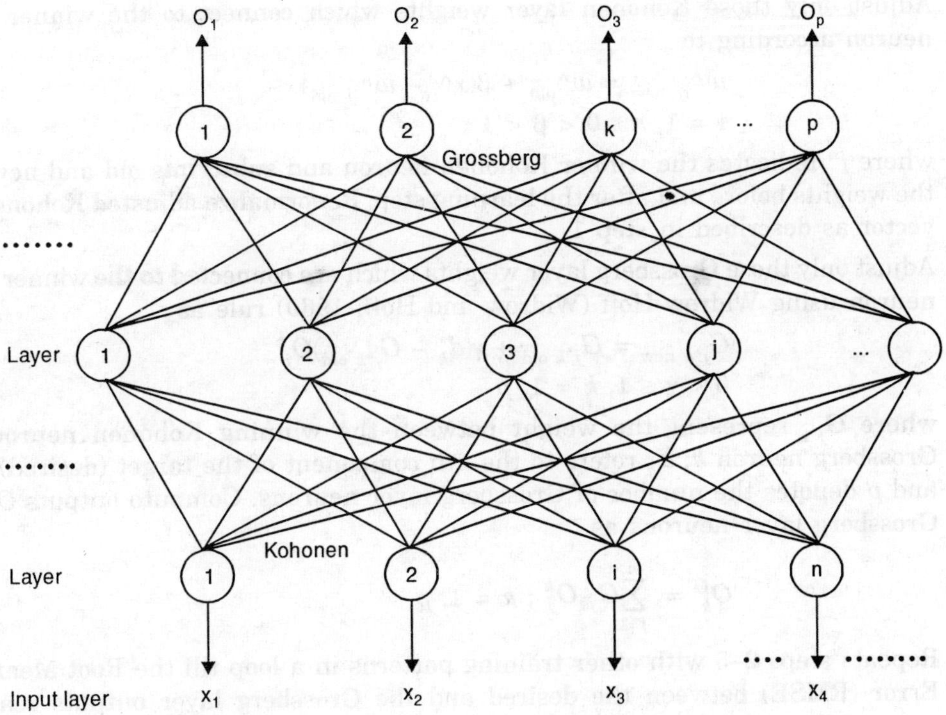

Fig. 4.9. *Schematic architecture of counterpropagation neural network.*

desired outputs. CPNN training results in the separation or classification of input patterns into different groups (classes) comprising similar patterns. The trained network then functions as the nearest-neighbour classifier. That is, when a new input pattern is presented to the network, it first finds that stored input vector which very closely resembles the applied pattern and then responds with the corresponding output. Although the detailed CPNN training procedure can be found at several places for the sake of completeness the training algorithm has been described in the following.

4.2.3 CPNN Training Algorithm

1. Normalize elements of an input vector $X = (x_1, x_2, \ldots, x_n)$ and randomly initialized kohonen layer weights w_{ij} as

$$X_i = \frac{x_i}{\left(\sum_{i=1}^{n} x_i^2\right)^{1/2}}; \quad wij = \frac{w_{ij}}{\left(\sum_{i=1}^{n} w_{ij}^2\right)^{1/2}}, \; j = 1, k \qquad \ldots(1)$$

   where $w^{\wedge}_{ij}$ and w_{ij} denote the unnormalized and normalized Kohnen layer weights. Compute outputs (O_j^x) of all Kohonen layer neurons as follows.

$$O_j^k = \sum_{i=1}^{n} w^{\wedge}{}_{ij} x^{\wedge}{}_{i}, \; j = 1, m \qquad \ldots(2)$$

2. Determine which of the m Kohonen neurons posses the largest output and declare that neuron as the competition winner.
3. Set the output of the winner Kohonen neuron equal to 1 the outputs of all other (nonwinning) Kohonen neurons are set to zero.

4. Adjust only those Kohonen layer weights which connect to the winner Kohonen neuron according to

$$w\hat{}_{ij\ new} = w\hat{}_{old} + \beta(x\hat{}_i - w\hat{}_{ij\ old}) \qquad ...(3)$$
$$i = 1, n : 0 < \beta < 1$$

where j^* indicates the winner Kohonen neuron and subscripts old and new refer to the weights before and after the learning step. Renormalize adjusted Kohonen weight vector as described in step 1.

5. Adjust only those Grossberg layer weights which are connected to the winner Kohonen neuron using Widrow-Hoff (Widrow and Hoff, 1960) rule as :

$$G_{j^*k\ new} = G_{j^*k\ old} + \gamma(d_k - G_{j^*k\ old})O_j^k \qquad ...(4)$$
$$0 < \gamma \leq 1,\ k = 1, p$$

where G_{j^*k} represent the weight between the winning Kohonen neuron j^* and Grossberg neuron k; d_k refers to the kth component of the target (desired) vector d and p denotes the number of Grossberg layer neurons. Compute outputs O_k^G of the Grossberg layer neurons as :

$$O_k^G = \sum_{j=1}^{m} G_{jk} O_j^k \ ;\ k = 1, p \qquad ...(5)$$

Repeats steps 2–5 with other training patterns in a loop till the Root Mean Square Error (RMSE) between the desired and the Grossberg layer outputs reaches the acceptable minimum as indicated by the proper classification of training patterns.

4.2.4 Theory of CPNN Classification

The input space to CPNN can be visualized as vectors of unit length distributed in an n-dimensional hypersphere. From vector algebra, the angle between two vectors is given by

$$\cos\theta = \frac{X.W}{|X||W|} \qquad ...(6)$$

Where the numerator is the scalar product of two vectors X and W with magnitudes denoted by $|X|$ and $|W|$ respectively. Expanding equation (6) and subsequently using equation (1) we can write.

$$\cos\theta = \frac{\sum_{i=1}^{n} x_i w_{ij}}{\left(\sum_{i=1}^{n} x_{i2}\right)^{1/2} \left(\sum w_{ij2}\right)^{1/2}} \qquad ...(7)$$

since the vectors X and W are normalized, [X] and [W] equals unity an hence the right hand sides of the equations (2) and (7) are identical. This indicates that the incoming sum to jth Kohonen neuron reflects the angle between the input vector and its weight vector for jth Kohonen neuron is defined as $[w_1, w_2, ..., w_n]$. During training, the weight adjustment specified by equation (3) has the effect of moving the weight vector W towards the input vector X. similarly, equation (4) tries to equate weight G_{l^*k} $(k = 1, p)$ with the target output vector d hence, at the end of training, the Grossberg layer weights would converge to the average values of the desired output and the weights between the input layer and a Kohonen neuron will be the average of those input patterns that would activate it. Consequently the converged weight vector W of a Kohonen neuron act as an exemplar (representative) vector to a group of input vectors lying close in its neighborhood. The training procedure will small β ensures that dissimilar input vectors activate different Kohonen neurons.

When the converged network is used to predict the class of a new input pattern, essentially the angle new vector makes with all the converged weight vectors gets computed (equations 2 and 7). The Kohonen neuron with weight vector making the least angle with the test vector wins the competition as it possesses the maximum output. This way the patterns belonging to one class or cluster consistently activate the same Kohonen neuron.

4.2.5 Fault Detection using CPNN

To valuate the learning and classification capabilities of CPNN for fault detection and diagnosis, we consider a representative model governing the dynamics of a no isothermal CSTR. The process represents a jacketed CSTR wherein an irreversible exothermic first-order reaction $A \longrightarrow B$ takes place. The reactor is fitted with three proportional control loops that control the outlet temperature, the reactor hold-up, and outlet concentration. The detailed schematic of this process has given by Venkatasubramanian et al.(1990). The governing process and controller equations are :

$$\frac{dV}{dt} = F_0 - F \qquad \text{...(8)}$$

$$\frac{dC_A}{dt} = \frac{F_0}{V}C_{A0} - \frac{F}{V}C_A - kC_A\,;\; k = \alpha \exp(\text{-EIRT}) \qquad \text{...(9)}$$

$$\frac{dT}{dt} = \frac{F_0 T_0}{V} - \frac{FT}{V} - \frac{\lambda k C_A}{{}_p C_p} - \frac{UA}{{}_p V C_p}(T - T_j) \qquad \text{...(10)}$$

$$\frac{dT_i}{dt} = \frac{F_j}{V_i}(T_{i0} - T_{j0}) + \frac{UA}{p_i V_i C_j}(T - T_j) \qquad \text{...(11)}$$

$$F_j = F_{j\text{-}k}\,(T_{set} - T) \qquad \text{...(12)}$$

$$F = F - k_L\,(V_{set} - V) \qquad \text{...(13)}$$

$$F0 = F_0 + k_A\,(C_{AO} - C_{AO}) \qquad \text{...(14)}$$

Where equations (8–11) describe the time evolution of reactor hold-up (V), reactant concentration (C_A), reactor temperature (T) and coolant temperature (Tj), respectively. The proportional control is affected via equations (12-14) wherein Fp, F_0 and F, respectively. denote the coolant, CSTR input and outlet flow rates.

4.2.6 Simulation of Faults

We consider a few but representative single faults which can occur during the steady-state operation of a CSTR when process parameters deviate by a fixed amount from their normal (or set) values. The specific faults which can influence the steady-state CSTR behavior have been identified (Venkatasubramanian et al, 1990; Watanabe et al, 1989) as : (*i*) input flow rate (Fo) high, (*ii*) input flow rate low, (*iii*) inlet concentration low, (*iv*) inlet temperature (To) high, (*v*) inlet temperature low, and (*vi*) decrease in heat transfer co-efficient (U) due to fouling. The inlet concentration can deviate if CSTR happens to be a downstream unit. We assume that this faults occur in a mutually exclusive manner. That is, out of seven only one type of fault can occur at any given time.

It can be easily seen from the equations (8–14) that any deviation I the model parameters would eventually affect the steady-state values of the state variables namely, (*i*) outlet reaction concentration(C_A), (*ii*) CSTR temperature (*T*), (*iii*) reactor hold-up (*V*), (*iv*) reactor output flow rate (*F*), (*v*) jacket coolant flow rate (*Fj*) and, (*vi*) coolant temperature (*Tj*). The magnitude of these state variables are generally available as measured data. The fault detection and diagnosis tasks involves fixing up the fault type and also the fault magnitude using the steady-state values of the state variables.

To generate input data for training, equations (8–14) were solved to obtain the steady-state values of the six state variables. The values of the model parameters are : $F_o = F_o$ = 1.5 m^3hr^{-1}, $F = F$ = 1.15 m^3hr^{-1}, $V = V_{set}$ = 1.35 m^3, $C_{Ao} = C_{Ao}$ = 8000 g-molm^{-1}, $T = T_{set}$ –333 K, $T_{jo} = T_o$ = 295 K, V_j = 0.1 m^3, α = 7.08 × 1010 hr^{-1}, C_j = 4 J (gmoloK)$^{-1}$, F_j = 1.4 m^3hr^{-1}, λ = –70000 J(gmol)$^{-1}$, R = 8.3262 J(gmolhr)$^{-1}$, E = 70000 J(gmol)$^{-1}$, U = 3 × 106 J(hrm^{2}K)$^{-1}$, p = 8 × 105 gmol(m^3)$^{-1}$, p_j = 106 gmol(m^3)$^{-1}$, k_c = 0.2 m^3(hr K)$^{-1}$, C_p = 3 J(gmol K)$^{-1}$, A = 25m^2, k_L = 10 hr^{-1} and k_a = 8.8 × 10^{-5} m^6(gmolhr)$^{-1}$. All the seven faulty process conditions were simulated separately. Each of the seven data sets so generated corresponds to 0.1–15% deviation (at the interval of 0.1%) from the normal value of the malfunction. Thus, each fault is represented by 150 patterns. Subsequently, all the seven data sets were combined to form a single input set for network training and the pattern consisting of the steady-state values of state variables under no fault conditions was added to this cumulative set. The data structure of the resultant training input set is given in Table 4.4. This set can be visualized as a matrix of size (1051.6) consisting of 1050 fault patterns representing seven faults and the remaining one portraying the normal process behavior. Table 4.5 lists the steady state values of the six state variables obtained using equations (8–14). Note that out of the 150 patterns of each fault covering 0.1–15% deviation range, the values corresponding to 5% and 15% deviations only are listed. However, Fig. 4.10 shows the plot of steady-state values of the reactor temperature (*T*) versus the outlet reactant concentration (C_A) corresponding to all the 1051 training input patterns.

Table 4.4. Data structure for network training and testing

Name of Fault	***Fault code***	***Training Data(inputs)***		***Test data(inputs)***	
		Pattern no(s).	***Deviation (%)#***	***Pattern no(s).***	***Deviation* %#***
1. Input flow rate high	F1	1–150	(+)0.1–15.0	1–1500	(+)0.01–15
2. Input flow rate low	F2	151–300	(–)0.1–15.0	1501–3000	(–)0.01–15
3. Inlet conc. High	F3	301–450	(+)0.1–15.0	3001–4500	(+)0.01–15.0
4. Inlet conc. Low	F4	451–600	(–)0.1–15.0	4051–6000	(–)0.01–15.0
5. Input temperature high	F5	601–750	(+)0.1–15.0	6001–7500	(+)0.01–15.0
6. Heat transfer coeff. Low	F6	751–900	(–)0.1–15.0	7501–9000	(–)0.01–15.0
7. Normal operation		1051			

* Percent deviation from the normal operating value of the parameter defined in column 2.

\# Training and Test data were generated at the deviation intervals of 0.1% and 0.01%, respectively.

Table 4.5. Magnitudes of state variables in presence of fault

Fault code	*Fault magnitude,%*	*Steady-state values of process variables*					
		T	C_A	V	F	T_i	F_j
F1	5	333.229	4260.650	1.335	1.207	330.492	1.445
	15	333.437	4393.390	1.367	1.322	330.612	1.487
F2	5	332.983	4115.119	1.344	1.092	330.350	1.396
	15	332.694	3953.730	1.332	0.997	330.182	1.338
F3	5	333.713	4243.623	1.346	1.114	330.770	1.542
	15	334.827	4316.734	1.339	1.043	331.400	1.765
F4	5	332.485	4122.381	1.353	1.185	330.060	1.297
	15	331.180	3943.535	1.360	1.256	329.285	1.036
F5	5	334.880	3923.135	1.350	1.150	331.429	1.776
	15	338.101	3448.366	1.350	1.150	333.174	2.420
F6	5	331.207	4477.732	1.350	1.150	329.302	1.041
	15	326.843	5126.579	1.350	1.150	326.559	1.686
	5	333.145	4184.539	1.350	1.150	330.312	1.429
	15	333.226	4172.284	1.350	1.150	330.048	1.445
Normal (no fault)	0	331.111	4189.655	1.350	1.150	330.424	1.422

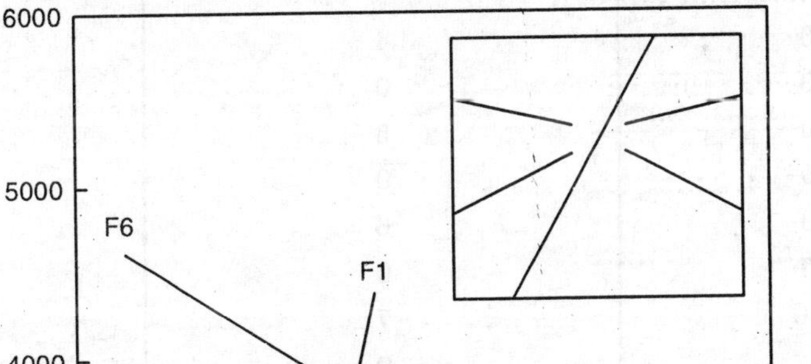

Fig. 4.10. *Reactor Temperature T.*

Figure 4.10. Plot showing the steady-state values of T versus C4 for all the seven faults. Inset shows the steady-state values corresponding to the fault number seven (F7). The steady-state with respect to the normal (no fault) process operation is shown by '*'. With a given training input pattern two fault characteristics, namely the fault type and the fault magnitude are associated. Therefore the desired network input or equivalently the desired Grossberg layer input vector (d) corresponding to each input vector consist of two elements (d_1, d_2) representating the fault number (type) and the fault magnitude respectively. The data structure of the desired Grossberg output vector is shown in table 4.6. Conventionally the deviation in process parameters within ± 5% threshold are considered to be normal and are not treated as faults. Therefore deviations upto 5% are assumed to be the cases of no fault and are represented by fault number 0 and fault magnitude 0 in table 4.6. The d_2 values in table 4.6 need further explanation. The pattern number 51–150 pertaining to the deviation range 5.1–15% are divided equally into 10 classes. These classes are assigned d_2 values from 6 to 15 (at unit increments) in a sequential manner indicating the approximate fault magnitudes. Other entries in table 4.6 can be interpreted analogously.

Table 4.6. Desired Grossberg layer outputs (d_1) corresponding to the training data

Pattern No(s).	*Fault Number (d_1)*	*Fault magnitude (d_2 %)#*
1–50	0	0
51–150	1	6.0–15.00
151–200	0	0
201–300	2	6.0–15.00
301–350	0	0
351–450	3	6.0–15.00
451–500	0	0
501–600	4	6.0–15.00
601–650	0	0
651–750	5	6.0–15.00
751–800	0	0
801–900	6	6.0–15.00
901–950	0	0
951–1050	7	6.0–15.00
1051	0	0

and 1% deviation interval

4.2.7 CPNN SIMULATION

In principle, 1051 training input patterns can be classifies in as many categories by using the same number of kohonen layer neurons. However, to keep the network size small, instead of choosing 1051 neurons in the kohonen layer we selected 106. This way the network can be made to learn 106 categories. Out of the 106 categories first 105 pertains to the faulty process behavior (fifteen fault classes separated by 1% intervals covering the deviation range 0.1–15% for each of the seven fault types) and the remaining one represents the normal process behavior. It suggests that a properly trained network should predict the fault magnitudes within 1% accuracy.

The CPNN architecture used for simulations comprises six neurons in the input layer to represent as many process variables, 106 neurons in the kohonen layer, and two neurons in the Grossberg layer to indicate the fault type and the fault magnitude respectively ($n = 6$, $m = 106$, $p = 2$). Initially, CPNN training was carried out exactly as described by algorithm steps 1–5. it was observed that the network does not classify the patterns properly when the weights begin with random values. For all the input patterns the same kohonen neuron was getting activated (winning). The observed phenomena is typical to CPNN and is known as stuck vector. To overcome the stuck vector problem we initialized the kohonen weight vectors to be same as the prototype input patterns. The set of 106 prototype vectors so chosen consist of 15 patterns each from seven fault classes and the last one indicating the normal process operation. The selected 15 patterns were those separated by 1% interval beginning to at 0.5% deviation. Due to this particular choice, the weight vector associated with each kohonen neuron, at the start of network training is located exactly at the center of the 1% fault deviation interval that the kohonen neuron is supposed to represent. After initializing the network weights as described above the stuck problem got solved. Thereafter, multiple training runs were performed to optimize the values of learning parameters β and γ; these were found to be 0.001 and 0.04, respectively. For such magnitudes the trained network classified the training data successfully *i.e.*, the network predicted all the seven fault types of the training data correctly. As intended, the fault magnitudes associated with the input patterns also were predicted within a percent accuracy. Figure 4.11 shows a representative plot of actual fault magnitudes versus the fault magnitudes learnt by the network at the end of training session. It can be seen that the network recognizes the fault magnitudes below 5% as no fault cases and emits 0 as the fault magnitude.

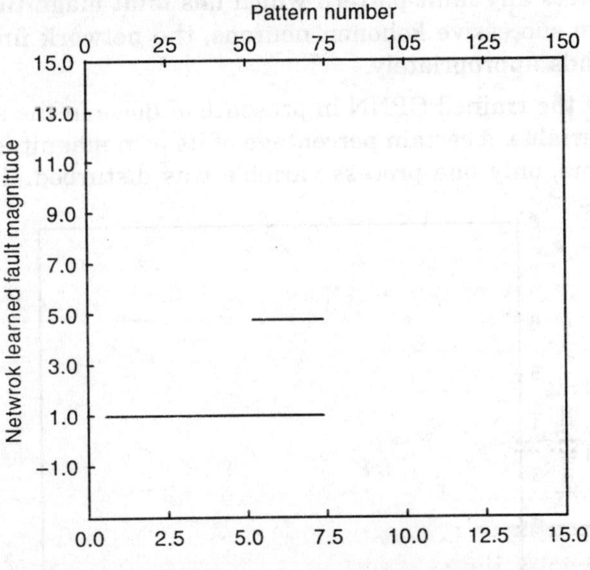

Fig. 4.11. *Representative plot of actual fault magnitudes versus the network learned fault magnitudes for patterns corresponding to fault No.1 (F1) of the training data. Upper x-axis shows the respective fault pattern numbers. Equivalent results are Obtained for other faults.*

The need for taking a somewhat large number (106) of neuron in the kohonen layer deserves an explanation especially in the context of EBP networks. In EBP network, there is no direct relationship between the number of neurons in the hidden layer and the number of classes the network can recognize. Therefore an EBP network even with few hidden neurons can learn and generalize the class information contained in the learning data. On the other hand, CPNN does not posses the interpolation and generalization abilities of the EBP networks but functions as a nearest neighbour classifier. Consequently, to a given input pattern, the trained networks assigns that learns class to which the input pattern is closest to. Thus, CPNN cannot represent any class which it has not learned explicitly during training. Moreover, in CPNN the number of kohonen layer neuron directly decides the number of classes the network can identify. This puts the restriction that to recognize m number of classes, as many kohonen neurons are essential. Since this study aims at detecting 105 fault patterns as also the normal process behavior that we selected 106 kohonen neurons. However, if lower (than 1%) accuracy in predicting the fault magnitudes can be tolerated, then it is possible to work with lesser number of neurons in the kohonen layer.

4.2.8 Results and Discussion

The data for rigorously testing CPNN's post-training classification ability was generated for all the seven faults at much smaller deviation intervals (0.01%) to cover the 0.01–15% fault magnitude range. The seven sets each compromising of 1500 patterns were combined to form a single test set, the structure of which is given in table 4d. The 10500 patterns so generated were applied to the network sequentially and the respective network outputs are shown in Fig. 4.12 and 4.13 as can be seen the network classifies the fault types with 100% accuracy. From Fig. 4.13 we can also observe that the network has predicted correctly all the fault magnitudes within 1% accuracy. With 106 kohonen neurons, the network has created as many fault classes each representing a specific fault number and fault magnitude. When the trained CPNN encounters any fault pattern which has fault magnitude lying between those represented by the two successive kohonen neurons, the network finds to which of the two is closer to and responds appropriately.

The robustness of the trained CPNN in presence of noise in the state variables also was tested. In each state variable, a certain percentage of its own magnitude was randomly added or subtracted. At a time, only one process variable was disturbed. The upper limit for the

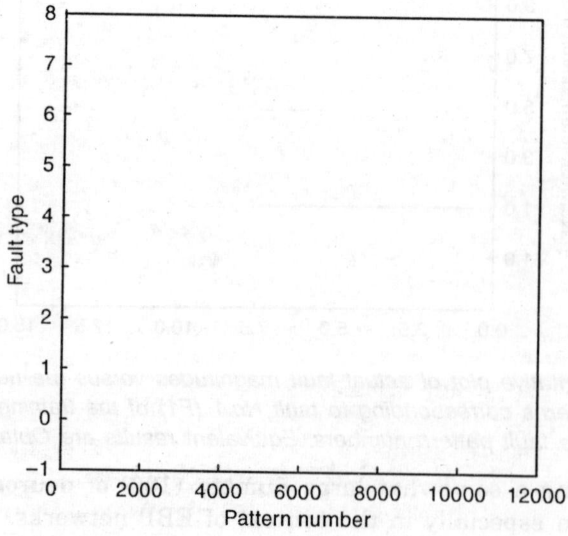

Fig. 4.12. *Plot showing the network predicted fault types for the test set.*

percent noise in the process variable tolerated by the trained network beyond which the network misclassified the fault types and/or the fault magnitudes are : *T*-0.18%, *Ca*-0.385, *V*-4.23%, *F*-0.74%, *Tj*-0.12% and *Fj*-4.21%. It is to be noted that the network will classify the fault correctly so long as the input vector in the presence of noise remain closer to the same weight vector as it would have in the absence of noise.

As compared to the EBP networks that have been used for detection and diagnosis of fault for similar systems the CPNN architecture used in this study contains large number of neurons in network's middle layer. However, even the large sized CPNN is computationally economic since : (*i*) in a single training step only those weights which are connected to the winner kohonen neuron need to be adjusted, (*ii*) evaluation of transfer function's derivatives (as in EBP algorithm) is not necessary since CPNN algorithm does not use derivatives for weight corrections, (*iii*) the approximate magnitudes of the optimal network weights are known a priori and therefore the network weights can be appropriately initialized before the network training begins and (*iv*) the trial and error approach involved in arriving at the optimal network structure is avoided since such an architecture is also known beforehand. Additional benefit in using CPNN methodology is that the training algorithm is simple to implement as compared to other neural network paradigms such as EBP, ART and RBF. However, unlike the EBP and the RBF networks, CPNN is restricted in its interpolation abilities; also it does not posses the stability plasticity properties of the ART based networks.

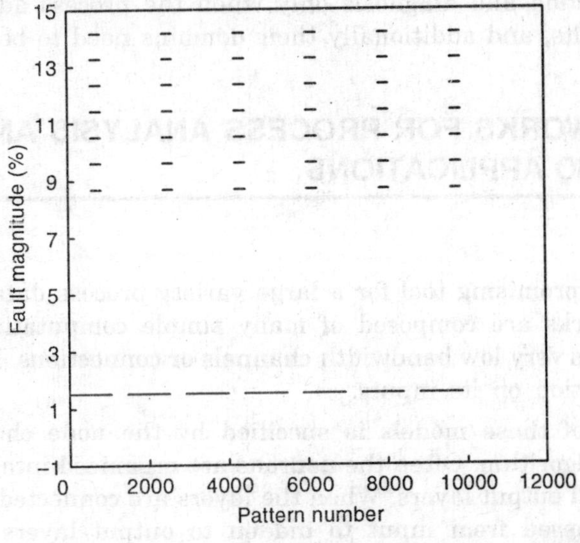

Fig. 4.13. *Plot showing the network predicted fault magnitudes for all the seven faults using the test set.*

4.2.9 Conclusions

This paper shows that the counterpropagation neural networks can be successfully employed for process fault detection and diagnosis purposes. The CPNNs are much superior to commonly used EBP networks in term of the training speed due to fewer computational steps also since the approximate magnitudes of the optimal normal weight can be guessed from the training data, the network weights can be appropriately initialized. As a result additional savings in the network training time can be realized. Moreover, the optimal CPNN structure can be fixed prior to the network training and, therefore, the trial and error approach involved in determining such architectures get avoided. CPNN's lack of the interpolation ability to some extent can be compensated by training the network with closely spaced data and by taking more kohonen neurons so that the networks learn additional classes to cover the same state space.

The CPNN strategy as elucidated in this paper can in principle be extended for multiple fault detection and diagnosis. However, as in the case of EBP networks the detection and diagnosis results may not be entirely satisfactory. If CPNN is used for multiple fault detection then the training data must explicitly contain patterns representing all the multiple faults that can occur in process operations. This will lead to a combinational explosion of training data if the number of multiple fault that can occur is large. Another problem which is generic in nature and thereby limits the diagnostic abilities of multiple fault detection methods is the nonlinear process behavior. For nonlinear systems, approximately same steady-state values of the process state variables can be realized as a result of several single and/or multiple fault combinations. Consequently it becomes difficult to attribute a point in the state space reached by the network input vector, to the occurrence of unique single or multiple faults. The problem cannot be fully addressed using relatively simple neural network formations such as EBP, CP or RBF. A notable success in this direction has been achieved by Watanabe et al. (1994) who using Hierarchical Artificial Neural Networks (HANN) could correctly diagnosis 93% double faults and 76%, triple faults. In essence CPNNs can be used for multiple fault detection and diagnosis only when the process admits finite and small number of multiple faults, and additionally their domains need to be clearly discernible.

4.3 NEURAL NETWORKS FOR PROCESS ANALYSIS AND OPTIMIZATION MODELING AND APPLICATIONS

4.3.1 Introduction

Neural networks are a promising tool for a large variety process data analysis procedures. Artificial neural networks are composed of many simple computational elements, nodes, locally interacting across very low bandwidth channels or connections. Each neuron performs a nonlinear transformation on its inputs.

The architecture of these models is specified by the node characteristics, network topology and learning algorithm. Often the neurons are organized into distinct layers, input, hidden or associated and output layers. When the layers are connected in a feedforward way (so that signals are passed from input to hidden to output layers without feedback or communication within a layer), the net is called a multilayered perception. Various architectures of neural networks have been suggested in literature. Neural networks in all categories address the need for rapid computation, robustness and adaptability. Neurals models require fewer assumptions and less precise information about the modeled system than do some more traditional techniques. Design of a neural system requires advance specification of relatively few fixed parameters. Many network variables can be set or reset by the data being processed, thus adapting to the specific needs of the current system state.

Neural networks are useful as modules in larger systems interacting with fuzzy logic, genetic algorithm and expert systems particularly well. The careful combination of techniques produce the most useful, robust system. Incorporation of neural network modules in an option that should be considered by simultanists in all application fields.

The neural network architectures of three distinct layers (input, hidden and output) and without hidden layers are connected by feedforward, weighted connections. The function of the input layer is to distribute values of input parameters into the net.

In the training phase a number of examples that are representative of the problem to be learned are provided to the net. By adapting its weights, the net learns the desired input-output relation. Neural networks typically learn to perform tasks by iterative error-minimization. The Generalized Data Rule (GDR) algorithm was used to train the network minimizing the sum of squares of the residual as well as the powell (SSQ) algorithm.

As the case studies are considered the processes of separation of butyl-acetate-butyl-alcohol-water system in interlinked industrial distillation columns.

The purpose of the present investigations is to evaluate the applicability of the neural network structures as a process data analyzer and optimization tool. Neural network learning models, operating within the computer simulation of complex chemical process may provide an opportunity to generate modify or verify expert knowledge in a synthetic environment.

4.3.2 Neural Network Models

Neural architecture are based on a common computing Threshold Logic Unit (TLU), shown in Fig. 4.14.

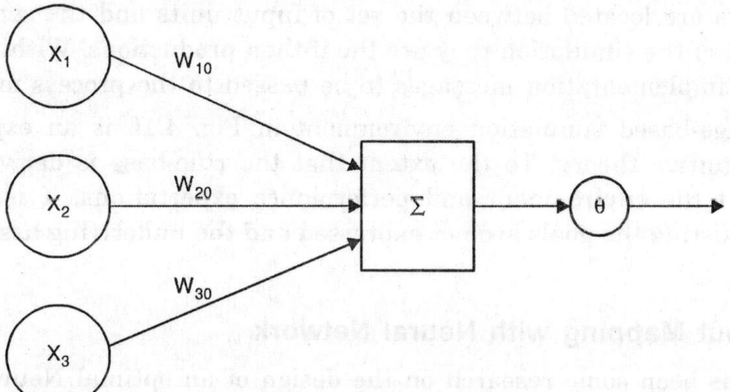

Fig. 4.14. *Threshold logic unit.*

With nodes associated with concepts and are weights representing similarity. The implementing element, TLU consist of a single concept node, all the input signals, and an output signal. TLU compute the function *W.X-T* for a series of input (*X*) and a unit threshold characteristic (*T*). Because these units implement linear surfaces within some multidimensional measurement space, they can be corrected to form multiple surfaces that partition the space into different decision regions. Training, or modification of the decision surface so that they maintain consistency with some known phenomenon, is realized by adjusting the weights and threshold to ensure that the appropriate unit activates for representative samples of a given population. Within a knowledge-based simulation a connectionist model may provide a number of advantages over traditional production system approaches. Many of these advantages relate to the inherent paricomony and coherence associated with network system in general.

Although network systems readily support automated learning, the link, between learning and parsimony is the development of a structure for characterizing an active goal-hierchy that represent a logical and coherent cognitive theory within some model. This neural architecture (Fig. 4.15) consists of three unit types : input (perception) units, internal (conceptual) units and output (action) units.

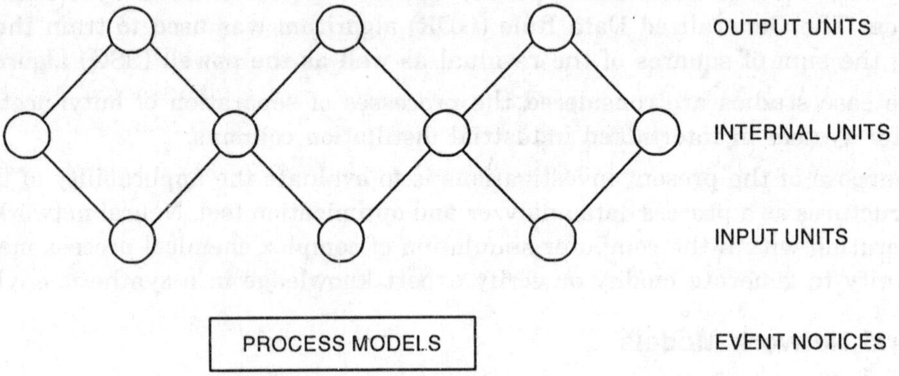

Fig. 4.15. *The connectionist simulation environment.*

Internal units are located between the set of input units and the set of output units. Within the context of the simulation they are the if-then productions. Within the simulation, outputs units are implementation messages to be passed to the process models.

The knowledge-based simulation environment in Fig. 4.15 is an expression of some control law or cognitive theory. To the extent that the rule-base is derived from a set of assumptions about the environment and performance expectations, it is a belief system. However, in the existing the goals are not expressed and the underlying assumptions are not evident.

4.3.3 Input-Output Mapping with Neural Network

Although there has been some research on the design of an optimal Neural Network (NN) structure it is still largely an art to determine the number of hidden layers and number of units in each hidden layer. The neural network structure is denoted as I × H × O, where I, H and O represent the number of input units and output units, respectively.

Most NNs use sigmoidal activations functions which make it possible for the neural network to perform a complicated input-output mapping through the backpropagation procedure. In essence a NN model is equivalent to a set of algebraic equations arranged in hierarchical order to form an input-output mapping. Changing the structure of an NN is nothing more than changing the hierarchical order of algebraic equations. Training an NN is just another way of estimating the parameters in the complex input-output transformation function formed by activation functions.

It is difficult to study the input-output transformation function of a NN with hidden layers(s). Without a hidden layer the NN output is a function of linear combination of the input variables.

4.3.4 Training a Feedforward Neural Network

The backpropagation training algorithm has been used successfully in training the NNs for wide applications. The backpropagation algorithm adjusts the weights in a feedforward NN consisting of several layers and an output layer. The goal is to reach the network to associate specific output states, call target states, each of several input states. Having learned the fundamental relationships between input and outputs, the NN can produce the correct output for a new previously unseen input. The backpropagation learning algorithm does not need too much computation time to obtain the correct weights if the training data is of small size. In other words if the relationships between input and outputs is simple, a set of weights is easy to obtain. Most often for complex problems relationships between input and outputs cannot be completely represented with a small amount of the training data set. Therefore the computation time required by the backpropagation is very large.

A popular configuration of neural network for backpropagation is a totally feedforward net. In the feedforward net inputs feeds up through hidden layers to an output layer. Each neuron form a weighted sum of the inputs from previous layers to which it is connected, adds a threshold value and produce a nonlinear function of this sum as its output value, Fig. 4.14. the output values serves as the input to the next layer to which the neuron is connected, and the processes is repeated until output values are obtained for the neurons in the input layer.

Thus each neuron performs :

$$Y_i^p = f\,(\Sigma w_{ij}\; x_i^p - \theta j) \qquad ...(1)$$

Where w_{ij} is the weight from neuron I to neuron j, w_{ij} can be positive or negative real number, and θi is the threshold of the jth neuron, p means the pth pattern. The $f(x)$ is a non linear function of activation that is often chosen to be of a sigmoidal form :

$$F(x) = (1/2)\ [1 + \tan\ h(x)] \qquad ...(2)$$

Is used in this analysis where tanh is his hyperbolic tangent. If d_i^p are the desired outputs and y_i^p are the output obtained from the output layer for the pth pattern. Neural nets are trained by minimizing the error function :

$$E = \sum_{p=1}\sum_{i=1}\left(d_i^p - y_i^p\right)^2 \qquad ...(3)$$

Where I indexes the number of neuron in the output layer, and p means the pth input pattern of the training set is presented on the input layer.

Minimizing the sum of squares of error is not always the best way of training a NN but for some applications it suffices (bulsari and saxen, 1991). Backpropagation by the generalized data rule, a kind of gradient descent method is one popular method.

The gradient descent was described by the following equations (4–9). The commonly used steepest descent procedure in minimizing E is to change wij and θi by Δwij and $\Delta\theta j$, where

$$\Delta wij = \frac{-dE}{dwij}\acute{n} \qquad ...(4)$$

$$\Delta\theta i = \frac{-dE}{d\theta_1}\acute{n} \qquad ...(5)$$

where η is the learning rate.

After simplification Δwij and $\Delta\theta j$ can be expressed as :

$$\Delta wij^p = \acute{\alpha}\, \Sigma\delta i^p yi^p + \acute{\alpha}\, \Delta wij^{p-1} \quad \text{...(6)}$$

$$\Delta\theta i = \acute{\alpha}\, \Sigma\delta i^p \quad \text{...(7)}$$

$$\delta i^p = (di^p - yi^p)\, yi^p\, (1 - yi)^p \quad \text{...(8)}$$

if the jth neuron is in the output layer, and

$$\delta i^p = yi^p\, (1 - yi^p)\, \Sigma\delta k^p wjk \quad \text{...(9)}$$

if the jth neuron is the hidden layer and k are overall neurons in the layer above neuron.

4.3.5 The Training Algorithms

Network training aims at achieving the least of errors, the errors measured as the difference between that calculated output and the desired output. In this investigation the powell method was used to calculate the weights in the neural which minimized the Sum of Squares of Errors (SSQ) as well as the backpropagation algorithm by the generalized delta rule-GDR method (Fig. 4.16). In the learning mode a set of training examples consisting of input/output vector pairs (x^p, d^p) is given. The objective is to select weights that minimize the sum of squared errors between the net prediction y^p and the desired output specified by the training examples d^p

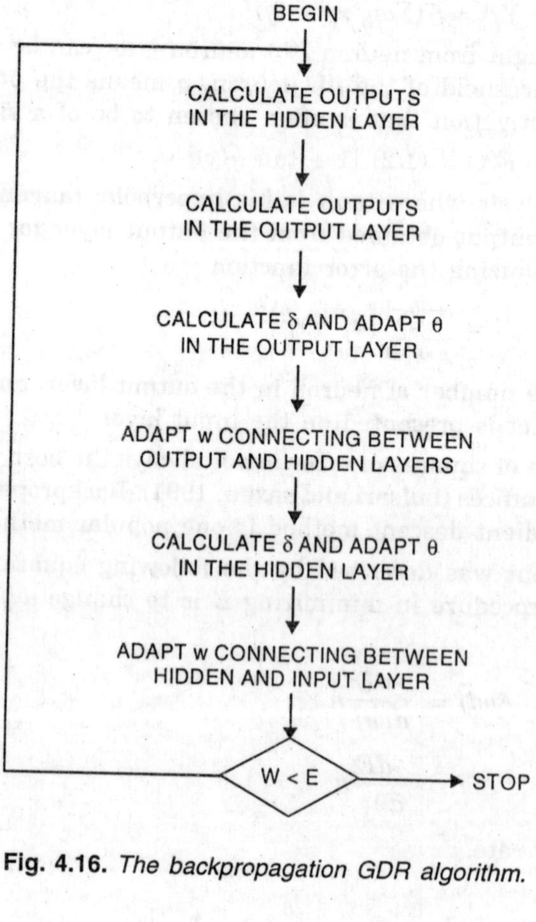

Fig. 4.16. *The backpropagation GDR algorithm.*

To begin learning, the network in initialized with small random weight in each branch. A training example is selected randomly, and the input vector x^p propagated through the network to get the predicted output y^p.$\acute{n}$ is called the learning rate which is equivalent to a step size, and $\acute{\alpha}$ which acts a momentum term to keep the direction of descent from changing too rapidly from step to step. On the first step the steepest descent direction is used ($\acute{\alpha} = 0$) :

Step 1 : Assign all neuron offsets (threshold) to small random values : θi.

Step 2 : Assign all weights to small random values : wij.

Step 3 : Repeat

For $p = 1$ to TP (TP is the total number of training patterns

For $j = 1$ to $n2$ ($n2$ is the number of neurons in the hidden layer)

Calculate neuron outputs in the hidden layer yi.

Endfor

For $k = 1$ to $n3$ ($n3$ is the number of neuron in the output layer).

Calculate neuron outputs in the outputs layer : yk

Calculate δk^p

$(\theta k^p) = \theta k^{(p-1)} + \Delta\theta k^{(p)}$

endfor

for $j = 1$ to n_2 and $k = 1$ to $n3$

$wjk^p = wjk^{(p-1)} + \Delta wjk^{(p)}$

endfor

for $j = 1$ to n_2

calculate δj^p

$\theta i^p = \theta i^{(p-1)} + \Delta\theta jL^{(p)}$

endfor

for $i = 1$ to n_1 and $j = 1$ to n_2

($n1$ is the number of neurons in the input layer)

$wij^p = wij^{(p-1)} + \Delta wij^{(p)}$

endfor

endfor

until ΔwE(E is the convergence criterion)

4.3.6 The Description of the Case Studies

In order to analyze the learning of NNs for the process classifier and optimization, two case studies were investigated. The process units involved in these examples are shown in Fig. 4.17.

Case Study No. 1

The first case study consist of a distillation column and liquid-liquid separator (heterogeneous azeotrope). The process units are shown in Fig. 4.17. The number of input neurodes Ni is equal to the number of input parameters Ni = 5 as shown in Fig. 4.18. $x1$, $x2$ and $x3$ are fraction of butylcaetate (1) butylalcohol (2) and water (3) in the feed from the waste streams of penicillin production. $\Delta p1$ is the pressure drop in the first column and $R1$ is the internal reflux ratio for the first column. The output layer consist of three neurods N0 = 3, corresponding to the three output variables :butylacetate composition in the upper phase of the separator (product1-upper layer), butylacetate composition in lower phase of separator (product1)-lower layer and butylalcohol composition (product 2) as shown in Fig. 4.18.

Case Study No. 2

As a second case study is considered the process of azeotropic distillation of butylacetate (1)-butylalcohol (2)-water (3) system in interlinked industrial distillation column as shown if Fig. 4.17. The number of input neurodes Ni is equal to the number of input parameters Ni = 8 as shown in Fig. 4.19. $x1$, $x2$ and $x3$ are fractions of butylacetate (1), butylalcohol (2) and water (3) in the feed from waste streams of penicillin production. $\Delta p1$ and $\Delta p2$ are pressure drops in the first and second columns, respectively. $R1$ and $R2$ internal reflux ratio for the first and the second columns, respectively, Rc is external reflux ratio. The output units consists of two neurodes according to output variables as shown in Fig. 4.19 the output variables are butylacetate composition (product1) and butylalcohol composition (product 2).

Analysis of the Learning and Discussion

In both case studies various NN models were explored to find the network architectures that give the least error during learning rate η and 0.0-0.9 for the momentum α were used in the learning phase. In the first case study the NN employed has five input nodes corresponding to the five variables of the system, and three output nodes corresponding to the three output variables. Various numbers of hidden units and training methods were explored and compared.

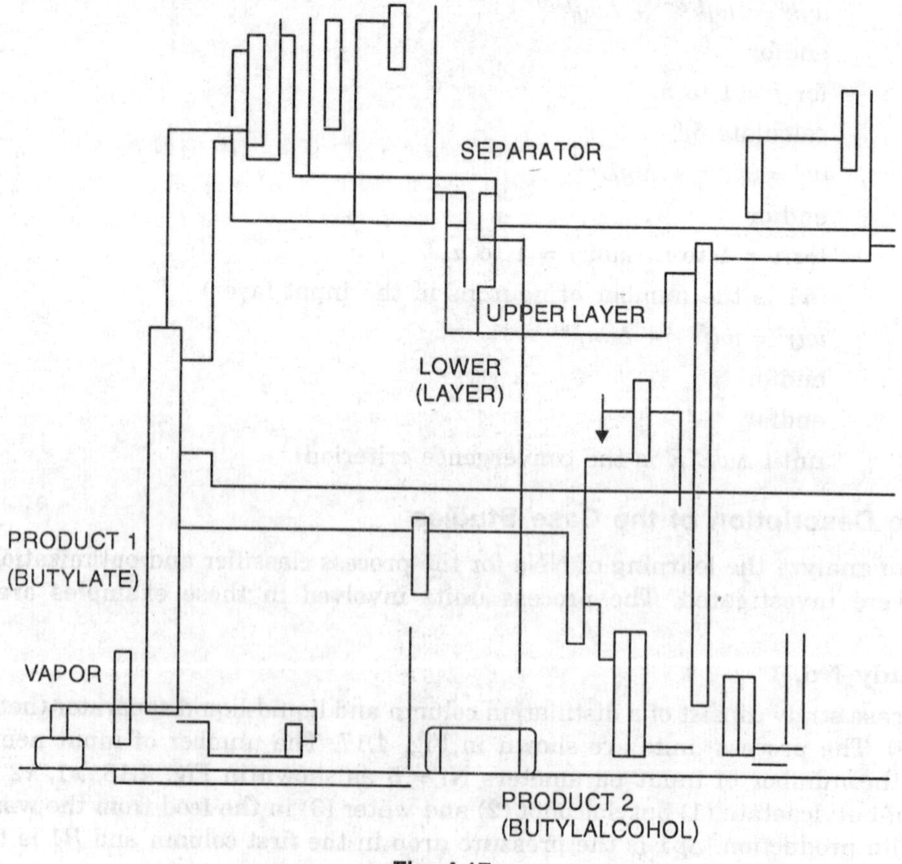

Fig. 4.17.

The training parameters are summarized in Table 4.7 in the second case study the NN employed has input nodes corresponding to the eight variables of the process and two output variables. Various numbers of hidden units and training methods were investigated as shown in table 4.8 figure 4.18 shows a sample network with two hidden units for the first case study initially set to be the same for different NN structures in figure 4.19.

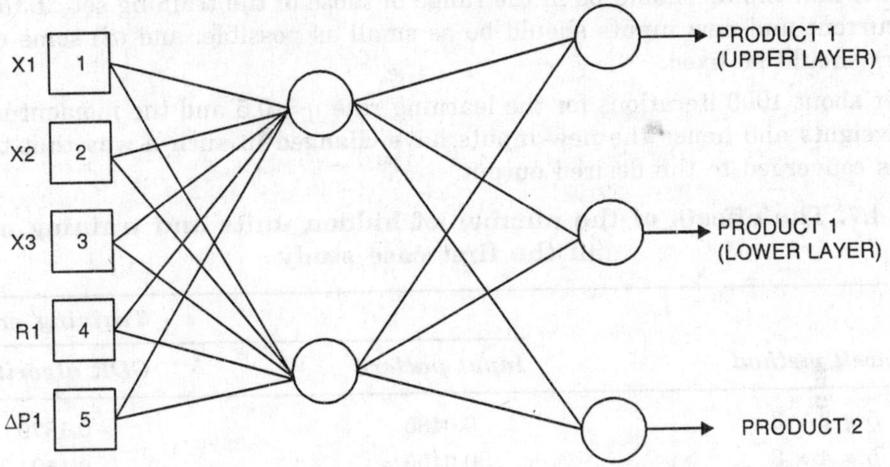

Fig. 4.18. *Trained neural network NN (5 × 2 × 3) for the case study No.1*

Figure 4.19 shows a sample network with three hidden units for the second case study initially set to be the same for different NN structures in table 4.8.

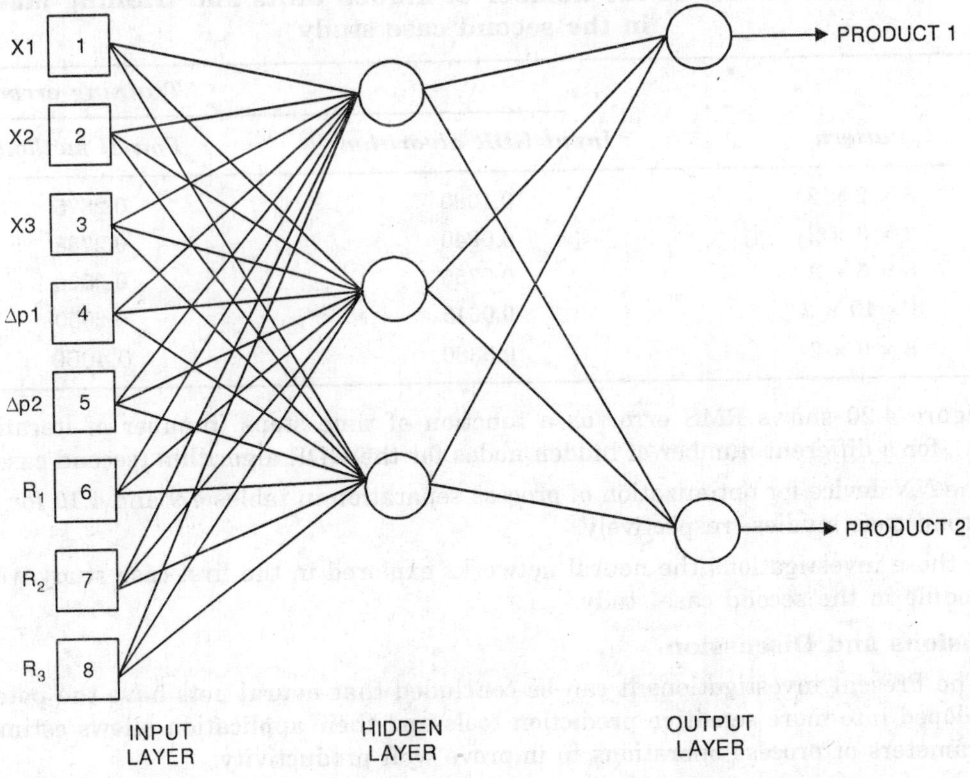

Fig. 4.19. *The neural network NN (8 × 2 × 2) for the case study No.2.*

The NN calculates on its own an optimal combination of input values. In such a case the net has to operate in reverse : given a desired higher production level. What are the corresponding input values ? This reverse computation tries to arrive at a Ni-D new input vector based on the desired No-D new output vector. This problem has an infinite number of solutions. Therefore the solution space has to be reduced by adding constraints : (*a*) the values of the new inputs should be in the range of those of the training set : *L* (*b*) difference between current and new inputs should be as small as possible; and (*d*) some of the input parameters should be fixed.

After about 1000 iterations for the learning rate $\eta = 0.5$ and the momentum α-0.9 the adaptive weights and hence the new inputs have changed in such a way that the network output has converged to the desired output.

Table 4.7. The effects of the number of hidden units and training methods in the first case study

		Training error
Powell method	*Input pattern*	*GDR algorithm*
5 × 2 × 3	0.0485	0.1879
5 × 4 × 3	0.0405	0.1591
5 × 6 × 3	0.0338	0.1325
5 × 0 × 3	0.1045	0.2380

Table 4.8. The effects of the number of hidden units and training method in the second case study

		Training error
Pattern	*Input GDR algorithm*	*Powell method*
8 × 2 × 2	0.1080	0.2875
8 × 3 × 2	0.0940	0.2788
8 × 6 × 2	0.0755	0.2500
8 × 10 × 2	0.0613	0.2050
8 × 0 × 2	0.3380	0.4060

Figure 4.20 shows RMS error as a function of time steps (number of iterations per pattern), for a different number of hidden nodes for the GDR algorithm (second case study).

The *NN* device for optimization of process separation in tables 4.9 and 4.10 for the first and second case studies, respectively.

In those investigations the neural networks explored in the first case study were used as a module in the second case study.

Conclusions and Discussion

From The Present investigations it can be concluded that neural nets have the potential to be developed into more sensitive prediction tools and their application allows estimation of the parameters of process operations to improve well productivity.

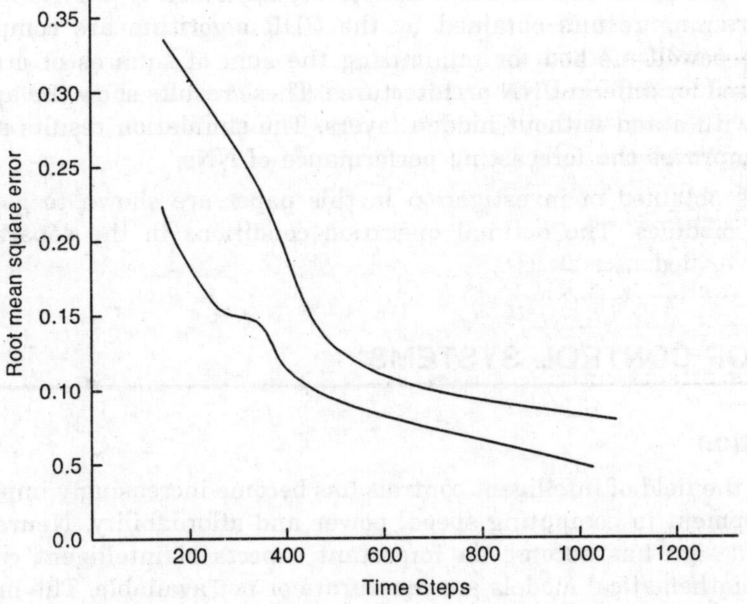

Fig. 4.20. *Training error as a function of time steps (second case study).*

Table 4.9. The outcome of the run with minimum error level for the first case study

Input parameter	*Current value*	*New value*
1. $x1$ vol%	58.43	59.00
2. $x2$ vol%	31.40	30.15
3. $x3$ vol%	10.17	10.00
4. $\Delta P1$ *Pa*	0.0785×10^5	0.0790×10^5
5. $R1$	0.50	4.25

Table 4.10. The outcome of the run with minimum error level for the second case study

Input parameter	*Current value*	*New value*
1. $x1$ vol%	59.00	59.55
2. $x2$ vol%	30.15	29.46
3. $x3$ vol%	10.00	9.34
4. $\Delta P1$ *Pa*	0.0790×10^5	0.0800×10^5
5. $\Delta P2$ *Pa*	0.1960×10^5	0.0750×10^5
6. $R1$	4.25	4.50
7. $R2$	0.25	1
8. $R3$	0.44	3.45

The aim of this investigation is to evaluate the applicability of NNs for industrial data analysis. The training results obtained by the GDR algorithm are compared with those obtained by the powell method for minimizing the sum of squares of errors. The results obtained are closed for different NN architectures. These results show the applicability of the NN structures with a and without hidden layers. The simulation results show that adding a hidden unit improves the forecasting performance of NNs.

The results obtained of investigation in this paper are shown to good effect of NNs combination as modules. The optimal operation conditions in the separation plant were experimentally verified.

4.4 DESIGN OF CONTROL SYSTEMS

4.4.1 Introduction

In recent years, the field of intelligent controls has become increasingly important due to the immense development in computing speed, power and affordability. Neural network based control system design has become an important aspects of intelligent control since it is effective when mathematical models are inaccurate or not available. The method provides a distinctive computational paradigm to learn (or to adapt) linear or nonlinear mappings from a prior data and knowledge without fully understanding the physical behavior of the system. Thus the method does not rely on models based on traditional analytic differential equations and since the models are developed using computers, the control design produces controllers, that can be implemented online.

The paper examines both the nonlinear multi-layered feed-forward architecture and the linear single-layer architecture of artificial neural networks for application in control system design. In the nonlinear multilayered feed-forward case, the two major problems are the long training process and the poor generalization. To overcome these problems, a number of data analysis strategies before training and several improvement generalization techniques are used. Basically, neural design entails constructing a controller not only to meet the performance objectives like rise time, overshoot, settling time, and state error, but also to satisfy neural network standard such as the low number of local minima, higher learning speed and better generalizations capability under stable conditions.

4.4.2 Architectures in Neural Networks

One of the major tasks in the design of a neural network is the selection of architecture and this choice depends on the nature of the problem. Inappropriate choice results into poor performance. The following are the commonly used neural network architecture for control system applications :

(*a*) *ADALINE Architecture (Adaptive Linear Element):* This architecture is a single layer with linear output. It is the simplest intelligent self-learning system that can adapt itself to achieve a given modeling task. Figure 4.21 is schematic diagram for such a network. Inputs connect directly to the outputs through a single layer of weights. It has a purely linear output unit; hence the network output y is a weighted linear combination of the inputs plus a constant term b_0, *i.e.,*

$$y = \sum_{i=1}^{n} w_i x_i + b_0 \quad \text{...(1)}$$

ADALINE is simple in structure, therefore inexpensive. It can classify only data sets that are linearly separable. Equation (1) classifies an exact linear model with $n + 1$ linear parameters, so we can employ least squares methods to minimize the error. However, most least-square methods require extensive calculation, which is not possible in a physical stem with simple components. Various methods have been developed to reduce calculation and speed up convergence, and these are discussed in the next section.

(b) *Feed-forward Neural Network Architecture* : This architecture is the most popular structure in practice due to its non-parametric, non-linear mapping between input and output. Networks with this architectures are known as universal approximators, including multilayer feed-forward neural networks employing sigmoidal hidden unit activations. These networks can approximate not only an uknown function but also its derivative. The feed-forward neural networks include one or more layer of hidden units between the input and output layers. As its name suggests, the output of each node propagates from the input to the output side. All connection point from input towards output. See figure 4.22.

Multiple layer of neurons with nonlinear activation functions allows this type of neural network to learn nonlinear and linear relationships between input and output vectors. Each input has an appropriate weighting W the sum of the weighted inputs and the bias B forms the input to the transfer function. Any differentiable activation function f may be used to generate the outputs. Three of the most commonly used activation function are purelin $f(x) = x$, log-sigmoid $f(x) = (1 + e^{-x})^{-1}$, and tan-sigmoid $f(x) = \tan h(x/2) = (1 - e^{-x})/(1 + e^{-x})$.

Both the hyperbolic tangent (Tan-sigmoid) and logistic (Log-sigmoid) functions approximate the signum and step functions, respectively, and yet provide smooth, nonzero derivatives with respect to the input signals. These two activation functions called squashing functions since their outputs are squashed to the range [0, 1] or [–1, 1]. They are also called sigmoidal functions because their –shaped curves exhibit smoothness and asymptotic properties.

The activation function f_h of the hidden units have to be differentiable nonlinear functions [typically, f_h is the logistic function or hyperbolic tangent function f_h (net) = tan h (net)]. If f_h is linear, then one can always collapse the net to a single layer and thus lose the universal approximation/mapping capabilities. Each unit of the output layer is assumed to have the same activation function.

The node function for the output layer is a weighted sum with no squashing functions. This is equivalent to a situation in which the activation function is a purelin function, and output node of this type are often called linear nodes.

4.4.3 Learning Algorithm

In this section a number of basic concepts necessary *i* the development of learning algorithms are presented and many of these algorithms are gradient-based. Learning in a neural network is normally accomplished through an adaptive procedure, known as a learning rule, whereby the weights of the network are incrementally adjusted so as to improved a predefined performance measure overtime. In other words, the process of learning is best viewed as an optimization process. More precisely, the learning process can be viewed as a "search" in a multidimensional parameter (weight) space for a solution, which gradually optimizes an objective (cost) function.

Gradient Based Methods

Gradient based methods searches for minima by comparing values of the objective function $E(\theta)$ at different points. The basic idea is to evaluate the function at points around the current search point and then look for lower values. In other words, the primary concern is to minimize the objective function $E(\theta)$ in the adjustable space $\theta = [\theta_1, \theta_2, \ldots, \theta_n]$ and to find a minimum point $\theta = \theta^*$. In general, a given function $E(\theta) = f(\theta_1, \theta_2, \ldots, \theta_n)$ is so complex that an iterative algorithm is often used to search the adjustable parameter space efficiently. In iterative descent methods, the next point θ_{new} is determined by a step down from the current point θ_{now} in a direction vector d given as :

$$\theta_{next} = \theta_{now} + \eta d$$

where η is some positively step size commonly referred to as the learning rate.

The principal differences between various descent algorithms lie in the first procedure for determining successive directions. Once the decision is reached all algorithms called for movement to (local) minimum point on the line determined by the current point θ_{now} and the direction d. That is, for the second procedure, the optimum step size can be determined by linear minimization as :

$$\eta^* = \arg(\min(\Phi\acute{\varnothing}(\eta)))$$

$$\eta > 0$$

where $$\acute{\varnothing}(\eta) = E(\varnothing_{new} + \eta d).$$

When the straight downhill direction d is determined on the basis of the gradient (g) of an objective function E, such descent methods are called gradient based descent methods. Gradient based descent methods is not highly regarded among the optimization methods mainly because of its slow rate of the convergence. The gradient never points to the global minimum except in the case where the error contours are spherical so many small steps are needed to arrive at the minimum.

Some common gradient methods are : steepest descent, Newton's method, Gauss-newton method, and Levenberg-Marquardt method. The latter method has proven useful in the design of control systems and we adopt it here.

Levenberg-Marquardt Method

The Levenberg-Marquardt algorithm can handle ill-conditioned matrices well, like nonquadratic objective functions. Also, if the Hessian matrix is not positive definite, the Newton direction may point towards a local maximum, or a saddle point. The Hessian can be changed by adding a positive definite matrix λI to H in order to make H positive definite.

Thus, $$\theta_{next} = \theta_{now} - (H + \lambda I)^{-1} g,$$

where I is the identity matrix and H is the Hessian matrix which is given in terms of Jacobian matrix J as $H = J^T J$. Levenberg-marquardt is the modification of the Gauss-Newton algorithm as

$$\theta_{next} = \theta_{now} - (J^T J)^{-1} J^T r = \theta_{now} - (J^T J + \lambda I)^{-1} J^T r.$$

The Levenberg-Marquardt algorithm performs initially small, but robust steps along the steepest descent direction, and switches to more efficient quadratic Gauss-Newton steps as the minimum is approached. This method combines the speed of Gauss-Newton with the everywhere convergence of gradient descent, and appears to be fastest for training moderate-sized feedforward neural networks.

Weight Update Algorithm

The reason for updating the weights is to decrease the error. The weight update relationship is

$$\Delta wij = \frac{\eta dE_p}{dw_{ij}} = \eta\,(d_{pi} - y_{pi})\,f_i x_j$$

where the learning rate η > 0 is a small positive constant. Sometimes η is also called the step size parameter.The Delta Rule is weight update algorithm in the training of neural networks. The algorithm progresses sequentially layer by layer, updating weights as it goes. The update equation is provided by the gradient descent method as

$$\nabla w_{ij} = w_{ij}\,(k+1) - w_{ij}(k) = -\eta \frac{dE_p}{dw_{ij}}$$

$$\frac{dE_p}{dw_{ij}} = -\,(d_{ij} - y_{pi})\,\frac{dy_{pi}}{dw_{ij}}$$

for linear output unit, where

$$y_{pi} = \sum_i w_{ij} x_i$$

and

$$\frac{dy_{pi}}{dw_{ij}} = x_i$$

so,

$$\nabla w_{ij} = w_{ij}\,(k+1) - w_{ij}\,(k) = \eta\,(d_{pi} - y_{pi})\,x_i$$

The adaptation of those weights which connects the input units and the *i*th output unit is determined by the corresponding error $e_i = \frac{1}{2}\sum_P \left(d_{pi} - y_{pi}\right)^2$

4.4.4 Training Data Analysis

A common complaint about back-propagation is the long training time. A typical raining session may require thousand of iterations. Large networks with large training sets might take days or weeks to be trained. Two training data analysis method, namely normalizing training set and initializing weights, and Principal Components Analysis (PCA) are intended to speed up the learning process.

The first method speeds up the training by choosing better solutions, by controlling the distribution of random initial weights and by avoiding sigmoid saturation problems that cause slow training.

The Principal Components Analysis (PCA) method can reduce the dimensionality of training data presented to a neural network without losing necessary information. It can speed up training significantly. One basis for selecting the initial weight distribution is to assume that the inputs have some statistical distribution and select the initial weight distribution so that the probability of saturating the node nonlinearity is small. Finding the optimal architecture of the neural network is as important as selecting an efficient learning algorithm. The total number of nodes also influences training speed. For a very large set of input variables with insufficient information, the network may not be able to estimate the relation very accurately. Using Principal Components Analysis (PCA) to analyze the data before applying to a neural network will help to overcome the above listed disadvantages.

PCA is a statistical technique that transforms a large set of correlated variables into a small set of uncorrelated variables containing most of the original information. It can be effectively used as part of the neural network training procedure.

4.4.5 Improving Generalization

The critical issue in developing a neural network is its potential for generalization. A network may be insufficiently complex and failed to fully detect the signal, leading to under fitting. A network that is too complex may fit the noise as well as the signal, leading to over fitting. Over fitting is especially dangerous because it can lead to predictions beyond the range of the training data. Over fitting can produce wild predictions even with noise-free data. Under fitting produces excessive bias in the outputs, whereas over fitting produces excessive variance. Over fitting can be remedied by using extra training data. When the amount of training data is fixed, three approaches to avoiding under fitting and over fitting, thereby getting good generalization, may be used :

(1) Selection of the model so that the size of weight as well as the numbers of weights, hidden units and layers, are appropriate to the number of training cases;

(2) Adding small amount of jitter (noise) to inputs during training to increase the effective number of training cases used;

(3) Performing cross-validation checks during training to determine when to stop.

Conclusion

The fundamentals of neural network based control system design are developed in this paper and are applied to intelligent control of the advanced flight propulsion control coupling (FPCC) aircraft. The results and applicability to the linearized lateral dynamics of the aircraft will be presented at the conference.

4.5. OTHER APPLICATIONS

There are many problems found in pulp and paper mills that have characteristics that make this problem difficult to handle from a control standpoint. Combination of a neural network system, a rule based system and/or a conventional computational system provides a tool to handle these problems with simplicity and effectiveness.

4.5.1 Control of Brown Stock and Bleach Washer

Brown Stock Washer is one of the subsystems of a pulp mill to separate clean pulp from black liquor obtained from a digester through a multi-stage countercurrent washing. The main variables affecting the process is input consistency in the **vat**, rpm of washer, input flow rate, temperature, vacuum and vat level etc.

Rudd used the NN to determine real time values for soda loss, washer mat consistency and washer mat unit density in brown stock washer, the former is used as soft sensor. The target is to control/stabilize the black liquor solids carried out by the pulp mat to the bleach plant. Results show a 25% reduction in standard deviation of the black liquor solids using an eight day trial. The controller also maintained larger disturbances in an automatic mode for the input variables. These values are used to control the washing operation. Data from a process domain is collected along with known results to develop training sets used to train a configured neural networks. The structural configuration of NN controller is shown in Fig. 4.21.

The NN based control strategy consists of dilution factor controller (DC), consistency (K), weight (w), speed (s) and flow controller (FC). NN controller (NNC) gets a signal for a set point or target value. The output signal from NNC goes to dilution factor controller which in turn sets out a signal to the flow controller in a cascading mode. The output signal from DC goes to control the flow of water to the filter mat.

4.5.2. Control of Refiner

Refining operation is essential to prepare desired quality of fibers. NN model can predict pulp quality at 10 s intervals and trains and tunes models in real time. It can also be used for estimating stock consistency using fiber properties, stock linear velocity, stock temperature, and dilution flows.

Kooi and Khorasani proposed a back-propagation NN as a controller to replace the self tuning regulator for providing a closed loop control of the energy in the woodchip refining processes. both static and dynamic. NN controller perform very well in emulating the self tuning regulator. For processes having a non minimum phase properties, the dynamic NN controller provides a satisfactory control compared to the self tuning regulator.

4.5.3 Modeling a Wood-chip Refiner

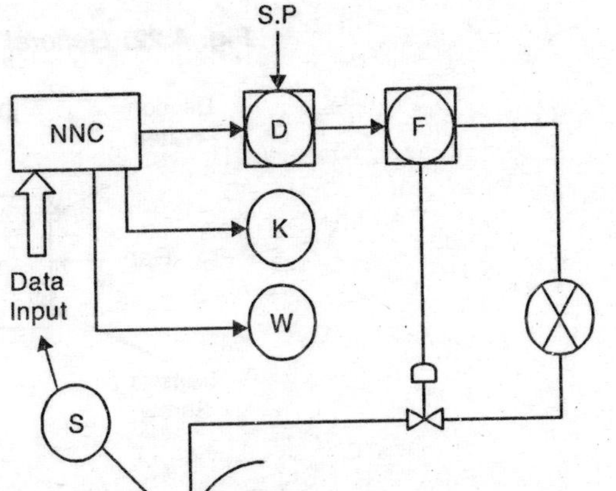

Fig. 4.21. *Neural network based control strategy.*

Refining is a mechanical process to convert raw materials to pulp fibers. A refiner consists of either two counter-rotating or one fixed and one rotating grooved plate with pressure exerted on one of them by hydraulic cylinder. A structure of a refiner is shown in Fig. 4.22, where wood-chips and dilution water are fed near the axis and are forced to move outwards between the plates by centrifugal and friction forces. Owing to mechanical actions and high pressure steam and friction , chips are broken down into fiber. Pulp refining is also a mechanical process to fibrilize the raw fiber so that fibers can be more flexible and conformable. The process can be accomplished by passing the stock through various kinds of equipments called pulp refiners or beaters. A diagrammatic sketch of the operation is shown in Fig. 4.23. As indicated above the stock after pulp fibrillations should have a desired degree of freeness(measured off-line in terms of °SR or CSF(Canadian standard freeness). Control of refiner will thus increase fiber quality, reduce energy consumption and minimize the fault occurring in the whole process.

As the freeness measurement is only taken every one or two hours in most paper mill OFF-LINE, such a long sampling period will not be suitable for ON-LINE control purposes, instead another control parameter called specific energy is used. This means that freeness is deterministic function of specific energy, thus is a function of S_e. Specific energy is defined as energy consumed per mass unit of wood fibers, and expressed as equal to motor load per oven-dry pulp mass flow. The various parameters in the system are transfer screw speed (u_T), the flow rate of dilution water, plate gap (*ud*), specific energy (*g*), motor load (*m*), disturbances (*d*) and plate gap (*ug*). The purpose of closed loop control for a refining process to manipulate *ut, ug,* and *ud* in order to control the process to achieve the desired *m, g* and consequently, the freeness (*F*). Using the weighted inputs obtained from the training, the feed-forward neural network can be used as a simulator to predict pulp quality like freeness, breaking strength, tear index and fiber length is predicted to change as one manipulates the two operating variables, namely, specific energy and refining consistency.

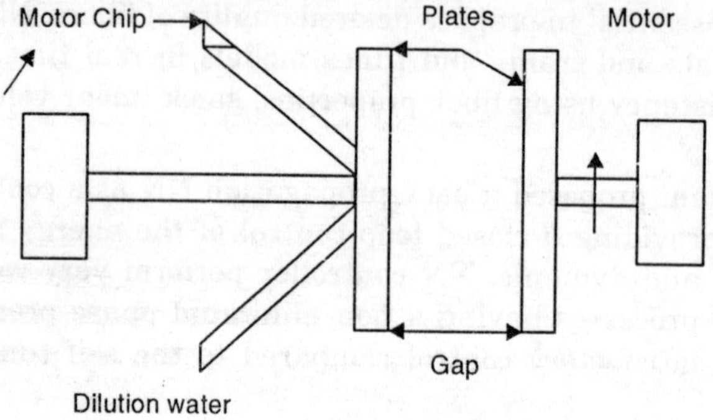

Fig. 4.22. *General structure of a refining process.*

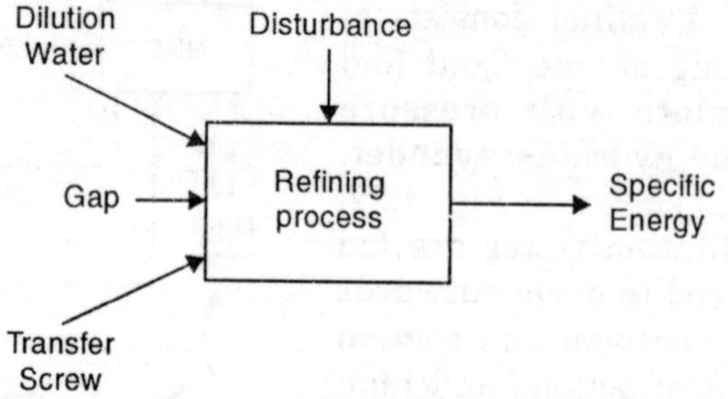

Fig. 4.23.

4.5.4 Modeling to the Retention Process in Papermaking

For paper making process the stock after refining need special treatment in stock preparation section of the paper machine, where internal sizing is done followed by addition of a host of inorganic and organic chemicals. These chemicals improve paper properties. The chemicals (clay, tale, soapstone, $CaCO_3$, TiO_2 etc. called fillers) and fibers should be retained on the wire as maximum as possible. This can be done by combination of physical entrapment and complex physico-chemical interactions generally instigated by the addition of polymeric retention aids and also by drainage aids. This means that the retention of fiber and filler on the wire section is an extremely difficult process to describe using derived physical equation only.

Rooke, presented a novel approach for modeling the retention of material on the papermaking wire using a combination of black box (neural networks) and physically derived models. ANNs model the complex evolution of the white water stock concentration very accurately, whilst the physical models of the blending chest, hydro cyclones and pressure screens are used to describe the head-box stock concentration.

4.5.5 Modeling Kappa Number in a Continuous Kamyr Digester

Kamyr digester is employed for converting raw materials (wood, bamboo, bagasse etc.) into pulp in a continuous manner, which necessitates sophisticated control of pulp parameters. In kraft pulping , pulp quality is generally measured by kappa number which is related to the lignin content remaining in the pulp. Inferential models for kappa number are developed using the methods of Partial Least Square Regression (PLS) and Neural Network (NN). B.S.Dayal et al. Investigated above technique to build empirical models for kappa number using historical data from an industrial continuous kamyr digester. A static model for kappa number based on the 21 input process parameters has been developed. No dynamics of any kind were taken into consideration.

4.5.6 Modeling Pulp Bleaching Process

The objective of bleach plant is to obtain the brightness (D) of pulp at a desired level while minimizing the use of bleaching chemicals like Cl_2, ClO_2 etc. There are various sequences of bleaching like CEH, CEDD, DEDED etc mainly used by paper mill. An ON-LINE measurement of D-stage brightness is desired for process control; however, because of sensor limitations, brightness is measured OFF-LINE by an hourly manual test. To ensure adequate pulp brightness, operators occasionally control to a higher than required brightness with a corresponding increased use of bleaching chemicals. The purpose of the model is to provide a real time indication of brightness so that operators can reduce chemical use. A bleach plant model has been developed using ANNIE (Artificial Neural Network Integrated Environment), in which data preparation, network topology selection, network training, evaluation, modification, code generation and simulation are integrated.

4.5.7 Prediction of Paper Properties

Curl is usually a paper defect and paper can be rejected if care is not taken during processing to eliminate curling. Paper "curl" can only be measured reliably OFF-LINE after manufacture, making it difficult to control. Peter et al predicted curl from parameters defining the current characteristics of a reel and the plant machinery using neural network techniques.

4.5.8 Modeling a Scrubber in a Paper Machine Ventilation System

Paper machines require a large quantity of hot dry air for the drying process. This air is used for the machine hood and pocket ventilation. After the drying process, the mixture of hot and evapourated water, which has a specific enthalpy several times greater than the air delivered to the drying hood, is conducted through the system of heat exchangers called recuperators. The last stage of the system of the heat exchangers usually represents a scrubber. Nenad et al studied feed-forward neural networks applied to estimate the outlet water temperature of the scrubber process. The networks are trained with data obtained from experiments carried out on two pilot scrubbers. The neural networks consisted of seven inputs and one output. The inputs were mass flow rate, temperature, inlet humidity of the supply air, mass flow rate of the water, inlet water temperature, height of the scrubber and water pressure in the nozzle. The output was the outlet water temperature from the scrubber.

4.6 PROBABILISTIC ARTIFICIAL NEURAL NETWORK FOR RECOGNIZING THE ARABIC HAND WRITTEN CHARACTERS

4.6.1 Introduction

A computer technology sub-field which has potential to be useful in a plurality of settings is automated recognition of textual information. This filed has been referred to generally as Optical Character Recognition (OCR). In general, an OCR machine reads machine printed/ hand written characters and tries to determine which character from a fixed set of the machine printed/hand written characters is intended to represent. The task of recognized characters can be broadly separated into two categories : the recognition of machine printed data and the recognition of hand written data Machine printed characters are uniform in size, position and pitch for any given font. In contrast, hand-written characters are non-uniform, they can be written in many different styles and sizes by different writers and by the same writers. Therefore, the reading of machine printed writing is a much simpler task than reading hand writing and has been accomplished and marketed with considerable success. The work presented in this study tries to demonstrate a framework for giving good recognition accuracy for off-line hand written Arabic characters input by developing a new system that can deal with Arabic hand written characters. So, our work tends to over look the following phases :

1. Studying the various techniques used in recognizing the hand written Arabic characters.
2. Considering moment invariant (order 3) method and Neural Networks (probabilistic Neural Network) for studying this problem.
3. Studying the problems of characters recognition techniques and make a little of comparisons between these techniques.
4. Developing a new recognition system technique to recognize hand written Arabic characters problems in order to overcome the problems that exist in the current technique.
5. Analyzing the recognized system from the proposed system with respect to the other recognized system obtained from other techniques. Finally, the proposed approach is trying to prove that using Probabilistic Neural Networks for recognizing hand written Arabic characters is better than other techniques since it overcomes all the problems in the previous techniques and it is suitable for handling all kind of problems in different fields. At the end, Arabic Hand Written Optical Character Recognition (AHOCR) is developed in the devices that use Arabic character recognition to process many documents automatically. AHOCR aims to convert document images to symbolic for modification, storage, retrieval, reuse and transmission. It helps the transition from book shelves and filing cabinets to the paper less world. Although there is no evidence yet of less paper, electronic document already abound[3, 4]. Also, this study aimed to document a frame work for giving good recognition accuracy to off-line hand written Arabic characters input. So, we propose an automatic prototype extraction method. Then, prototypes are used to train a document-specific OCR system to perform character recognition on document images of the same or similar quality and typesetting. Finally, we say that our contribution provides : a moment method, type of neural network algorithm probabilistic (PNN) which make use of as much information as possible from the character bit maps and labels to estimate character widths, character location, etc and match/ no match probabilities.

4.6.2 Related Works of Hand Written Arabic Character Recognition Systems

Machine simulation of human reading has been the subject of intensive research for almost three decodes. A large number of researches are concerned with Latin, chiness and Japanese characters. However, little work has been conduct on the automatic of Arabic characters because of its complexity of text. The main objective of this section is to present the state of Arabic character recognition research throughout the last two decades. The previously related work can be described as :

Hierarchical rule based approach : Sheik and Al- Taweel[5] assumed a reliable segmentation stage which divide letters into the four groups of position (initial, media, final and isolated). The recognition system depends on a hierarchical division by the number of strokes. One stroke letters were classified separately from two stroke letters ...etc. Ratios between extreme and position of dots in comparison to the primary stroke were defined heuristically on the data set to produce a rule-based classification.

Segmented structural analysis approach : Al- Emami and Usher[6] used a structural analysis method for selecting features of Arabic characters. The classifications use a decision tree. In preprocessing, some of the features extracted during the segmentation process were direction codes, slops and presence of dot flags. A new input needed to search three decision trees for the primary stroke and also for the upper and lower dots. The system was trained on 10 writers with a set of 120 postal code words with a total of 13 characters. They use one tester who had a recognition rate of 86%.

Structural and fuzzy approach : Amin and Bouslama presented a hybrid system that combine structural and fuzzy techniques. Structural analysis discriminated between various letter classes to be recognized and fuzzy logic allowed for variability in people hand writing within the same class. Sampling was done on the same class and on the input data points by comparing tangent angles at various points along the line. End points were kept automatically. The first point that had a tangent difference bigger than a threshold became next sampled point. The authors chose basic shapes such as curves, loops, lines and dots as good feature for discrimination between letter classes. These were constructed using geometric and structural relationship between the sampled points. After fuzzifying the features, fuzzy "If-Then rules" were created heuristically by the authors followed by a study of the data set. These fuzzy rules could distinguish letters from combination of the fuzzy features and allowed for fuzzy membership to cover the variability in hand written between authors.

Template matching and dynamic programming approach : Alimi and Ghorbel showed how to minimize error in an off-line recognition system for isolated Arabic characters using template matching and dynamic programming with assumed segmentation. The reference bank of prototypes was prepared after smoothing, normalization and coding the data coordinates into a parametric representation of angles. When new data was presented to the system, the distance between the prototype and the new data string was minimized using dynamic programming. The number of prototypes was varied to see the effect on recognition rates. More prototypes give better accruing.

Artificial neural networks classifiers : Haraty and El- Zabadani present a system for recognition of handwritten Arabic text using neural networks. Their work builds upon previous work that dealt with the vertical segmentation of the written text. However, they faced some problems like overlapping characters that share the same vertical space. They tried to fix that problem by performing horizontal segmented and the second one performs the horizontal segmentation. Both networks use a set of features that are extracted using a heuristic program. The system was tested and the rate of recognition obtained was 90%. This strongly supports the usefulness of proposed measures for handwritten Arabic text.

Optical character recognition system : The goal of Optical Character Recognition (OCR) is to classify optical patterns (often contained in a digital image) corresponding to alphanumeric or other characters. The process of OCR involves several steps including : segmentation, feature extraction and classification. Firstly, for the classification process, there are two steps in building a classifier : training and testing. These steps can be broken down further into sub-steps. From Fig. 4.24, we see that the training phase is structured from three sub phases given by preprocessing, feature extraction and model estimation. On the other hand, for the testing phase, this phase contains also three sub phases given by : pre-processing, feature extraction and classification. Secondly, for the OCR Pre-processing process; preprocessing is primarily used to reduce variations of characters. In OCR systems, preprocessing includes the connection of segmentation and normalization as shown in Fig. 4.25. Pre-processing receives a first binary image of a plurality of characters. Pre-processing is generally consists of a series of image to image transformation. The pre-processing steps often performed in OCR are : Scanning, Binarization, Noise Removal, Segmentation and Normalization. Thirdly, with regard to feature extractor, this step is the key issue of character recognition. Feature extraction abstracts high level information about individual patterns to facilitate recognition. A wide variety of approaches have been proposed to capture the distinctive feature of machine characters. These approaches fall into one of two categories :

(1) global analysis which contains techniques as moments and mathematical transforms.

(2) Structural analysis in which efforts are aimed at capturing the essential shape features of characters generally from their skeletons of contours.

Fourthly, with regard to recognizer (classifier), there are three categories of character classifiers : neural network approach, statistical approach and structural approach. Fifthly,

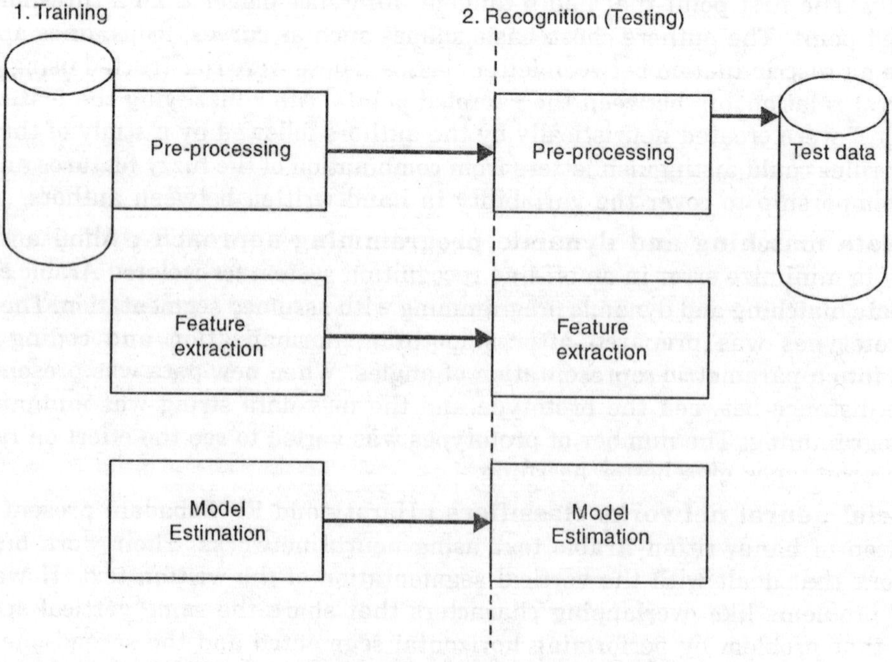

Fig. 4.24. *Pattern classification process.*

for the final phase of OCR which is postprocessor, the post-Processor is designed to supplement the recognition process to improve the accuracy of the process. The post-process examines the bitmap generated by the recognizer and makes a determination as to the validity of the selection made by the recognizer. In one embodiment, gross structural feature.

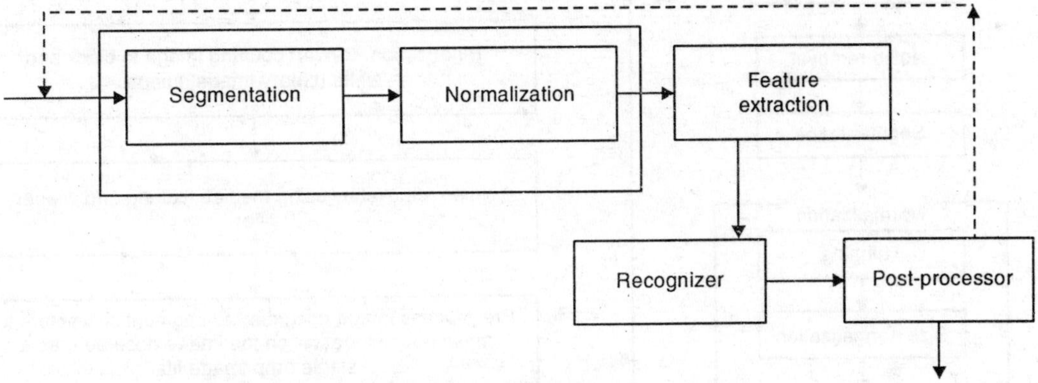

Fig. 4.25. *Flow diagram for optical character recognition system.*

Such as character strokes and contours contained in the bitmap fed-to the post-processor by the recognizer are used for this purpose. The post-processor use various techniques to distinguish one character from another. For example, the geometry/topology of an image (*e.g.*, bitmap) can be used to distinguish characters represented by the image. Geometric/topological features include.

(*i*) Loops such that appear in the handwritten letters.

(*ii*) Straight lines which appear in such handwritten letters as.

(*iii*) Endpoints and

(*iv*) Intersections.

4.6.3 The Proposed Handwritten Arabic Character Recognition System (AHOCR)

Handwritten Arabic character recognition system (AHOCR) aims to convert images document to text. The main objective of this section is to introduce a novel method of off-line handwritten Arabic character recognition used to construct AHOCR. In AHOCR, after moving the document from a storage location to a digital scanner, for each image document scanned at 300 dpi, the output is formatted image with ('bmp' : windows Bitmap (BMP), 'jpg' or 'jpeg', Joint Photographic Expert Group (JPEG) and adequate results are obtained with this quality, the scanner generates image document or a selected portion of the image document. The scanner then applies the image to a recognition system according to the invention. The AHOCR recognition system as shown in Fig. 4.26 includes a Geometric Moments Invariant (GMI) for feature extraction and Probabilistic Neural Network (PNN) for recognition. Recognizer can process the image received from the scanner to determine all of the character written on the document that was scanned. In general, the recognition system generates data representative of each character on the document and passes that data as output to a buffer memory. The central computer typically controls and/or initiates other aspects of the operations such as storage, retrieval, reuse and transmission. It helps the transition from bookshelves and filling cabinets to the paperless. The main components of AHOCR are : Pre-processor, feature, extractor and recognizer, classifier. The first stage of our proposed AHOCR is called

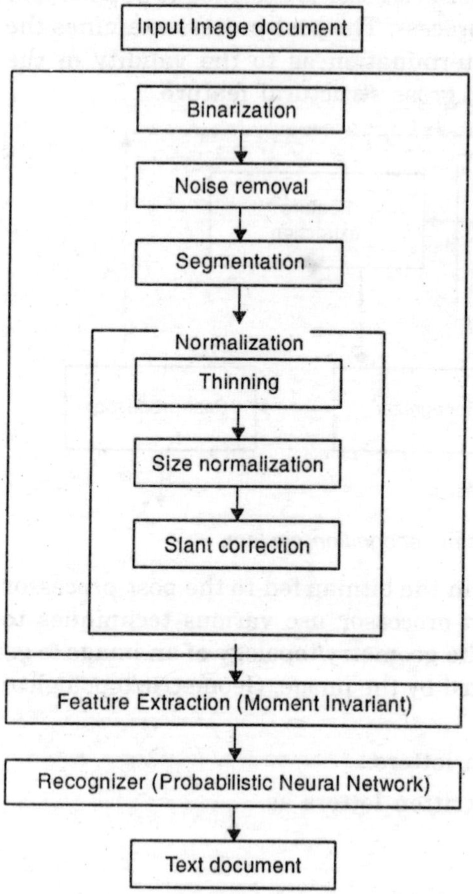

Fig. 4.26. *Flow diagram for the proposed handwritten Arabic character recognition system (AHOCR).*

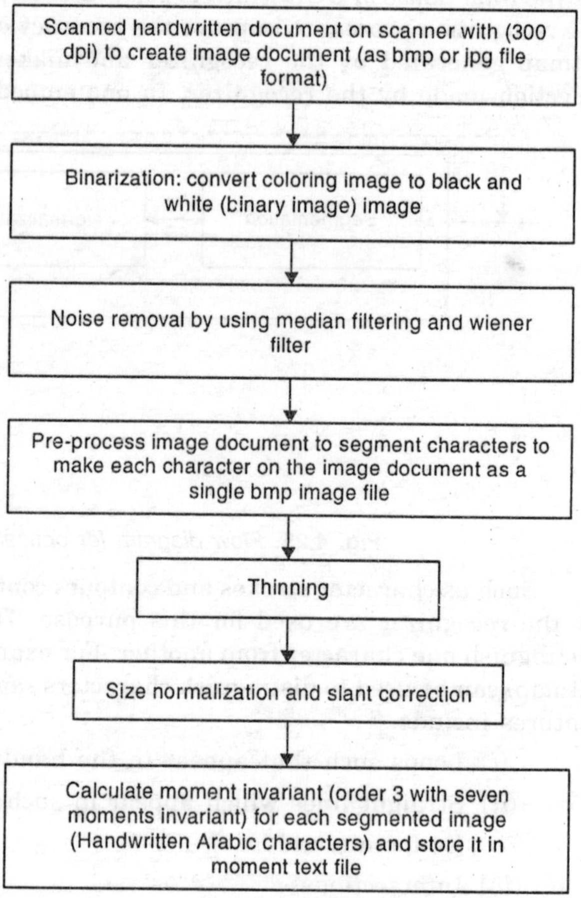

Fig. 4.27. *Operation executed on image document to create database for Arabic handwritten invariant moment.*

pre-process. This stage is structured from various phases given by : Binarization, noise removal, segmentation and normalization. The second stage is called character feature extraction operation of AHOCR. This stage is subdivided into the following phases : Geometricmoment invariant, moment invariant for Arabic character of AHOCR, neural network classifier operation of AHOCR, probabilistic neural network structure, probabilistic neural network classifier of AHOCR, Creating database for Arabic Handwritten Invariant moment of our proposed approach as well as operation concepts is shown in Fig. 4.27.

4.6.4 Experimental Results of AHOCR for Handwritten Arabic Text Document

Our experiments were conducted on the Arabic handwriting of 25 independent writers document shown in Fig. 4.28. These documents were then processed. The experiments were done on 3 disjoint data sets given by :

1. Training (37800) = 20 volunteers × 5 iterations × 378 characters 2. Validation (3780) = 10 volunteers × 378 characters 3. Test (764) (5 volunteers with different number of characters in each document). The Validation set was composed of characters that were

same authors that were totally seen in the training process. The test set was written by 5 authors that were totally unseen in the training process. There are two procedures done in our experiments : training and testing. The trial trained on the training set and tested on the validation test.

سورة الفاتحة

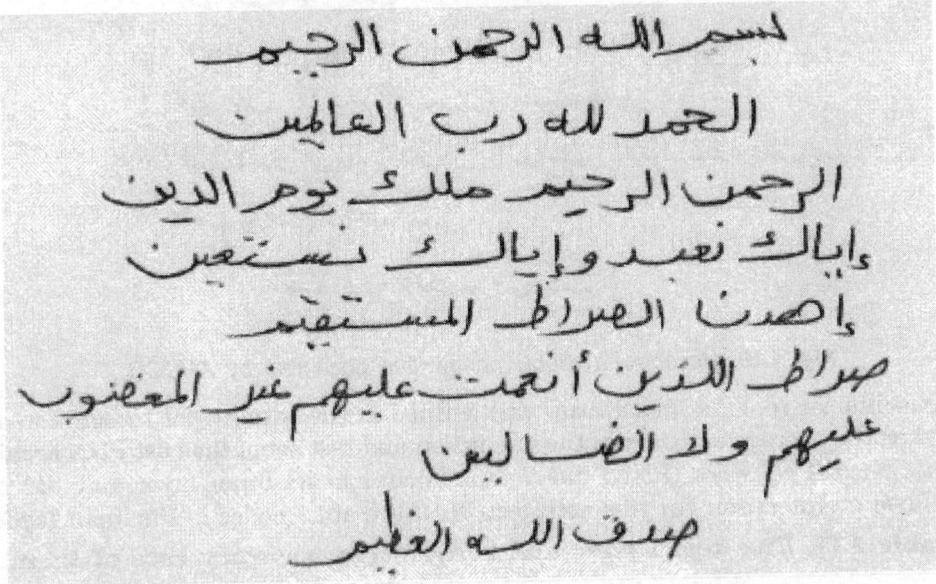
بسم الله الرحمن الرحيم
الحمد لله رب العالمين
الرحمن الرحيم ملك يوم الدين
إياك نعبد وإياك نستعين
إهدنا الصراط المستقيم
صراط الذين أنعمت عليهم غير المغضوب
عليهم ولا الضالين
صدق الله العظيم

Fig 4.28. *Arabic handwritten document written by the first test writer.*

The experiment was to simply train the probabilistic neural network architectures on the training set and test on all three sets. The results are become the baseline for letter optimization.

For each of the seven moment value of input data (image character) as described in Table 4.11, 142 output nodes (141 for Arabic characters, kart node for reject result). In the output layer, we take the advantage of the fact that final values range from 0 to 1. Given this, we can interpret each output of a node in the output layer as a confidence level for each possible output. So, each node in the output layer represents a possible Arabic character being recognized. The output layer is set to reorganize 142 possible outputs : (– 0 --9), (+, – , *, 1, =, !, ., ;, ?) and not recognized. After running our algorithm with a learning rate of = 0.9, we found that choosing an error goal for probabilistic architecture during the 8000 epoch's probabilistic training time will improve : the accuracy across training, validation and test (Table 4.12). The best probabilistic for recognition accuracy is the probabilistic three layers neural networks architecture. For training, it recorded a recognition accuracy rate of 99%. For validation, it had recognition accuracy rate of 98%. For test, it had a recognition accuracy rate of 96% and the average recognition accuracy rate is 97%. Looking at a breakdown of the test set results (Table 4.11), we notice that five test writers had a good accuracy rate as shown in Fig. 4.29.

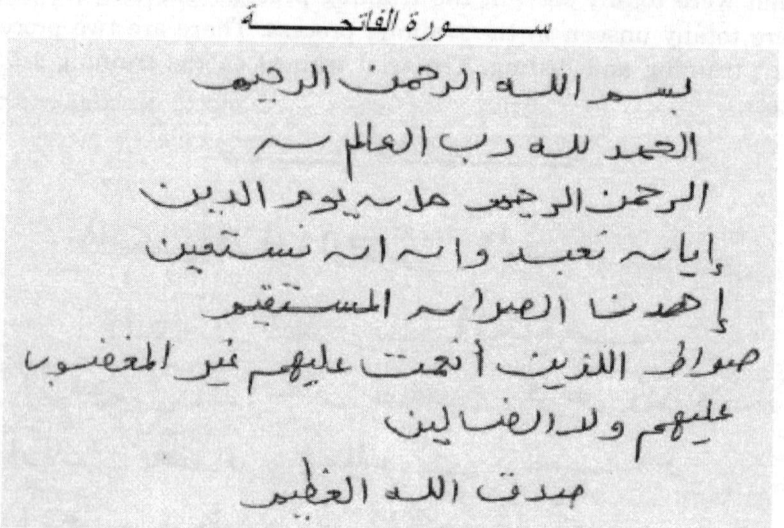

Fig. 4.29. *Recognized Arabic handwritten document by AHOCR.*

The baseline for recognition accuracy was defined as the baseline for recognition accuracy was defined as the average accuracy of the validation and test set of the best PNN architecture. Probabilistic Neural Network (PNN) has 7 input nodes in its input layer and 142 nodes in its output layer architecture. For this architecture, there are 7 nodes in the input layer (node).

Table 4.11. Five test writer and recognition accuracy rate of them

Writer	*Error rate*	*Accuracy*	*Rate*
21	4%		96%
22	5%		95%
23	3%		97%
24	3%		97%
25	5%		95%
Average test accuracy rate			96%

Table 4.12. Recognition accuracy results for text Arabic character

Train recognition	*Validation recognition*	*Test recognition*	*Average*
Accuracy rate	Accuracy rate	Accuracy rate	Accuracy rate
22	5%		95%

4.7 IMAGE PROCESSING

The role of input is vital to recognize objects. It forms a part of computer vision. The object have to be acquired, digitized and further processed to provide useful information. Image acquisition is done using image sensors like point sensors, linear sensors and two dimensional sensors. The analog information on the intensity of image is passed through digitizers and suitable utilities for pre-processing.

The process of edge enhancement permits the elimination of irrelevant information in the digitized images, thus facilitating the recognition of objects. In edge enhancement, image processing is done by edge detection where it separates the object form its background and extracts the contour of the object.

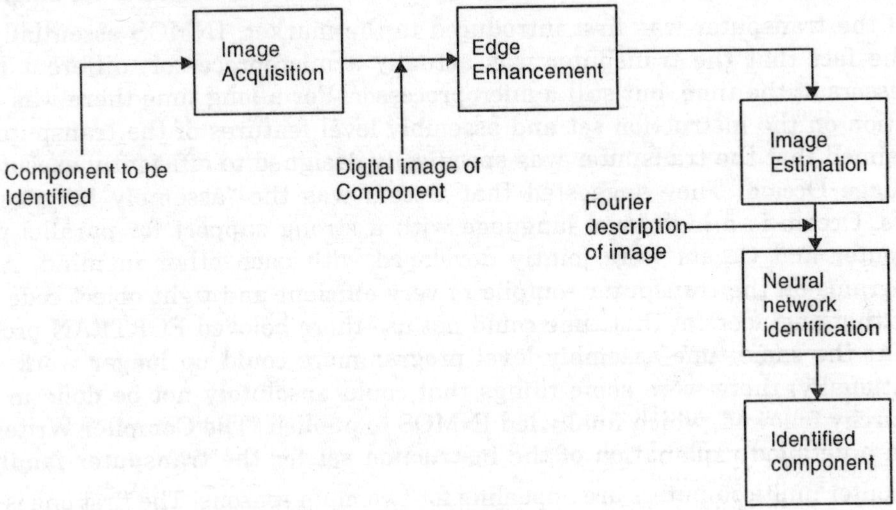

Fig. 4.30.

4.8 TRANSPUTERS

4.8.1 A Brief Background

The transputer was introduced to the world in 1985 by INMOS limited. The transputer was a VLSI chip, and at that time was heralded as a revolution in the world of computing. The transputer is essentially a high performance microprocessor. One of its most significant features is its ability to perform multitasking in hardware, and its sub micro-second context switching. Context switch time denotes the time it takes for a higher priority task to preempt a lower priority task, and start executing. Communication between processes is also provided by hardware, both for internal data transfers, and transfers between different processors. The first processor in the transputer series was T414 and boasted an unprecedented speed of 10 MIPS (millions of instructions per second), with the capability of multitasking in hardware. Dedicated on chip link controllers allowed for communications between processes running on different processors (transputers), with a minimal processor overhead. The T414 is a 32-bit processor with 2K on-chip RAM and four interprocessor links, capable of addressing upto 4Gbytes of external memory using multiplexed address and data lines.

Since then, other processors have been developed by INMOS. T212 : A 16-bit version of the T414 with 2K of onboard RAM and a 64K address range. Using separate address and data buses.

- M212 : A T212 with two of the four links replaced by a built-in disc controller circuit.
- T800 : Essentially, a revamped T414 with a floating point co-processor integrated on the chip, more instructions, and on-chip RAM increased to 4K. This is one of the more

popular transputers sice it combines high performance floating point processing (1.5 MFLOPS) with the possibilities of parallel processing.

- T222 : A T212 with 4K of on chip RAM.
- T425 : An updated T414 with debugging instructions added such as for single stepping.
- T801 : A T800 with separate address and data lines for faster memory access.
- T805 : An updated T800 with debugging instructions added such as for single stepping.

When the transputer was first introduced to the market, INMOS essentially forgot to mention the fact that the transputer was actually a microprocessor, different from other microprocessors at the time, but still a microprocessor. For a long time there was also a lack of information on the instruction set and assembly level features of the transputers. In fact INMOS claimed that the transputer was specifically designed to efficiently execute the high level language Occam. They suggested that Occam was the "assembly language" for the transputers. Occam is a high level language with a strong support for parallel processing. The transputer and Occam were jointly developed with each other in mind. As a result Occam programs on the transputer compile to very efficient and tight object code. However, this meant that engineers at that time could not use there beloved FORTRAN programming language. At the same time assembly level programmers could no longer work at the low level. Additionally, there were some things that could absolutely not be done in Occam. A state of anarchy followed, which finally led INMOS to publish "The Compiler Writer's Guide", which gave a detailed explanation of the instruction set for the transputer family.

Transputer multicomputers are appealing for two main reasons. The first one is flexibility, both in the implementation of user-configurable networks, and in a growing software base, which includes, among other languages, C, C++, Occam, Pascal, Modula-2 and Prolog. The second reason is affordability. Oneand four-transputer boards are now available for most popular personal computers and workstations, making transputer-based multiprocessors available for as low as $450 per node, bringing the exploration of parallel programming within the reach of most universities and colleges, and even individuals.

Processes and Concurreny in the transputer. The transputer uses processes as the basic software building block and provides the direct implementation of a process in hardware. A process is an independent computation (or a sequence of computations) that communicates with other processes. This communication on the transputer is achieved by explicitly defined channels. A process itself may consist of subprocesses by time-sharing.

The transputer provides a number of links which support point-to-point communications between transputers, hence allowing processes to be distributed over a network of transputers. Therefore, it is possible to build a system with a network of transputers, with each transputer in the system executing a set of processes and each transputer capable of communicating with others on the network. It should be noted however that each transputer can only communicate directly with another physically connected transputer.

It is the ability to specify a hardwired fuction as a process which provides the architectural framework of transputers the capability to be used in highly specialized and diverse applications.

Transputer Harware Description. The transputer is a component designed to exploit the potential of VLSI technology. This technology allows for a large number of identical components to be manufactured cheaply. For this matter it is desirable to be able to implement a concurrent system using identical components. As mentioned earlier the transputer is a high performance microprocessor which has been designed to facilate interprocess and interprocessor communication. The transputer architecture defines a family of programmable VLSI components.

A Programmable Device Transputer systems can be designed and programmed using a variety of different languages including assembly level mnemonics, occam, concurrent Ada, and concurrent versions of C and C++. A Multitasking processor with Memory on a single chip.

The transputer processor supports multitasking, and enforces two levels of priority for concurrent tasks.

Besides allowing the creation of parallel applications where communication and computation functions can be implemented cleanly in separate modules, the multitasking feature provides us with the opportunity to start experimenting with parallelism in a shared memory environment. Almost every operation that a transputer performs involves interfacing with memory. By providing on chip memory this interface time has been greatly reduced.

4.8.2 Links and Channel Communication

Transputers communicate with each other via high-speed serial links. The small number of communication wires required and the simplicity of the protocol makes the networking of transputers simple and in most-cases user configurable. This feature allows for the easy evaluation of various network configurations such as rings, meshes, hypercubes, or trees. At the software level, the hardware links are defined as channels. Hence, while transputers communicate with each other via links, the tasks residing in them communicate through channels. Because the transputer implements communication primitives at its lowest level (in microcode), and because the access to the serial links is memory-mapped, the transputer offers a powerful feature to the programmer; primitive supporting the communication between tasks residing on different neighboring transputers can also be used to allow tasks residing on the same transputer to communicate. In other words, tasks residing on the same transputer can communicate by sending a message to each other with the same primitive they would use to exchange messages with a task residing on a neighboring transputer. This powerful feature allows the programmer to study first hand some of the complex issues dealing with mapping and folding parallel applications to small networks.

4.8.3. Virtual Channels

Virtual channels are a technique for circumventing the limited-fanout of the multi-computer nodes. While a node may be physically limited to four Input/Output links, as is the case for the transputer, a software or hardware routing mechanism can be introduced to allow the transfer of message between different transputers as if they were connected by a channel, even though they may not be directly connected to each other, and their four links may already be connected to other transputers. Hence a virtual path can be created between arbitrary pairs of nodes. This feature, invisible to the programmer, offer a powerful medium for implementing arbitrary networks that can be dynamically configured and modified.

Hence a transputer circuit contains a processor, a small amount of memory, a co-processor, and four highspeed bi-directional links. Although such simple a list may not be impressive, the elegant design of the transputer provides a rich environment for parallel processing.

Worth mentioning is the fact that combining these entities on a single silicon chip was not a technological breakthrough in itself. Other companies, such as Intel or Motorola had introduced versions of their popular 8-bit processors with local memory and interfacing hardware. The novelty was the combination of several factors. One of the most important factor was the introduction of a high-level language, occam whose features were directly supported by the transputer hardware. and that made the transputer a building block for parallel computers. The second prominent factor was the ease with which transputers could be connected to each other with as little as a few electrical wires.

The four bi-directional input/output (I/O) ports of the transputer are designed to interface directly with the ports of other transputers, very much like the pegs on top of Lego blocks fit directly in their bottom cavities. This feature allows for several transputers to fit on a small footprint, with very little extra logic circuits, making it possible to easily fit four transputers with some memory on a PC daughter board (ISA bus), or microchannel board.

4.8.4 IMS T800 Architecture

The IMS T800, with its on-chip floating point unit is only 20% larger in area than the T414. This small size and high performance design emerges from a careful note of silicon economics. The IMS T800 architecture is similar to that of the T414. However, in addition to the memory, links, Central Processing Unit (CPU), and the external memory interface, it includes a Floating Point Unit (FPU), which operates concurrently and under the control of the CPU. Figure 4.31 shows a block diagram for the T800.

The IMS T800, like the T414 operates at two priority levels. The FPU stack is duplicated so that when the T800 switches from low to high, none of the states in the FPU are written to memory. This reduces the worst-case response significantly. Furthermore, duplication of the register stack enables the floatingpoint arithmetic to be used in an interrupt mode.

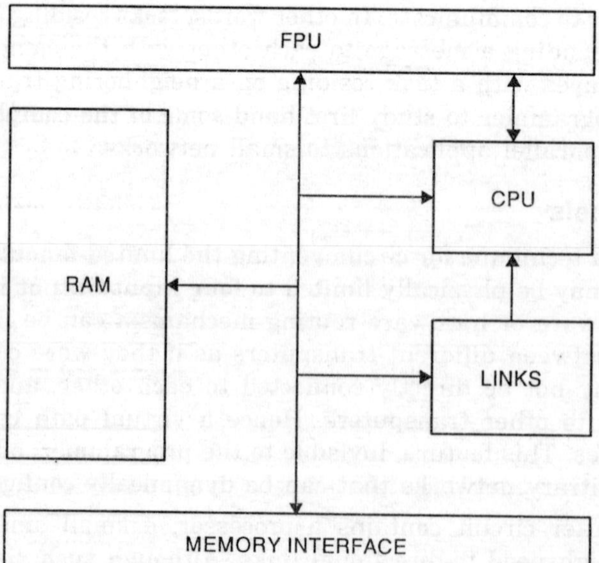

Fig. 4.31.

4.8.5 Instruction Set Overview

This section presents a discussion on the instruction set for the T414. The T414 has 100 instructions which can be grouped as follows :

- 16 addressing and memory acces instructions
- 6 branching and program control
- 41 arithmetic and logical
- 12 process scheduling and control
- 16 inter-process communication
- 9 miscellaneous.

4.8.6 Addressing and Memory Access Instructions

There are two ways of addressing memory; namely to specify the address as a fixed offset from the address in the workspace pointer or the A register. Specifying the address as a fixed offset in the workspace pointer is called "local access", since the workspace pointer conventionally points to an area of memory used to hold the local variables for a procedure. Specifying the address as a fixed offset in the A register is called "non-local access". Instructions are provided for reading and writing bytes or blocks of bytes to and from the memory using the above mentioned addressing schemented to by the workspace pointer.

Instruction	*Brief Description*
LDL n	Load Local. Loads a word into Reg A which lies at an offset of n words from the address pointed to by the workspace pointer.
STL n	Store Local. Stores a word from Reg A to the memory location which lies at an offset of n words from the address pointed to by the workspace pointer.
LDNL n	Load Non-Local. Loads a word into Reg A which lies at an offset of n words from the address pointed to by the A Register.
STNL n	Store Non-Local. Stores a word from Reg A to the memory location which lies at an offset of n words from the address pointed to by the A Register.
LDLP n	Load Local Address. Loads into the reg A the effective address that is calculated instead of the contents of the address.
LDNLP n	Load Non-Local Address. Loads into the reg A the effective address that is calculated instead of the contents of the address.
LB	Load Byte. Loads the byte at the address contained in Reg A into Reg A thus overwriting the previous contents of Reg A.
SB	Store Byte. Stores the byte contained in the bottom eight bits of Reg B in the memoiry location specified by the address contained in Reg A.
MOVE	Move Message. Copies a block of bytes from the address in Reg C to the address in Reg B. The number of bytes to be moved is specified in Reg A.
WSUB	Word Subscript. Increments the address in Reg A by the number of words specified in Reg B.

BSUB	Byte Subscript. Increments the address in Reg A by the number of bytes specified in Reg B.
WCNT	Word Count. Breaks the address in Reg A into word address and the byte offset components, storing them in Regs A and B respectively.
BCNT	Byte Count. Multiplies the value in Reg A by the number of bytes in a word.
AJW n	Adjust Workspace. Increments the workspace pointer by n.
GAJW n	General Adjust Workspace. Exchanges the contents of the workspace pointer and Reg A.
LDPI	Load Pointer to Instruction. Calculates an address, which consists of the current value of the IP incremented by the contents of Reg A and then stores this value in Reg A.

4.8.7 Branching and Program Control Instructions

The transputer provides only has six instructions for altering the flow of control of the program, which brings it close to being a RISC processor.

Instruction	*Brief Description*
CJ n	Conditional Jump. Examines the contents of Reg A. If the contents are 0 (zero), the IP is incremented by n. The value in A is popped in either case.
J n	Jump. Increments the IP by n.
LEND	Loop End. Used to implement deterministic loops. Reg A has the displacement which is subtracted from the IP if the instruction succeeds. Reg B has the address of a two word control block. Each time the instruction is executed the contents of the first word are incremented, and the second decremented. If the value in the second word is greater than the first the branch is taken by replacing the contents of IP with (IP - contents of Reg A).
CALL n	Call. Decrements the workspace pointer by four words, stores the contents of C, B, A and the IP at these memory locations, and then increments IP by n.
RET	Return. Load the IP with the contents of the workspace pointer and increments the workspace pointer by 4 words.
GCALL	General Call. Exchanges the contents of Reg A and the IP.

4.8.8 Arithmetic and Logical Instructions

Instruction	*Brief Description*
REV	Reverse. Swaps the contents of Regs A and B.
LDC n	Load Constant. Loads n in A and pushes the previous contents of Reg A to B previous contents of B to C and losing the previous contents of C.
MINT	Minimum Integer. Pushes the constant MinInt onto the evaluation stack.
ADC n	Add Constant. Adds n to the contents of A.
ADD	Signed Addition. A <= A + B. Error flag is set on overflow.
SUB	Signed Subtraction
MUL	Multiply
DIV	Divide
REM	Remainder
SUM	Unsigned Addition
DIFF	Unsigned Subtraction
PROD	Unsigned Multiplication
FMUL	Fractional Multiply
EQC n	Equals Constant. Compares n with the contents of A.If they are equal true (1) is stored in A otherwise a false (0) is stored in A.
GT	Greater Than. If B > A, A <= true (1) else A <= false (0).
CSUB0	Check Subscript from Zero
CCNT1	Check Count from One
AND	Bitwise AND
OR	Bitwise OR
XOR	Bitwise XOR
NOT	Complement
SHL	Shift Left
SHR	Shift Right
LADD	Long Add
LSUM	Long Sum

LSUB	Long Subtract
LDIFF	Long Difference
LMUL	Long Multiply
LDIV	Long Divide
LSHL	Long Shift Left
LSHR	Long Shfit Right
XDBLE	Extend to Double. Converts a single word value into a double word value.
CSNGL	Check Single. Sets the error flag if the value cannot be squeezed into a single word value.
XWORD	Extend to Word
CWORD	Check Word
NORM	Normalize. Normalizes the double word in BA by shifting it left until the top bit is set.
CFLERR	Check Floating Poinjt Infinity or Not A Number (NAN).
LDINF	Load Single Length Infinity.
POSTNORMSN	Post Normalize Correction.
ROUNDSN	Round Single Length Floating Point Number.
UNPACKSN	Unpack Single Length Floating Point Number.

The last five instructions are not included in the T800 transputer, since it has a floating point co-processor.

4.8.9 Process Scheduling and Control Instructions

The transputer has built in mechanisms to support the concurrent execution of processes. Processes may be operated at two levels of priority. Two queues of active processes are maintained, a high priority process queue and a low priority process queue. A process can be in one of four states : executing, waiting. To execute (it is in one of the active process queues), waiting for a timer event (it is in a timer queue) or waitng for a communication event (it is not in any queue). A high priority process will continue to execute untill it terminates or waits for a timer or communication event to take place. In this case if there are any other high priority processes waiting to be executed, the process from the head of the high priority process queue is scheduled. If there are no high priority processes waiting to execute the next low priority process will be scheduled. A low priority process can be preempted by a high priority process at any time. Low priority processes are time-sliced. If a low priority process executes a loop end (LEND) or a Jump(J) instruction, and it has been executing for more than its time-slice period then it is descheduled and placed at the end of the low priority process queue. The low priority process at the head of the queue will commence execution until the nect time-slice or it is preempted by a high priority process.

4.8.10 Inter-Process Communication Instructions

Inter-Process communication is carried out using channels. A channel is an abstract connection between exactly two processes. One process sends a stream of bytes down the channel to another process, which reads and stores them. If a process tries to send data to another process which is not ready, then the sending process will be descheduled until the receiving process becomes ready, and thus synchronization is achieved.

For two processes running on the same transputer, a channel is implemented by using a word somewherein memory that is shared by the two processes. This word is referred to as the channel word. Before any communication can take place this word must be inialized to MinInt (Minimum Integer). This with the transputer's signed address space is interpreted as the lowest address in memory. This address can never be the address of a valid workspace. The channel word would normally be initialized by the parent process of two communicating children. When a process tries to communicate, it examines the contents of the channel word. If the contents are MinInt, the other process is not ready, so it stores the process descriptor in the channel word and deschedules. The IP is stored in location -1 of its workspace and the address of the data to be transferred from or to at location -3. When the other process is ready, it examines the contents of the channel word, finds a valid process descriptor and concludes that the other process is ready. It transfers the block of bytes and restarts the other process. All this is implemented within the microcode of the transputer and hence is extremely fast and efficient. For two processes running on two separate transputers, the two transputers must be connected by hardware INMOS links. Here the communication via channels is taken care of via the hardware within the transputers themselves. When a process on one transputer is ready to send data out to another process on another transputer, the sending process is descheduled. Hardware determines when the other transputer is ready, and transfers the data using Direct Memory Access (DMA), after which the sending process is rescheduled. While this is happening other processes may be executed. At machine code level it appears the same as the former case; the same instructions are used. The distinguishing factor is that in external communication the address of the channel word passes as a parameter in one of the first few locations of memory. The microcode instruction detects the address in one of the reserved locations and pass their parameters on the link hardware for the associated with that address.

Instruction	*Brief Description*
STARTP	Start Process. Adds a new process to the back of the active process queue. Reg A holds the address of the workspace that the new process will use and Reg B holds the offset from IP that the new process will execute. The new process is set at the same priority as the current process and the current process will continue execution with the next instruction.
ENDP	End Process. Conditionally terminates the process. It decrements a count in memory. If this count is non-zero it terminates (the next active process is taken and the current process is not added to the end of the queue) otherwise the process continues but at a different execution address and workspace counter. It takes one parameter, an address in Reg A. This address points to the workspace of the parent process. At location 0 in this workspace is the restart address for the parent process, location 1 holds the count of the child processes. If this count decrements to zero the workspace pointer is set to the value in the A register and its IP to the value pointed to by Reg A.

STOPP	Stop Process. Stops the current process. This process is not added back to the end of the queue. The next active process is scheduled.
STOPERR	Stop On Error. Same as STOPP, but only if the error flag is set.
RUNP	Run Process. Starts a new process. Reg A has the process descriptor. A process descriptor is the address of the workspace for that process with the bottom bit set to the priority of that process. (A workspace lies on a word boundary making the last few bits unused for address specification). Based on the priority the process is added to the end of the appropriate queue. The IP for that process is set to one word below the workspace address.
STHF	Store High Priority Front Pointer
STHB	Store High Priority Back Pointer
STLF	Store Low Priority Front Pointer
STLB	Store Low Priority Back Pointer
SAVEH	Save Low Priority Queue Registers.
SAVEL	Save Low Priority Queue Registers.
LDPRI	Load Priority. Loads 0 or 1 into A based on the priority of the current process.

To illustrate the backpropagation algorithm, let's choose a network and apply it to a particular problem. To begin, we will use the 1-2-1 network that we discussed earlier in this chapter. For convenience we have reproduced the network in figure 4.32. Next we want to define a problem for the network to solve. Suppose that we want to use the network to approximate the function :

$$G(p) = 1 + \sin\left(\frac{\pi}{4}p\right) \quad \text{for } -2 \le p \le 2$$

To obtain our training set we will evaluate this function at several value of p.

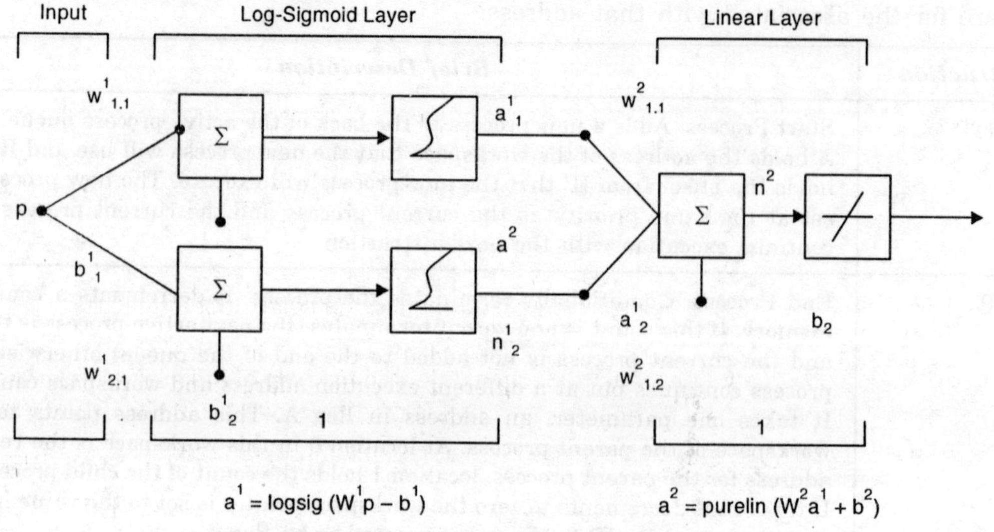

Fig. 4.32. *Example Function Approximation Network.*

Before we begin the backpropagation algorithm we need to choose some initial values for the network weights and biases. Generally these are chosen to be small random values. For now let's choose the values.

$$W^1(0) = \begin{bmatrix} -0.27 \\ -0.41 \end{bmatrix},\ b^1(0) = \begin{bmatrix} -0.48 \\ -0.13 \end{bmatrix},\ W^2(0) = [0.09 - 0.17],\ b^2(0) = [0.48]$$

The response of the network for these initial values is illustrated in figure 4.33, along with this sine function we wish to approximate.

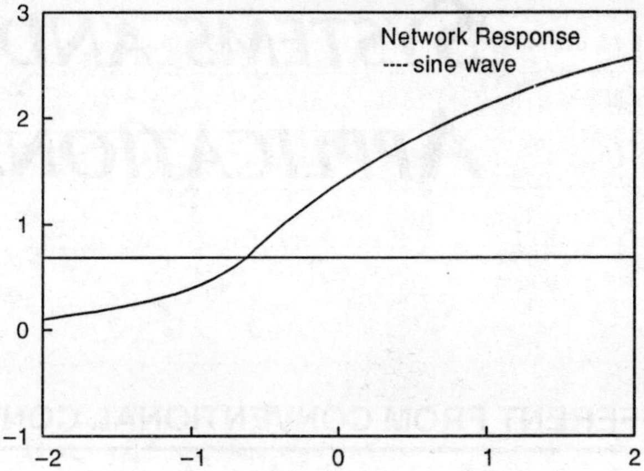

Fig. 4.33. *Initial Network Response.*

Now we are ready to start the algorithm. For our initial input we will choose $p = 1$:

$$a^0 = p = 1$$

The output of the first layer is then

$$a_1 = f_1 = (W_1 a_0 + b_1) = \text{logsig}\left[\begin{bmatrix} -0.27 \\ -0.41 \end{bmatrix}[1] + \begin{bmatrix} -0.48 \\ -0.13 \end{bmatrix}\right] = \text{logsig}\left[\begin{bmatrix} -0.75 \\ -0.54 \end{bmatrix}\begin{bmatrix} \dfrac{1}{1+e^{0.75}} \\ \dfrac{1}{1-e^{0.54}} \end{bmatrix}\right] = \begin{bmatrix} 0.321 \\ 0.368 \end{bmatrix}$$

EXERCISE

1. Explain counter propagation neural network. Give its algorithm.
2. What do you meant by Vapour Liquid Equilibrium (VLE) ? Make a model of the VLE system using matlab software.
3. Make a program for prediction VLE data in matlab.
4. How to train the network in unsupervised manner (simulink tool in matlab) ? Train the network with the data given in table 4f.
5. How to optimize the industrial production data with the help of artificial neural network ? How many transfer functions can be used for that purpose ? Give their significance.
6. Make a program for backpropagation GDR algorithm using matlab software.

□□□

Chapter 5

FOUNDATION OF FUZZY APPROACHES SYSTEMS AND ITS APPLICATIONS

5.1 HOW IS FL DIFFERENT FROM CONVENTIONAL CONTROL METHODS ?

Fuzzy Logic (FL) incorporates a simple, rule-based IF X AND Y THEN Z approach to a solving control problem rather than attempting to model a system mathematically. The FL model is empirically-based, relying on an operator's experience rather than their technical understanding of the system. For example, rather than dealing with temperature control in terms such as "SP = 500F", "T < 1000F", or "210C < TEMP < 220C", terms like "IF (process is too cool) AND (process is getting colder) THEN (add heat to the process)" or "IF (process is too hot) AND (process is heating rapidly) TBEN (cool the process quickly)" are used. These terms are imprecise and yet very descriptive of what must actually happen. Consider what you do in the shower if the temperature is too cold : you will make the water comfortable very quickly with little trouble. FL is capable of mimicking this type of behavior but at very high rate.

5.2 HOW DOES FL WORK ?

FL requires some numerical parameters in order to operate such as what is considered significant error and significant rate-of-change-of-error, but exact values of these numbers are usually not critical unless very responsive performance is required in which case empirical tuning would determine them. For example, a simple temperature control system could use a single temperature feedback sensor whose data is subtracted from the command signal to compute "error" and then time differentiated to yield the error slope or rate-of-change-of-error, hereafter called "error-dot". Error might have units of degs F and a small error considered to be 2F while a large error is 5F. The "error-dot" might then have units of degs/min with a small error-dot being 517/min and a large one being 15F/min. These values do not have to be symmetrical and can be "tweaked" once the system is operating in order to optimize performance. Generally, FL is so forgiving that the system will probably work the first time without any tweaking.

FL was conceived as a better method for sorting and handling data but has proven to be a excellent choice for many control system applications since it mimics human control logic. It can be built into anything from small, handheld products to large computerized process control systems. It uses an imprecise but very descriptive language to deal with input data more like a human operator. It is very robust and forgiving of operator and data input and often works when first implemented with little or no tuning.

5.3 WHY USE FL ?

Fuzzy logic is used because:

1. It offers several unique features that make it a particularly good choice for many control problems.
2. It is inherently robust since it does not require precise, noise-free inputs and can be programmed to fail safely if a feedback sensor quits or is destroyed. The output control is a smooth control function despite a wide range of input variations.
3. Since the FL controller processes user-defined rules governing the target control system, it can be modified and tweaked easily to improve or drastically alter system performance. New sensors can easily be incorporated into the system simply by generating appropriate governing rules.
4. FL is not limited to a few feedback inputs and one or two control outputs, nor is it necessary to measure or compute rate-of-change parameters in order for it to be implemented. Any sensor data that provides some indication of *a s*), stem's actions and reactions is sufficient. This allows the sensors to be inexpensive and imprecise thus keeping the overall system cost and complexity low.
5. Because of the rule-based operation, any reasonable number of inputs can be processed (1–8 or more) and numerous outputs (1–4 or more) generated, although defining the rulebase quickly becomes complex if too many inputs and outputs are chosen for a single implementation since rules defining their interrelations must also be defined. It would be better to break the control system into smaller chunks and use several smaller *FL* controllers distributed on the system, each with more limited responsibilities.
6. FL can control nonlinear systems that would be difficult or impossible to model mathematically. This opens doors for control systems that would normally be deemed unfeasible for automation.

5.4 HOW IS FL USED ?

1. Define the control objectives and criteria : *What am I trying to control ? What do I have to do to control the system ? What kind of response do I need ? What are the possible (probable) system failure modes ?*
2. Determine the input and output relationships and choose a minimum number of variables for input to the FL engine (typically error and rate-of change-of-error).

3. Using the rule-based structure of FL, break the control problem down into a series of IF X AND Y THEN Z rules that define the desired system output response for given system input conditions. The number and complexity of rules depends on the number of input parameters that are to be processed and the number fuzzy variables associated with each parameter. If possible, use at least one variable and its time derivative. Although it is possible to use a single, instantaneous error parameter without knowing its rate of change, this cripples the system's ability to minimize overshoot for a step inputs.
4. Create FL membership functions that define the meaning (values) of Input/Output terms used in the rules.
5. Create the necessary pre- and post-processing FL routines if implementing in S/W, otherwise program the rules into the FL H/W engine.
6. Test the system, evaluate the results, tune the rules and membership functions, and retest until satisfactory results are obtained.

5.5 LINGUISTIC VARIABLES

In 1973, Professor Lotfi Zadeh proposed the concept of linguistic or "fuzzy" variables. Think of them as linguistic objects or words, rather than numbers. The sensor input is a noun, *e.g.*, "temperature", "displacement", "velocity", 'flow", 11pressure", etc. Since error is just the difference, it can be thought of the same way. The fuzzy variables themselves are adjectives that modify the variable (*e.g.*, "large positive" error, "small positive" error "zero" error, ft small negative" error, and "large negative" error). As a minimum, one could simply have "positive", "zero", and "negative" variables for each of the parameters. Additional ranges such as "very large" and "very small" could also be added to extend the responsiveness to exceptional or very nonlinear conditions, but aren't necessary in a basic system.

FL does not require precise inputs, is inherently robust, and can process any reasonable number of inputs but system complexity increases rapidly with more inputs and outputs. Distributed processors would probably be easier to implement. Simple, plain-language IF X AND Y THEN Z rules are used to describe the desired system response in terms of linguistic variables rather than mathematical formulas. The number of these is dependent on the number of inputs, outputs, and the designer's control response goals.

5.6 MATRIX RULES

In the last article the concept of linguistic variables was presented. The fuzzy parameters of error (command- feedback) and error-dot (rate-of-change-of-error) were modified by the adjectives "negative", "zero", and "positive". To picture this, imagine the simplest practical implementation, a 3-by-3 matrix. The columns represent "negative error", "zero error", and "positive error" inputs from left to right. The rows represent "negative", "zero", and positive" "error-dot" input from top to bottom. This planar construct is called a rule matrix. It has two input conditions, "error" and "error-dot", and one output response conclusion (at the intersection of each row and column). In this case there are nine possible logical product (AND) output response conclusions. Although not absolutely necessary, rule matrices usually have an odd number of rows and columns to accommodate a "zero" center row and column region. This may not be needed as long as the functions on either side of the center overlap somewhat and continuous dithering of the output is acceptable since the "zero" regions correspond to "no change" output responses the lack of this region will cause the system to continually hunt for "zero". It is also possible to have a different number of rows than columns. This occurs when numerous degrees of inputs are needed. The maximum number of possible rules is simply the product of the number of rows and columns, but definition of all of these rules may not be necessary since some input conditions may never occur in practical operation. The primary objective of this construct is to map out the universe of possible inputs while keeping the system sufficiently under control.

5.7 APPLICATIONS OF FUZZY LOGIC CONTROL SYSTEM IN PROCESS INDUSTRY

5.7.1 Temperature Control

Process

The first STEP IN Implementing FL is to decide exactly what is to be controlled and how. For example, suppose we want to design a simple proportional temperature controller with an electrical heating element and a variable-speed cooling fan. A positive signal output calls for 0–100 percent heat while a negative signal output calls for 0–100 percent cooling. Control is achieved through proper balance and control of these two active devices.

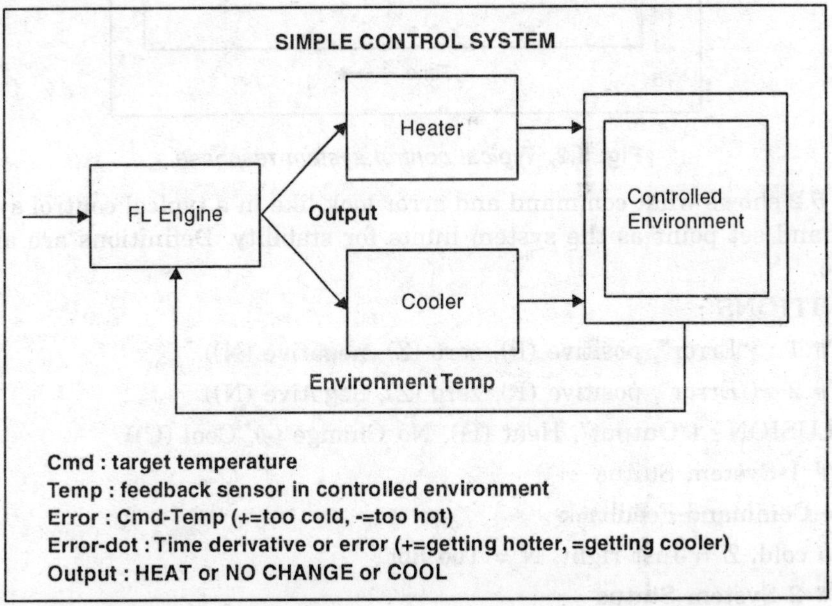

Fig. 5.1. *A simple block diagram of the control system.*

It is necessary to establish a meaningful system for representing the linguistic variables in the matrix. For this example, the following will be used :

"*N*" = "negative" error or error-dot input level

"*Z*" = "zero" error or error-dot input level

"*P*" = "positive error or error-dot input level

"*H*" = "Heat" output response

"_" = "No change" to current output

"*C*" = "Cool" output response

Defining the minimum number of possible input product combinations and corresponding output response conclusions using these terms. For a three-by- three matrix with heating and cooling output responses, all nine rules will need to be defined. The conclusions to the rules with the linguistic variables associated with the output response for each rule are transferred to the matrix.

What is being Controlled and How

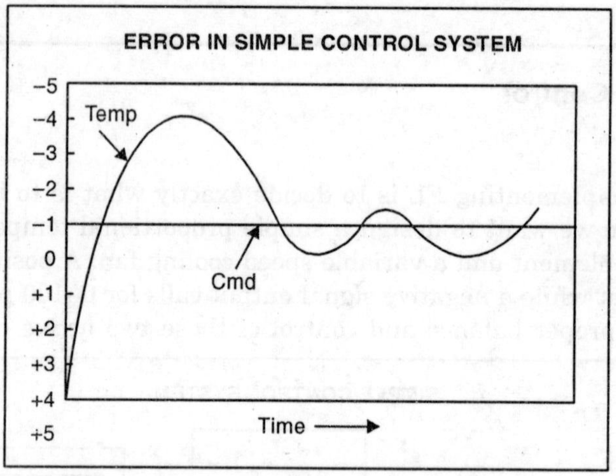

Fig. 5.2. *Typical control system response.*

Figure 5.2 shows what command and error look like in a typical control system relative to the command set point as the system hunts for stability. Definitions are also shown for this example.

DEFINITIONS :

INPUT# 1 : ("Error", positive (P), zero (Z), negative (N))

INPUT# 2 : ("Error", positive (P), zero (Z), negative (N))

CONCLUSION : ("Output", Heat (H), No Change (-), Cool (C))

INPUT# 1 System Status

Error = Command-Feedback

P = Too cold, Z = Just right, N = Too hot

INPUT# 2 System Status

Error-dot = d (Error)/dt

P = Getting hotter Z = Not changing N = getting colder

OUTPUT Conclusion and System Response

Output H = Call for heating - = don't change anything C = Call for cooling.

Block Diagram of Temperature Control System in Simulink

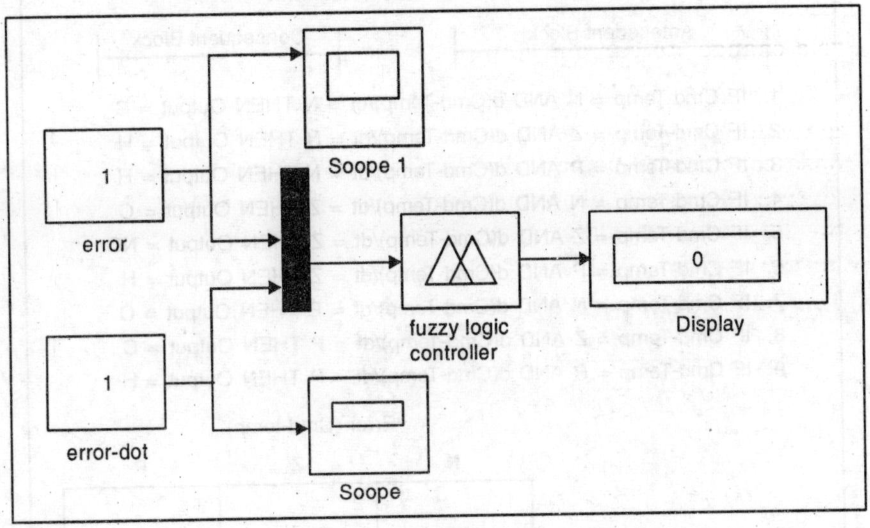

Fig. 5.3

No. of inputs = 2

Input 1 = error

Input 2 = error-dot

No. of output = 1

Output = temperature

Triangular membership function for each input and output

Operating Rules

Linguistic rules describing the control system consist of two parts; an antecedent block (between the IF and THEN) and a consequent block (following THEN). Depending on the system, it may not be necessary to evaluate every possible input combination (for 5-by-5 and up matrices) since some may rarely or never occur. By making this type of evaluation, usually done by an experienced operator, fewer rules can be evaluated, thus simplifying the processing logic and perhaps even improving the FL system performance.

After transferring the conclusions from the nine rules to the matrix there is a noticeable symmetry to the matrix. This suggests (but doesn't guarantee) a reasonable well-behaved (linear) system. This implementation may proved to be too simplistic for some control problems, however it does not illustrate the process. Additional degree of error and error-dot may be included if the desired system response call for this. This will increase the rule base size and complexity but may also increase the quality of the control. Figure 5.4 shows the rule matrix derived from the previous rules.

Linguistic variables are used to represent an FL system's operating parameters. The rule matrix is a simple graphical tool for mapping the FL control system rules. It accommodates two input variables and expresses their logic product (AND) as one output response variable. To use, define the system using plain-English rules based upon the inputs, decide appropriate output response conclusions.

Rule Structure and Rule Matrix

Antecedent Block | Consequent Block

1. IF Cmd-Temp = N AND d(Cmd-Temp)/dt = N THEN Output = C
2. IF Cmd-Temp = Z AND d(Cmd-Temp)/dt = N THEN Output = H
3. IF Cmd-Temp = P AND d(Cmd-Temp)/dt = N THEN Output = H
4. IF Cmd-Temp = N AND d(Cmd-Temp)/dt = Z THEN Output = C
5. IF Cmd-Temp = Z AND d(Cmd-Temp)/dt = Z THEN Output = NC
6. IF Cmd-Temp = P AND d(Cmd-Temp)/dt = Z THEN Output = H
7. IF Cmd-Temp = N AND d(Cmd-Temp)/dt = P THEN Output = C
8. IF Cmd-Temp = Z AND d(Cmd-Temp)/dt = P THEN Output = C
9. IF Cmd-Temp = P AND d(Cmd-Temp)/dt = P THEN Output = H

Error-(Cmd-temp)

Error-(d(cmd-Temp)/dt)	N	Z	P
N	1 C	2 H	3 H
Z	4 C	5 NC	6 H
P	7 C	8 C	9 H

Fig. 5.4. *The rule structure.*

Membership Functions

The membership function is a graphical representation of the magnitude of participation of each input. It associates a weighting with each of the inputs that are processed, define functional overlap between inputs, and ultimately determines an output response. The rules use the input membership value as weighting factors to determine their influence on the fuzzy output sets of the final output conclusion. Once the functions are inferred, scaled, and combined, they are defuzzified into a crisp output which drives the system. There are different memberships functions associated with each input and output response. Some features to note are :

SHAPE triangular is common, but bell, trapezoidal, have shine and, exponential have been used. More complex functions are possible but require greater computing overhead to implement. HEIGHT or magnitude (usually normalized to 1) WIDTH (of the base of function"), SHOULDERING (locks height at maximum if an outer function. Shouldered functions evaluate as 1.0 past their center) CENTER points (center of the member function shape) OVERLAP (N and Z, Z andP, typically about 50% of width but can be less).

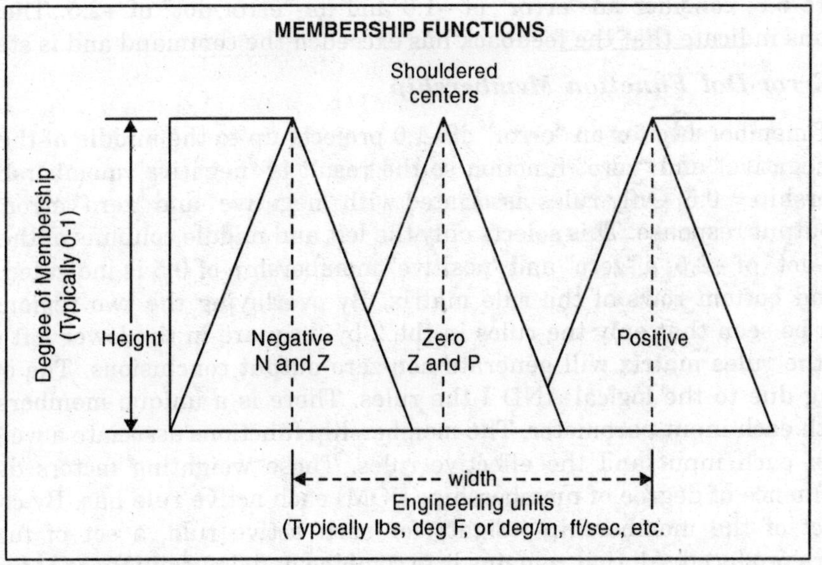

Fig. 5.5. *The features of a membership functions.*

Figure 5.5 illustrates the features of the triangular membership function which is used in this example because of its mathematical simplicity. Other shapes can be used but the triangular shape lends itself to this illustration.

The degree of membership (DOM) is determined by plugging the selected input parameter (error or error-dot) into the horizontal axis and projecting vertically to the upper boundary of the membership function (s).

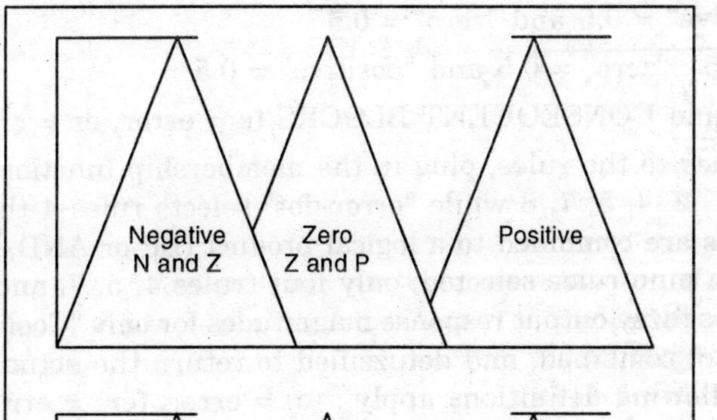

Fig. 5.6. *A sample case.*

In Figure 5.6, consider an "error" of --1.0 and an "error-dot" of +2.5. These particular input conditions indicate that the feedback has exceeded the command and is still increasing.

Error and Error-Dot Function Membership

The degree of membership for an "error" of –1.0 projects up to the middle of the overlapping part of the "negative" and "zero" function so the result is "negative" membership = 0.5 and "zero" membership = 0.5. Only rules associated with "negative" and "zero" error will actually apply to the output response. This selects only the left and middle columns of the rule matrix. For an "error-dot" of +2.5, a "zero" and "positive" membership of 0.5 is indicated. This selects the middle and bottom rows of the rule matrix. By overlaying the two regions of the rule matrix, it can be seen that only the rules in the 2-by-2 square in the lower left corner (rules 4, 5, 7, 8) of the rules matrix will generate non-zero output conclusions. The others have a zero weighting due to the logical AND I the rules. There is a unique membership function associated with each input parameter. The membership functions associate a weighting factor with values of each input and the effective rules. These weighting factors determine the degrees of influence of degree of membership (DOM) each active rule has. By computing the logical product of the membership weights for each active rule, a set of fuzzy response magnitudes are produced. All that remains is to combine and defuzzify these output responses.

Putting it all Together. As inputs are received by the system, the rule base is evaluated. The antecedent (IF X AND Y) blocks test the inputs and produce conclusions. The consequent (THEN Z) blocks of some rules are satisfied while others are not. The conclusions are combined to form logical sums. These conclusions feed into the inference process where ach response output member function's firing strength (0 to 1) is determined.

Data summary from previous illustrations :

Input Degree of Membership

"error" = –1.0. "negative" = 0.5 and "zero" = 0.5

"error-dot" = +2.5 : "zero" = 0.5 and "positive" = 0.5

ANTECEDENT and CONSEQUENT BLOCKS (e = error, er = error-dot or error-rate)

Now referring back to the rules, plug in the membership function weights from above. "Error" selects rules 1, 2, 4, 5, 7, 8 while "error-dot" selects rules 4 through 9. "Error" and "error-dot" for all rules are combined to a logical product (LP or AND, that is the minimum of either term). Of the nine rules selected, only four (rules 4, 5, 7, and 8) fire or have non-zero results. This leaves fuzzy output response magnitudes for only "Cooling" and "No_Change" which must be inferred, combined, and defuzzified to return the actual crisp output. In the rule list below, the following definitions apply : (e) = error, (er) = error-dot.

1. If (e<0) AND (er<0) then Cool 0.5 and 0.0 = 0.0
2. If (e=0) AND (er<0) then Heat 0.5 and 0.0 = 0.0
3. If (e>0) AND (er<0) then Heat 0.0 and 0.0 =0.0
4. If (e<0) AND (er = 0) then Cool 0.5 and 0.5 = 0.5
5. If (e=0) AND (er = 0) then No_chng 0.5 and 0.5 = 0.5
6. If (e>0) AND (er = 0) then Heat 0.0 and 0.5 = 0.0
7. If (e<0) AND (er>0) then Cool 0.5 and 0.5 = 0.5
8. If (e=0) AND (er>0) then Cool 0.5 and 0.5 = 0.5
9. If (e>0) AND (er>0) then Heat 0.0 and 0.5 = 0.0

The inputs are combined logically using the AND operator to produce output response values for all expected inputs. The active conclusions are then combined into a logical sum for each membership function is computed. All that remain is to combine these logical sums in a defuzzification process to produce the crisp output.

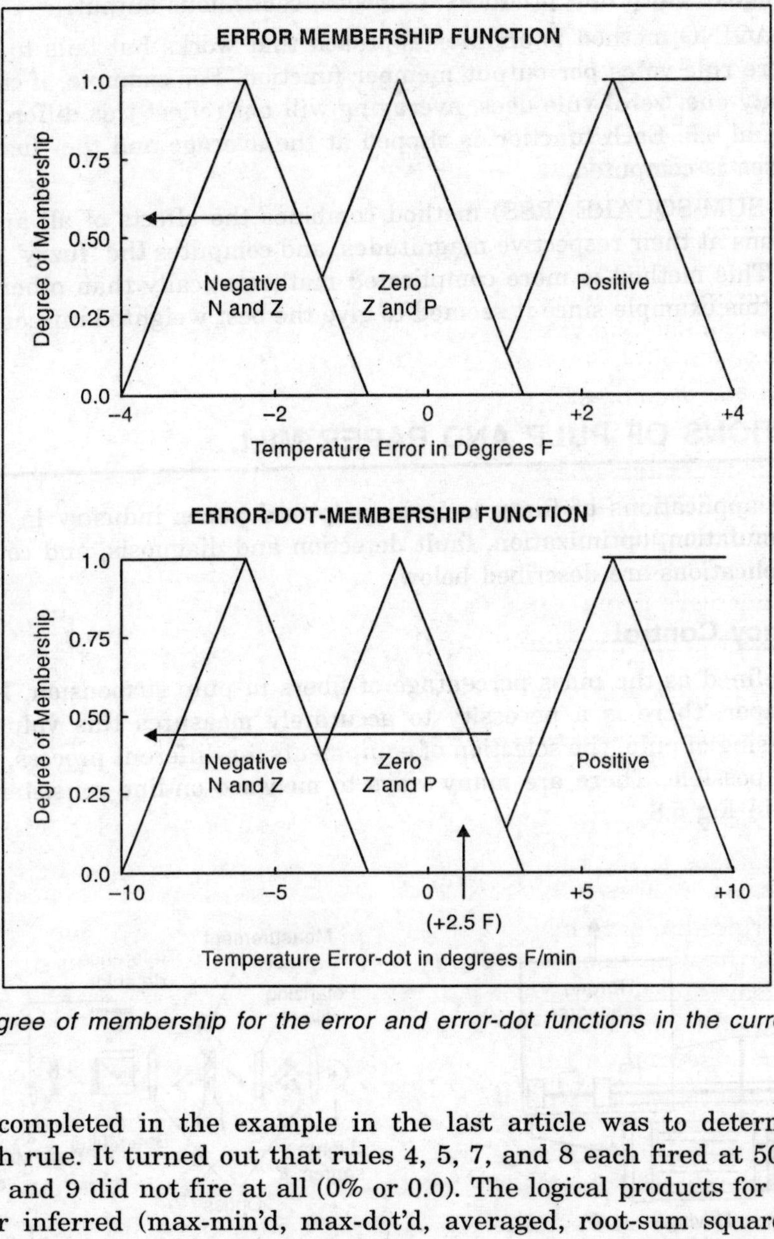

Fig. 5.7. *Degree of membership for the error and error-dot functions in the current example.*

Inferencing

The last step completed in the example in the last article was to determine the firing strength of each rule. It turned out that rules 4, 5, 7, and 8 each fired at 50% or 0.5 while rules 1, 2, 3, 6, and 9 did not fire at all (0% or 0.0). The logical products for each rule must be combined or inferred (max-min'd, max-dot'd, averaged, root-sum squared, etc.) before being passed on to the defuzzification process for crisp output generation. Several inference methods exist.

The MAX-MIN method tests the magnitudes of each rule and selects the highest one. The horizontal co-ordinate of the "fuzzy centroid" of the area under that function is taken as the output. This method does not combine the effects of all applicable rules but does produce a continuous output function and is easy to implement.

The MAX-DOT or MAX-PRODUCT method scales each member function to fit under its respective peak value and takes the horizontal co-ordinate of the "fuzzy" centroid of the composite area under the function (s) are shrunk so that their peak equals the magnitude of their respective function ("negative", "zero", and "positive"). This method combines the influence of all active rules and produces a smooth, continuous output.

The AVERAGING method is another approach that works but fails to give increased weighting to more rule votes per output member function. For example, if three "negative" rules fire, but only one "zero" rule does, averaging will not reflect this difference since both averages will equal 0.5. Each function is clipped at the average and the "fuzzy" centroid of the composite area is computed.

The ROOT-SUM-SQUARE (RSS) method combines the effects of all applicable rules, scales the functions at their respective magnitudes, and computes the "fuzzy" centroid of the composite area. This method is more complicated mathematically than other methods, but was selected for this example since it seemed to give the best weighted influence to all firing rules.

5.8 APPLICATIONS OF PULP AND PAPER MILL

There are many applications of fuzzy logic in pulp and paper industry in the areas like modeling and simulation, optimization, fault detection and diagnosis, and control. Some of the potential applications are described below.

5.8.1 Consistency Control

Consistency is defined as the mass percentage of fibers in pulp suspension. For processing pulp to make paper, there is a necessity to accurately measures this value. If it is not controlled, processing of pulp, the selection of equipments for different process, the formation of paper are not possible. There are many ways to measure on-line consistency of a pulp. These are given in Fig 5.8.

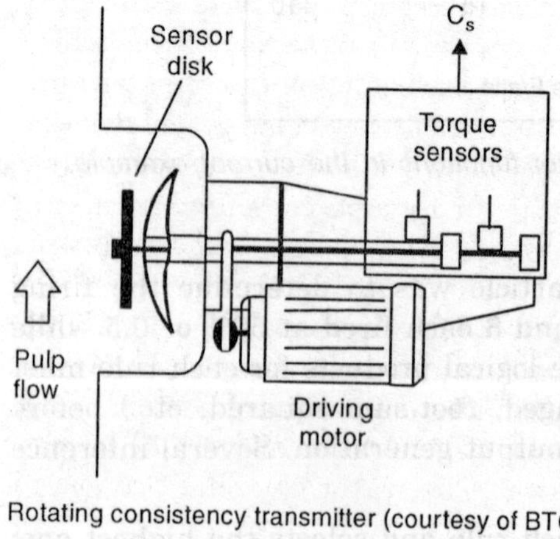

Rotating consistency transmitter (courtesy of BTG).

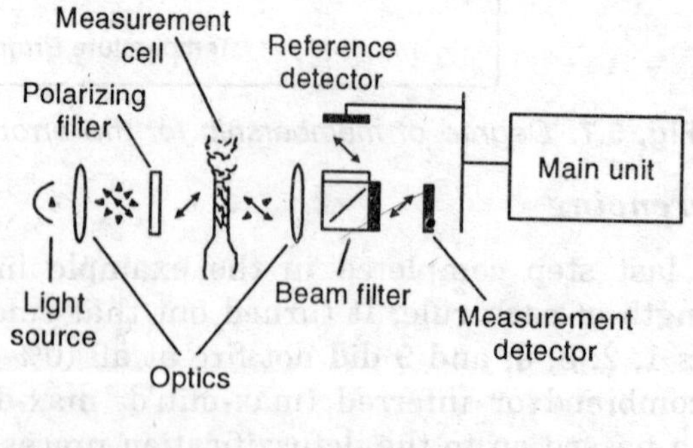

Principle of depolarization consistency measurement (courtesy of Valmet Automation Inc.).

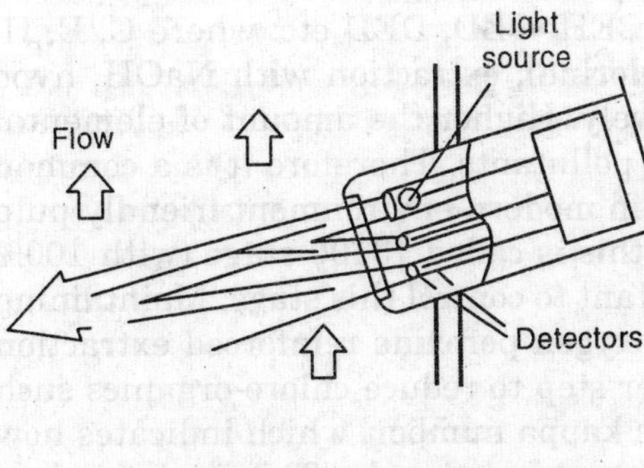

Back-scattering principle for consistency measurement (courtesy BTG).

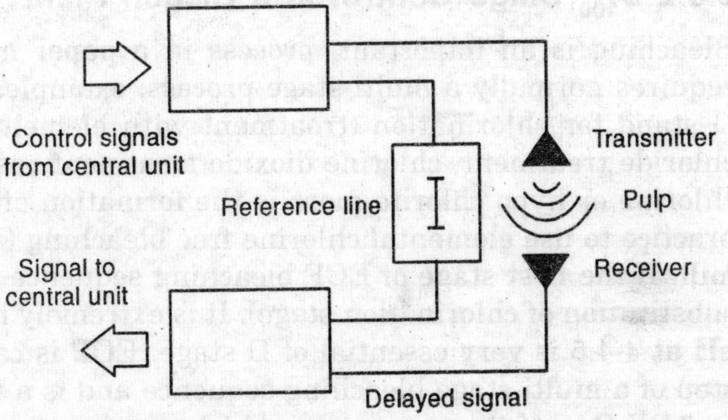

The principle of microwave consistency measurement principle (courtesy Valmet Automation Inc.)

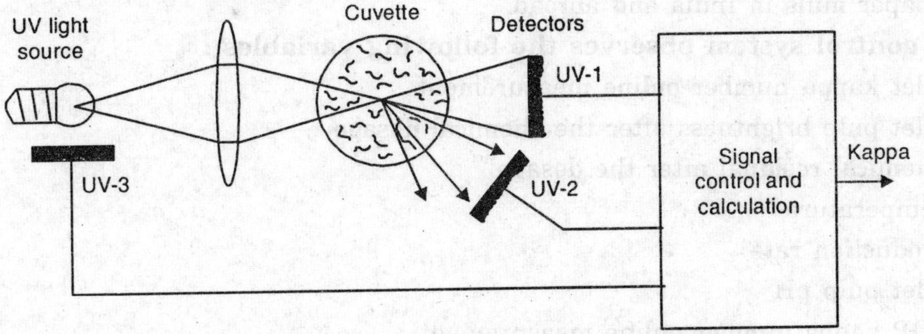

Kappa Measurement Principle (Courtesy STFI)

Fig. 5.8. *Consistency control.*

The control of consistency includes dilution step with addition of water or extra addition of pulp with many possible loops like feed-forward, feed-back, feed-backfeed-forward, feedback cascaded, ratio control etc.

There are many ways to control consistency in a fiber line of a paper mill accurately. The application of feedforward and adaptive gain of a PID controller can achieve satisfactory control. Consistency control is a good candidate for fuzzy logic control. One unique attribute of fuzzy logic control (FLC) is its ability to handle process nonlinearities. This is not true for PID control. The consistency process is easy to simulate and allows one to pre-tune the FLC. This way dividends as the fuzzy logic control is more difficult to tune compared to a PID controller. There was one significant consideration in applying FLC to consistency control. The consistency control strategy using fuzzy logic is shown in Fig. 5.3. The mixed water flows in to a sedimentation tank where the turbid part of water is cohered with the aid of PAC and settled to the bottom. The treated water finally flows into a filtration tank producing clean water. Chlorine i's added for the sterilization of the water. The main control problem of a human operator in this process is to determine the amount of PAC to be added so that the turbidity of the treated water is kept below a certain level. The water cleaning process is shown in Fig. 5.7.

5.8.2 D_{100} Stage Control in a Bleach Plant

Bleaching is an important, process in a paper mill to produce bright and white paper. It requires normally a multi-stage process, examples are CEH, CED, DED etc. where C, E, H, D stand for chlorination (treatment with elemental chlorine), extraction with NaOH, hypo chloride treatment, chlorine dioxide treatment respectively. Higher the amount of elemental chlorine or hypo chlorite more is the formation of AOX pollutants. Therefore it is a common practice to use elemental chlorine free bleaching (ECF) in modern environment friendly pulp mill. If the first stage of ECF bleaching sequence is D, this is called 13100 stage (with 100% substitution of chlorination stage). It is extremely important to control this stage. Maintaining pH at 4-4.5 is very essential of D stage. EOP is called oxygen peroxide reinforced extraction step of a multi stage bleaching sequence and is a further step to reduce chloro-organics such as AOX One of the parameters which requires control is kappa number, which indicates how much lignin (or other chromophores) still remains in the treated pulp. This is defined as number of milliliters tubes of KMn04 consumed per gram of OD pulp under specified conditions. Online measurement of kappa number has been made possible and is now being practiced in many paper mills in India and abroad.

The control system observes the following variables :

- Inlet kappa number online measurement
- Inlet pulp brightness after the chemical dosage
- Chemical residual after the dosage
- Temperature
- Production rate
- Inlet pulp pH
- EOP kappa number online measurement.

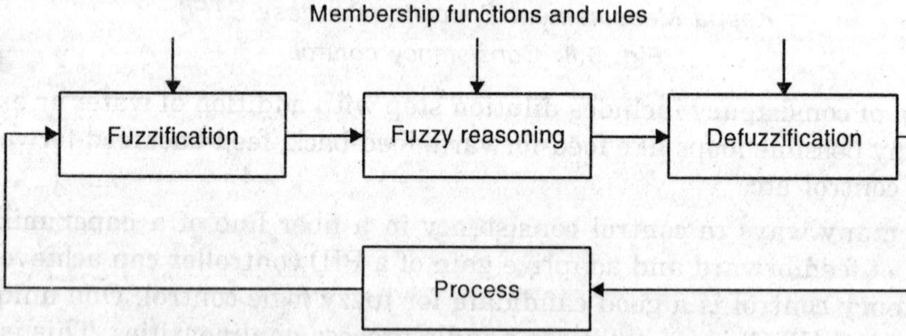

Fig. 5.9. *Fuzzy logic control structure.*

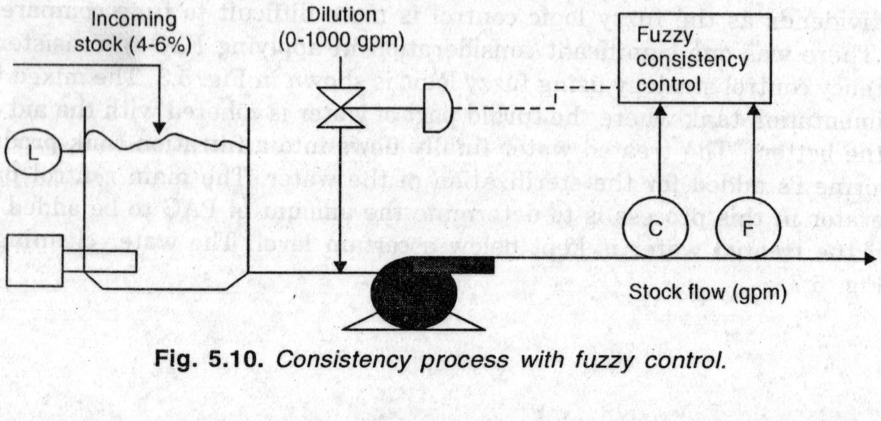

Fig. 5.10. *Consistency process with fuzzy control.*

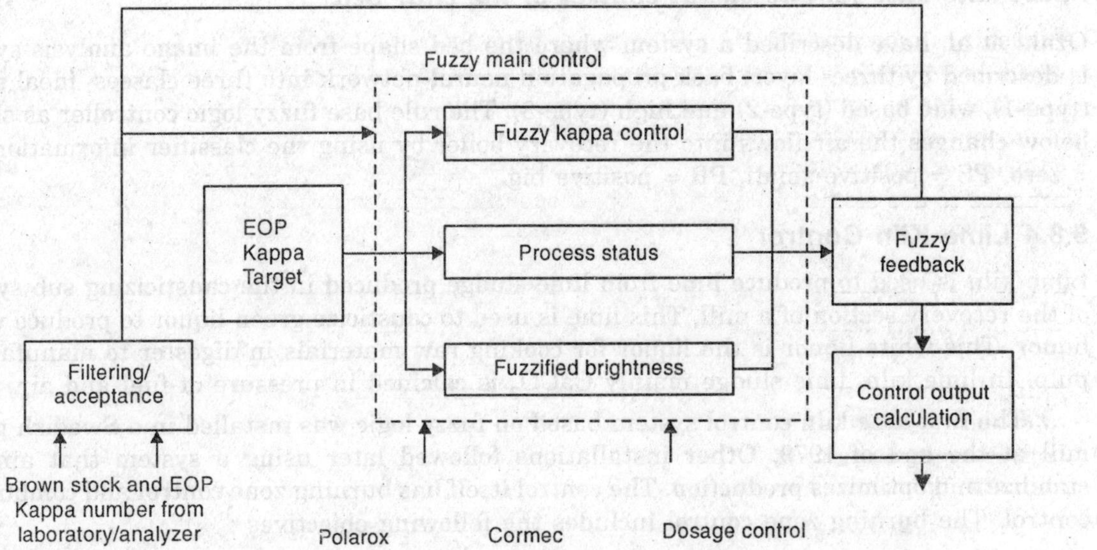

Fig. 5.11. *Structure of the fuzzy logic based bleaching control strategy.*

The control strategy is shown in Fig. 5.11 Fuzzy logic control uses rules such as the following :" if kappa number is increasing, brightness is decreasing, and pH is increasing, then more chlorine dioxide is necessary". Application is modular and hierarchical and therefore easy to use and maintain. The control output is a set point to the dosage controller. The feed forward part uses kappa measurement and brightness and excess chemical sensors before the bleaching stage with inlet pulp pH, COD and conductivity measurements, if available. The feedback controller compares the set point and the actual value for the EOP kappa number and calculates the correction to the feed forward control.

5.8.3 Recovery Boiler Control

The recovery furnace is used to burn the concentrated black liquor, after the liquor is processed in concentration step. The black liquor of solid content 65% or higher is sprayed in the furnace and undergoes combustion. The carbonaceous char resulted due to incineration forms a bed called char bed, the conditions of which is to be maintained. It must be symmetric and uniform. The char reduces the Na_2SO_4 to Na_2S.

This consists of

- Bed condition and symmetry control
- Temperature profile control
- Char bed shape control.

Monitoring bed material and energy balances, bed temperatures, and emission controls the bed conditions and symmetry in the recovery boiler. Corrective actions taken will influence air flows and liquor spraying[1]. Symmetry control can also use fire-room cameras and image processing. Good results using fuzzy logic control in symmetry control are available. The temperature profile in the recovery boiler requires control so that the bed temperature remains sufficiently high to obtain high reduction, this means that burning occurs at the lower part of the furnace. In addition to reduction, this is also good for bed reactions, thermal efficiency, emissions and fouling of heat surfaces.

Fuzzy rule base for the visual control of the char bed

Ozaki et al. have described a system where the bed shape from the image analysis system is described by three- layer, back propagation neural network into three classes- ideal shape (type-1), wide based (type-2) and high (type-3). The rule base fuzzy logic controller as shown below changes the air flows into the recovery boiler by using the classifier information, ZO = zero, PS = positive small, PB = positive big.

5.8.4 Lime Kiln Control

Lime kiln is used to produce lime from lime sludge produced in the causticizing sub system of the recovery section of a mill. This lime is used to causticize green liquor to produce white liquor. This white liquor is the liquor for cooking raw materials in digester to manufacture pulp. In lime kiln, lime sludge mainly $CaCO_3$ is calcined in pressure of fuel and air.

The first lime kiln control system based on fuzzy logic was installed in a Swedish paper mill at the end of 1979. Other installations followed later using a system that aims to stabilize and optimizes production. The control itself has burning zone control and combustion control. The burning zone control includes the following objectives :

- Control very cold kiln
- Stabilize temperatures
- Correct quality
- Optimize production

Combustion control aims for the following :

- Control very high CO
- Control low O_2
- Control exit temperature
- Control high O_2.

A fuzzy expert system application for lime kiln control in rotary lime kiln has made significant improvement in increasing capacity to an extent 16.5%, white liquor production capacity to 6.8%. Approximate 10% energy saving and decreasing the residual carbonate level by about 1% has been achieved.

5.8.5 Quality Control in Stock Preparation

Pulp quality determination is essential to manufacture right quality of paper to meet customer demands. Fuzzy logic controller has become very important in quality control of fiber in the stock preparation section of paper machine. Pulp quality includes many morphological as well as process parameters such as mean fiber length, fiber width/diameter, specific refining energy and freeness values. These parameters are usually measured and controlled around mechanical device called refiners. The process is usually called refining. The fuzzy logic strategy based on freeness and mean fiber length control with specific energy using on-line freeness and fiber length analyzers is available. Two fuzzy controllers are used in cascaded mode. Multi variable fuzzy quality controller was tested at the refiner line as an advisory controller. It does not control the process itself Operators must fulfill the suggestion of the controller, The fuzzy freeness control notices freeness level changes much earlier than operators react to them. The first controller observes the fiber length and smoothly begins to raise freeness set point if fiber length starts to become too short. The controller checks if the fiber length allows reduction of the freeness set point. The second controller keeps freeness on a desired level by changing the set point of total specific energy. The controllers use floating averages of on-line freeness and fiber length measurements. The control strategy is shown in Fig. 5.12.

Another publication' discusses the application of intelligent methods in refiner control. Their system consists of the following :

- Thermodynamic model that calculates the blow line consistency every 10 s.
- Neural network model that predicts pulp quality at 10 s intervals and trains and tunes models in real time.
- Fuzzy logic control for freeness and fiber length that moves all refiner gaps simultaneously.
- Rule based system for power saving analysis and maximizing refiner production during off-peak time.
- Rule-based monitoring of stability of the refining process.

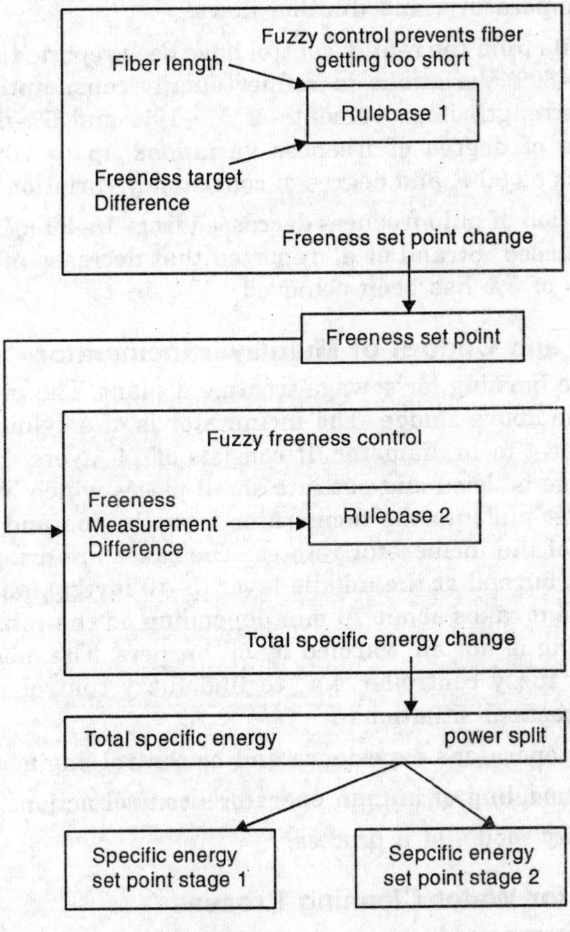

Fig. 5.12. *Control strategy of fuzzy quality control.*

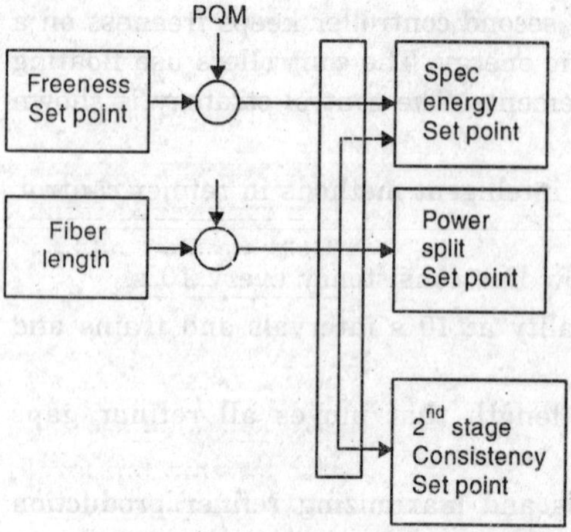

Fig. 5.13. *Quality control strategy.*

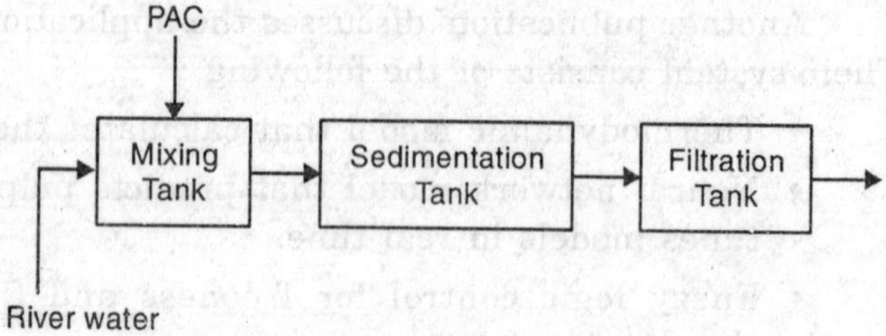

Fig. 5.14. *Water cleaning process.*

Neural network model for estimating stock consistency using fiber properties, stock linear velocity, stock temperature, and dilution flows.

The following benefits from the refiner control have been reported . Consistency variations have decreased by 50%–80%.Variations in refiner energy consumption decreased by 30%–70%. Tear and tensile strength improvements of 5%–10% and 5%–15%, respectively have been reported. Decrease of degree of freeness variations up to 70%, variations in other quality variables as much as 80%, and degree of consistency variation 35% have been shown.

The standard deviation of pulp freeness decreased from 15–30 mL to 3–10 mL. Variation in fiber length also decreased. Strand et al' reported that decrease of freeness variations by 75% and energy savings of 5% has been achieved.

5.8.6 Fuzzy Modeling and Control of Multilayer Incinerator

This is applied for sludge burning for sewage treatment plant. The multilayer incinerator is a furnace for burning the above sludge. The incinerator is of a cylindrical type, with about 20 m in height and about 4 m in diameter. It consists of 14 layers. Before its treatment in the incinerator, the sludge is dried and cut into small pieces which are called sludge cakes. The sludge cakes are first put into the incinerator from the top and then fall down to the lower layers as the axis of the incinerator rotates. The cakes are dried at upper layers with heat energy (1–4 layers), burned at the middle layer (5–10 layers), and become ashes at the lower layers. The treatment takes about 70 min depending on the rotation speed of the axis. The heat source of burning is hot air warmed by oil burners. The most important problems is a method to design a fuzzy controller, *i.e.*, to find fuzzy control rules. There are three applicable methods in practical situations :

- Based on human operator's experience and or control engineer's knowledge.
- Based on fuzzy modeling of human operator's control actions.
- Based on the fuzzy model of a process.

5.8.7 Fuzzy Modeling for Water Cleaning Process

Fuzzy identification of systems and its applications to modeling and control have been reported by Takagi and Sugeno for the above process. This process is used for any industry including pulp and paper. In this process, turbid river water first come into a mixing tank where chemical products called Poly aluminium chloride (PAC) and also chloride are put and mixed in the water. Then

Present and future trends

Most of the integrated pulp and paper mill in India are increasingly applying DCS system for many operations and processes including mill wide control. There is a continuous trend of using fuzzy logic control application in pulp and paper industry as DCS supplier adding this capability to their system. Three categories of potential control applications are :

- Basic regulatory control Supervisory control
- Decision support logic

The possibility of regulatory control loop in pulp and paper industry exists where the performance could be enhanced. The candidates of paper industry operate for chip bin level control, blow heat accumulator pressure control output temperature control for heat exchanger, pH control in any area of paper making and effluent treatment plant, chip bin temperature control (used in presteaming chip in continuous digester), main steam temperature (boiler) control, pressure control of dryer sections on paper machine, and consistency control. Some of the applications of supervisory control are control of combustion in recovery boiler and its production rate, causticizing plant, power plant, integrated digester vessel level and level for twin vessel continuous digester installation, automatic grade change in a paper machine, tie line, excess oxygen control, kappa control for continuous digester.

The use of FL for decision support has many potential uses. In these applications FL is substituted for Boolean logic. Basically it maps all of the variables that can influence the desired index to a single fuzzy variable. These are fuzzy variables that can be used for trigger actions. Some examples are

- Black out prediction index (recovery boiler)
- Plug movement index for chip or pulp flow in continuous digester
- Shrinks, swirl index (boiler drum level)
- Boiler leak index (recovery boiler)
- Total reduced sulphur (TRS),override index (lime kiln)
- Stability index (boiler, kiln) etc.

CONCLUSION

Fuzzy logic control has become an indispensable tool today to the subsystems of paper mill, which are difficult to control. Inaccuracies and uncertainties are very common in chemical process industry, pulp and paper industry in particular. In this industry the fuzzy concept has already been used in regulatory control, supervisory control as well as to provide decision logic to solve intricate problems. The examples are consistency control in fiber line, chlorine-dioxide stage in a bleach plant, shape of bed, its symmetry and temperature profile in recovery boiler, pulp quality control in stock preparation plant, lime kiln control, waste sludge incineration and water purification process. The potential strength of fuzzy logic control has been highlighted to solve the complex process control problems of pulp and paper industry. Significant benefits have been accrued out of this applications to the paper mill personnel.

EXERCISE

1. How is Fuzzy Logic different from control methods ?
2. How does Fuzzy Logic work ?
3. Why do we need Fuzzy Logic ?
4. What is linguistic variables ?
5. How is Fuzzy Logic used ?
6. What are the applications of Fuzzy Logic control system in process industry ?
7. Explain the applications of pulp and paper mills.
8. Differentiate between recovery boiler control and lime kiln control.

□□□

3. What is learning/ training process ? Give the classification of artificial neural network learning processes. Differentiate between supervised and unsupervised learning with some aspects.
4. Define the following terms :
   - Membership function
   - Fuzzy sets
   - Linguistic variable
5. Differentiate between neural networks and fuzzy logic system.
6. The input to a single-input neuron is 5.0, its weight is 3.5 and its bias is –2.
   (*i*) What is the net input to the transfer function ?
   (*ii*) What is the neuron output ?
7. What is the output of the neuron of solved Q. 6. If it as the following transfer functions ?
   (*i*) Hard limit
   (*ii*) Linear
   (*iii*) Log-sigmoid.

□□□

Chapter 6 ARTIFICIAL NEURAL NETWORK CONTROLLER

6.1 INTRODUCTION

A complex network system may contain a neural network which controls or influences its processes. This network is termed as control neural network. It can be built out of a domain model based on domain knowledge. More than one network can be involved in the domain structure. Barton, Sutton and Anderson developed the first neurocontrol scheme. Their system involved two networks, both of which were simple table lookups. Action and critic networks were clearly distinguish in their neurocontrol theory. Their approach has nourished a substantial line of research on neurocontrol. Lapedes and Farber developed another scheme which consisted of a master network and a slave network; the former set the weights for the latter.

Control decides the next action. This decision is based on the current situation and the goals to be pursued. Such information is described in the database or the working memory. The database is non-monotonic, since an action when executed may change it.

When there is more than one goal to be accomplished, the controller must determine the dependencies among goals and order them properly. In planning system, there are different ways to order goals. An old approach is to use a linear stack, which processes goals by the 'last in first out' order. A blackboard-based model deals with goals in an asynchronously parallel manner. There are various heuristic approaches for ordering goals. The goal with the highest priority score is visited first. In the data driven control action is based on the currently processed goal; and in the mixed approach, the action is based on the currently processed goal; and in the mixed approach, the action is based on the current situation and the currently processed goal. The mixed control strategy is more efficient than the other two since it offers bidirectional search for the solution.

6.2 SCHEMES FOR NEUROCONTROL

Models of dynamic systems and their inverses have immediate utility and control. In the control literature, a number of well established and deeply analyzed structures (schemes) for the control of nonlinear systems exist. Such models are made available in the form of neural networks which have been trained. The following control schemes, from the mainstream control theory viewpoint are of much importance.

- *Supervised control* : There are many control situations where a human provides the feedback control action for a particular task and where it has been proven difficult to design an automatic controller using standard control technique. In some situations, it is desirable to design an automatic controller which mimics the action of the human. Neural networks provide a possibility of this.
- *Direct inverse control* : This scheme utilizes an inverse system model. The inverse model is simply cascaded with the controlled system and the composed system results in an identity mapping between the desired response and the controlled system output. Thus the network acts directly as a controller in such configuration. Direct inverse control is common in robotics application. This approach relies heavily on the fidelity of the inverse controller. Absence of feedback leads to lack of robustness. This problem can be overcome to some extent b using online learning.
- *Model reference control* : Here the desired performance of the closed-loop system is specified through a stable reference model M which is defined by its input-output pair $\{r(y), y^r(t)\}$. The control systems attempts to match the plant output $y^p(t)$ with that of the reference model output *i.e.,*

  $\lim_{t\to\infty} \| y^r(t) - y^p(t) \| \le \varepsilon$ for some specified constant $\varepsilon \ge 0$.
- *Predictive control* : In the realm of optimal and predictive control methods, the 'receding horizon technique' has been introduced as a natural, computationally feasible feedback law. In this approach, the neural network model predicts the future plant responses over the specified horizon. The predictions supplied by the networks are passed to a numerical optimization routine which attempts to minimized a specified performance criterion in the calculation of a suitable signal.
- *Optimal decision control* : In this application, the state space is partitioned into regions corresponding to various control situations. The realization of a control surface is accomplished through a training procedure. Since the time-optimal surface in general is nonlinear, it is necessary to use architecture capable of approximating a nonlinear surface. One of the possibilities is to quantize the state space into elementary hypercube in which the control action is assumed constant. The process can be carried out with linear vector quantization architecture. It is then necessary to have another network as a classifier. If continuous signals are required, standard back-propagation architecture can be used.
- *Adaptive linear control* : A Hopfield network may be utilized as a dynamic controller for a linear system. In this case elements of various structure theories are utilized to construct the controller. Hence, it is robust, it is possible to include adaptation through standard methods. The Hopfield network can also be used as a part of the adaptation mechanism. In this case, the network is included in the adaptation path and is used to minimize square-error rates of all the states simultaneously. Here, the output of the network represents the parameters of a linear model for the plant.

- *Adaptive control using a generic index (Reinforcement learning control)* : This kind of network makes use of low quality feedback signal, while the performance measure for a supervised system is defined in terms of a set of targets by means of a known error, reinforcement learning addresses the problem using any measure whose value can be supplied to the learning algorithm. Instead of trying to determine the target controller outputs from the target plant responses, one tries to determine target controller outputs that would lead to an increase in the measure of plant performance.

6.3 BRIEF OVERVIEW OF CONTROL SYSTEM CONCEPTS

6.3.1 Static and Dynamic Systems

The concepts of transfer characteristics, transfer functions and feedforward and feedback control are discussed below, as these are related to neurocontrollers. Solutions to a control problem depend directly on the precision with which the characteristics of the process are known. For example, in a single channel control problem, if the plant input is a scalar variable, the process if known can be described by a relationship between the plant actuating signal and the plant response. In general, this relationship is expressed as P, where P is the process transfer function. It has the form $P(s)$ where s is the complex variable. Plants are basically of two types. The static or the nondynamic plant is the one where the transfer function $P(s)$ is independent of s and reduces to simple functional relationship between the actuating signal and the response. For such plants, the transfer function becomes the transfer characteristics. In case of dynamic plants, they cannot be characterized by constants, not even by complex time-variant functions because their responses, being solutions of differential or integro-differential equations, are function of time. The transfer function for such plant is defined as the ratio between the integral transforms of the output and the input signal. The Laplace transform is the most commonly used transforms to express the input and output signals of linear plants. The significance of the transfer characteristics in system and control theory is based on the fact that the response of a static system to an arbitrary excitation can be computed as a product of its transfer characteristics and of the excitation. Similarly the transform of the response of a dynamical system can be expressed as a product of the transfer function and transform of the excitation.

6.3.2 Open-loop Configuration

For a plant that is completely known, any desired relationship between input and response can be realized by a simple open-loop control configuration as shown in Fig. 6.1. the feedforward controller consist of two parts connected in cascade. The second one cancels the process transfer function because its own transfer function has been chosen as the inverse of the non

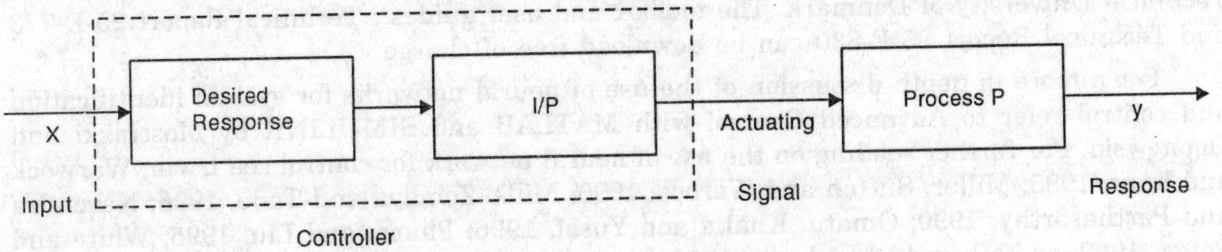

Fig. 6.1. *Inverse Feedforward Method of Control.*

process transfer function. In addition, the front part of the controller introduces the desired overall transfer function of the controller and the plant, equal to *D*. Thus the controller's transfer function should be equal to D/P. This approach is known as the inverse control since the most essential part of the controller provides the inverse of the plant's transfer function.

In this approach involving the cascade connections of the controller driving the plant and involving feedback; a neurocontroller that acts as the plant inverse need to be designed. Inverse control method cannot be relied upon when the transfer function varies during the course of operation or when $P(s)$ is not completely known during system design.

6.3.3 Feedback Control

It is a thumb rule to turn to feedback control systems to circumvent any or both of the above mentioned limitations. One of the most common feedback arrangements is shown in Fig. 6.2.

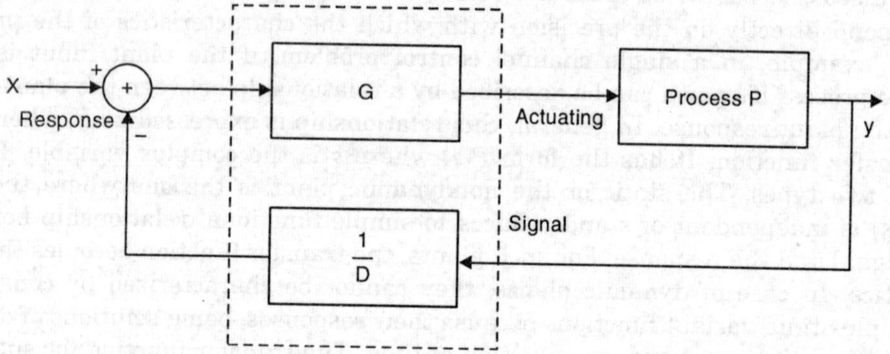

Fig. 6.2. *Feedback Control.*

For high and fixed loop gains, the output is independent of the plant transfer function, $P(s)$. Therefore, the use of feedback provides a useful means of overcoming both the parameter variation of the plant and ignorance of the transfer characteristics. These observations hold true for non-dynamic plants too.

In the processing sections, we shall see the various phases involved in designing a neurocontroller scheme, and plant identification schemes using neural networks.

There are user supplied MATLAB toolkits that implement neural network based system identification and control paradigms :

The NNSYSID Toolbox is located at : http ://kalman.iau.dtu.dk/Projects/proj/nnsysid.html and the NNCTRL Toolkit is at : http ://www.iau.dtu.dk/Projects/proj/nnctrl.html.

These toolbox were developed by Magnus Morgaard of the Institute of Automation, Technical University of Denmark. The toolbox and user guides : Technical Report 95-E-773 and Technical Report 95-E-830 can be download free of charge.

For a more in depth discussion of the use of neural networks for system identification and control refer to Advanced Control with MATLAB and SIMULINK by Moscinski and Ogonowski. For further reading on the use of neural network for control see Irwin, Warwock and hunt, 1995; Miller, Sutton and Werbos, 1990; Mills, Zomaya and Tade, 1996; Narendra and Parthasarthy, 1990; Omatu, Khalid and Yusof, 1996; Pharm and Liu, 1995; White and Sofga, 1992; or Zbikowski and hunt, 1996.

There are five general methods for implementing neural network controllers (Werbos pp. 50–65, in Miller Sutton and Werbos 1990) :

1. Supervised Control
2. Direct Inverse Control
3. Neural Adaptive Control
4. Back-propagation Through Time
5. Adaptive Critic Method.

6.3.4 Supervised Control

In supervised control, a neural network is trained to perform the same actions as another controller (mechanical or human) for given inputs and plant conditions. After the neural controller is trained, it replaces the controller.

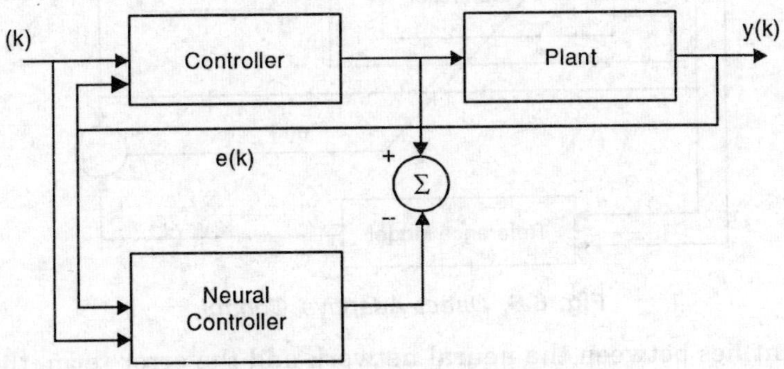

Fig. 6.3. *Neural Controller Training.*

6.3.5 Direct Inverse Control

In Direct Inverse Control, a Neural Network is trained to model the inverse of a plant. This modeling is similar to the system identification problem.

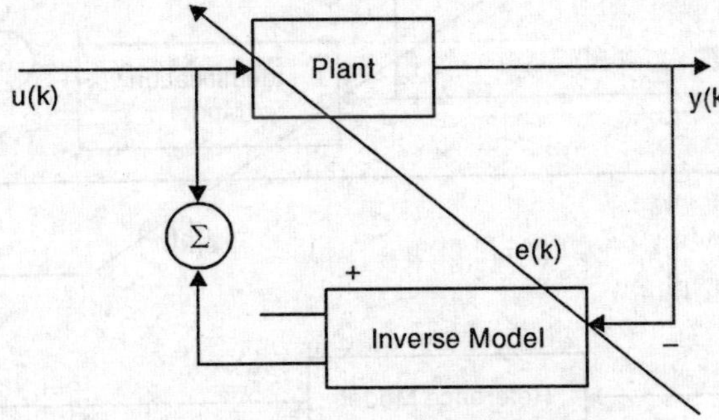

Fig. 6.4. *Inverse System Identification.*

After the neural network learns the inverse model, it is used as a forward controller. This methodology only works for a plant that can be modeled or approximated by an inverse function $(F^{-1}) = 1$ the output $(y\ (k))$ approximates the input $(u\ (k))$.

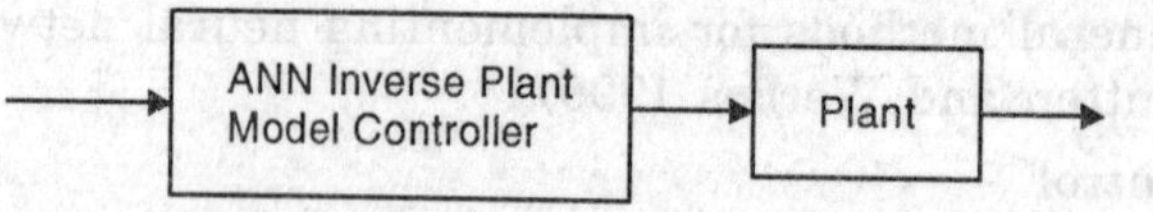

Fig. 6.5. *Direct Inverse Control.*

6.3.6 Model Referenced Adaptive Control

When the plant model changes with time due to wear, temperature affects, etc., neural adaptive control may be the best technique to use. Model Referenced Adaptive Control (MRAC) adapts the controller characteristics so that the controller/plant combination performs like a reference plant.

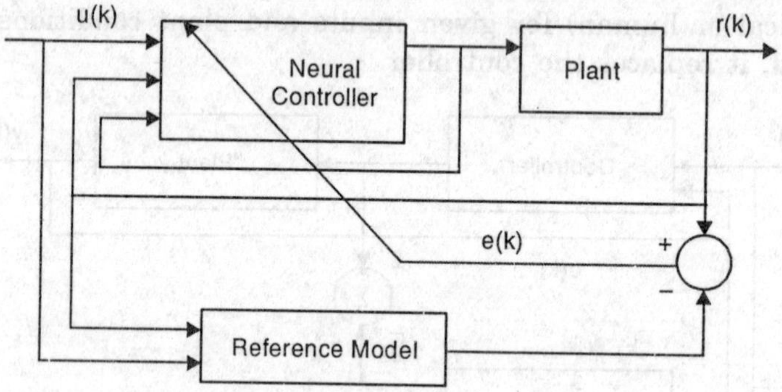

Fig. 6.6. *Direct Adaptive Control.*

Since the plant lies between the neural network and the error term, there is no method to directly adjust the controllers weights to reduce the error. Therefore, indirect control must be used.

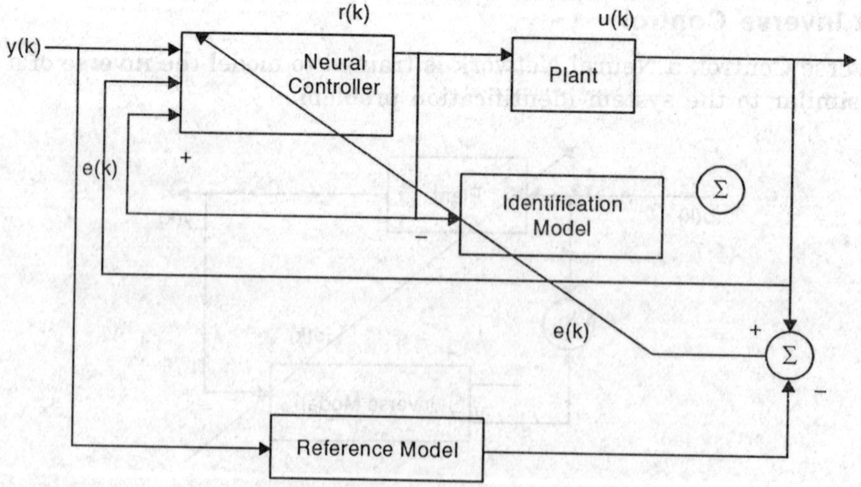

Fig. 6.7. *Indirect Adaptive Control.*

In indirect adaptive control an ANN identification model is used to model the non-linear plant. If necessary, this model may be updated to track the plant. The error signal can now be back propagated through the identification model to train the neural controller so that the plant response is equal to that of the reference model. This method uses two neural networks, one for system identification and one for MRAC.

6.3.7 Back Propagation Through Time

Back propagation Through Time (BPTT) can be used to move a system from one state to another state in a finite number of steps (if the system is controllable). First a system identification neural network model must be trained so that the error signals can be propagated through it to the controller, then the controller can be trained with a BPTT paradigm.

6.3.8 Generalized Delta-Rule Algorithm and its Application to Fault Diagnosis

Many of the growing number of more sophisticated training algorithms use both the internal threshold and sigmoid threshold functions. One particularly useful example is the delta-rule algorithm, which is a gradient-descent learning technique (described previously in Equations 2.17 through 2.20). This algorithm is more efficient than the vanilla backpropagation algorithm, requiring a fraction of the training iterations, and it incorporates both types of threshold values.

6.4 SYSTEM IDENTIFICATION

The task of both conventional and neural network based system identification is to build a mathematical model of a dynamic system based on empirical data. In neural network based system identification, the internal weights and bias of the neural network are adjusted to make the model outputs similar to the measured outputs. Conventional methods use empirical data and regression techniques to estimate the coefficients of different equations (ARX, ARMAX) or state space representations.

6.4.1 ARX System Identification Model

A dynamic model is one whose output is dependent on past states of the system which may be dependent on past inputs and outputs. A static model's output at a specific time is only dependent on the input at that time. The basic conventional dynamic model is the difference equation and the most common difference equation form is the ARX model : Autoregressive with Exogenous Input model which is sometimes called the Equation Error Model. This model uses past inputs and outputs to predict current outputs. For example, examine the following ARX model.

$$Y(t) + a_1 y(t-1) + \ldots + a_{na} y(t-n_a) = b_1 u(t-n_b) + e(t)$$

The co-efficient are represented by the set : $\theta = [a_1\, a_2 \ldots a_{na},\, b_1\, b_2 \ldots b_{nb}]$. The designer sets the structure and a regression technique is used to solve for the co-efficients. This for can be visualized as

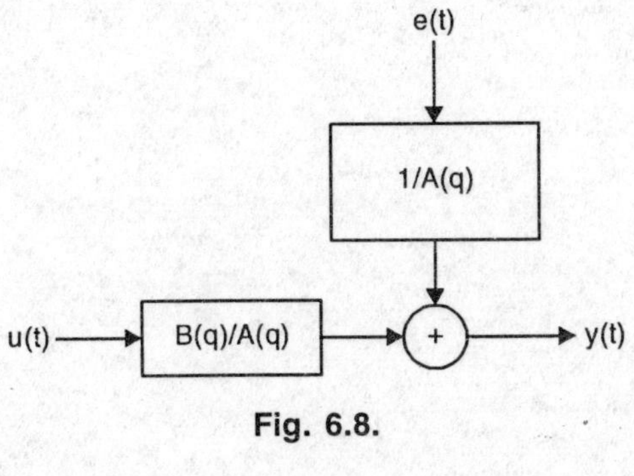

Fig. 6.8.

where :

$A(q) = 1 + a_1 q^{-1} \ldots a_{na} q^{-na}$

$B(q) = b_1 q^{-1} \ldots b_{nb} q^{-nb}$

And :

$Y(t) = [B(q)/A(q)]\ u(t) + [1/A(q)]\ e(t).$

This model assumes that the poles (roots of $A(q)$) are common between the dynamic model and the noise model. This model is a linear model, one of the major advantages of using neural networks is their non-linear approximating capabilities.

EXERCISE

1. Differentiate between classical controller and artificial neural network controller.
2. How to design artificial neural network controller with the help of MAtlab software ?
3. What is adaptive linear control ?
4. What do you mean by Open Loop Configuration ? Explain.

□□□

INDEX

□□□